Social Marketing

SOCIAL MARKETING

Strategies for Changing Public Behavior

PHILIP KOTLER

EDUARDO L. ROBERTO

THE FREE PRESS
A Division of Macmillan, Inc.
NEW YORK

Collier Macmillan Publishers
LONDON

The Free Press
A Division of Macmillan, Inc.
866 Third Avenue, New York, N.Y. 10022

Collier Macmillan Canada, Inc.

Printed in the United States of America

printing number
1 2 3 4 5 6 7 8 9 10

Library of Congress Cataloging-in-Publication Data

Kotler, Philip.

  Social marketing.

  1. Social marketing. I. Roberto, Eduardo L. II. Title.
HF5415.122.K68 1989   658.8   89-45735
ISBN 0-02-918461-4

*T*his book is dedicated to all those tireless workers in health organizations, environmental organizations, government organizations, and international bodies, such as WHO, AID, UNICEF, and the World Bank, who unselfishly give their time and energy to help the world's people achieve a better, safer, and more satisfying life.

With love to Nancy, Amy, Melissa, Jessica, Joel, Neil, and Milton.—PK

With love to Corrie, Sharon, Elaine, Ardy, and Cherry.—ELR

Contents

PART FOUR
MANAGING SOCIAL MARKETING

Preface

Every nation in the world is experiencing social problems that its citizens and government are attempting to solve. Solving social problems involves social change—changing the way individuals and groups lead their lives by transforming adverse or harmful practices into productive ones, changing attitudes and values in communities and entire societies, and creating new social technologies that usher in desired changes and elevate the quality of people's lives.

Virtually all societies in these closing years of the twentieth century are wrestling with an acceleration and intensification of social change. Long-standing ideologies, such as Marxism, are weakening in the face of social and financial crises. Authoritarian political systems are undergoing massive changes, sometimes in the direction of democratization. In Third World countries, new ideas and practices, stimulated by global communications, are disrupting existing social orders. There is a "revolution of rising expectations." More people in more societies are eager for social change—for changes in their ways of life, their economies and social systems, their lifestyles, and their beliefs and values—than ever before.

In the past, massive changes were brought about by force and violence, through war and revolution. It is hoped that in the future, students of social change may look at the final decade of the twentieth century as a time when the balance of social change by exchange and persuasion versus social change by violence started to shift in favor of planned, voluntary, and nonviolent change.

Many modern societies are powered by a belief in democracy,

rationality, and progress. The dominant idea is that social and individual life can be shaped, changed, and improved by rational action—by individuals, by groups of people working together voluntarily, by the government, or by a combination of citizen and governmental action.

Social change campaigns arise among people who are intent on directing, shaping, and controlling change. Therefore, social change can be viewed as taking two forms: changes that occur spontaneously, that take place in the course of life without deliberate planning or rational human intervention, and changes that are planned and engineered by human beings to achieve specific agreed-on objectives and goals. In democratic societies, for the most part, planned social change is brought about by the concerned action of governments and citizens. The assumption is that leaders must win the consent of the governed to make major changes, although some democratic governments have ''engineered'' consent from the governed, manipulating the public in devious or heavy-handed ways. Insofar as democratic societies often seek to limit the scope and power of governments, changes undertaken voluntarily, by individuals and groups that are formed to promote social change, assume a prominence and, indeed, legitimacy in the conduct of social life. In these instances, citizen/voluntary action is valued as a legitimate alternative to ''big government.''

This book examines the art and science of promoting planned, targeted social change. It highlights successful social change campaigns that have been launched by governments, by a combination of governments and citizens, and by citizens themselves. It probes the hows and whys of failed campaigns and the conditions of successful ones.

Its theme is that knowledge, techniques, and technologies now exist to organize and implement effective social change programs, in virtually every area of social concern, both locally and nationally. Social change campaigns can achieve their objectives of influencing, determining and changing ideas and practices. The lessons of successful social change campaigns in modern, industrialized nations and in developing nations can be utilized to launch sought-after social changes in all nations of the world, even in those that still resist the notion that social change is possible and achievable through human intervention and purpose. Bringing about life-improving social change is the challenge and goal of social marketing.

Acknowledgments

Every book is the product of far more people than the authors themselves. As authors, we owe a great debt to many past and present scholars who have thought and written deeply about the human condition and the ways to improve the lot of humanity. And our debt is owed no less to the leaders and doers who have initiated and led major social campaigns to improve the human condition.

We owe a considerable debt to individuals and organizations who have discussed their social marketing campaigns with us and who have asked for our advice and participation in developing social marketing strategies.

We owe a debt to our colleagues at Northwestern University and the Asian Institute of Management for our many helpful discussions of the problems of social change and progress. We specifically want to thank Martin McCarthy and Jill Grace for their critical comments on an early version of the manuscript.

We owe a major debt as well to Neil G. Kotler, who reviewed our manuscript and made important suggestions about the scope and point of view and who helped us craft the manuscript into its present form. His appreciation of the possibilities of social change is the outcome of his service as a volunteer in the U.S. Peace Corps in Ethiopia in the mid-1960s.

We want to acknowledge the help of specific individuals on our staffs in preparing the manuscript: Marion Davis, Ellen Fishbein, Marcia Lind, and Andrea Siegel.

We want to thank Robert Wallace, Laura A. Rosenfeld, and Edith Lewis of The Free Press for their patience and support during the long process of researching this book. We also want to thank the Henry Foundation for its generous support of some of the research costs.

Finally, and most importantly, we want to thank our families for giving us the time, feeding, and care to develop this "labor of love."

Philip Kotler
Evanston, Illinois

Eduardo L. Roberto
Manila, Philippines

ONE

UNDERSTANDING
SOCIAL MARKETING

1

The Nature and Role
of Social Campaigns
to Change Public Behavior

Numerous potential solutions have been proposed for the myriad social problems with which the world is grappling and, typically, there are disagreements on how best to solve problems as diverse as illiteracy, drug and alcohol abuse, teenage pregnancy, the spread of AIDS, and poor nutrition. Often, solutions bring calls for launching a social campaign to change public attitudes and behavior. Social campaigns designed to change public behavior abound. For example, on a single day in January 1989, several press releases were issued in Chicago to describe the launching of the following social campaigns:

The Harvard School of Public Health has announced important new developments in a national media campaign against drunk driving spearheaded by a unique alliance of Harvard, Hollywood, Madison Avenue and the broadcast networks. The project's goal is to change American social norms regarding drinking and driving and thereby reduce alcohol-related traffic deaths. . . . One of the project's immediate objectives is to promote widespread adoption of the ''designated driver'' concept. Dr. Jay Winsten, the project's head, said: ''In planning the project, we were impressed by the striking contrast between American and Scandinavian practices. When a Swede drives to a party and is offered an alcoholic beverage, it is typical to respond, 'No thanks, I'm driving.' When a Swedish couple goes out for the evening, they routinely discuss 'Who's driving tonight?' and the implications are clear—the 'designated driver' doesn't drink. In contrast, the American norm is to drink and drive. By the time American teenagers are 16–18 years old, a majority say they have been a passenger when the driver was drunk. On weekend nights after 10:00 P.M., over 8% of drivers on the U.S. roads are seriously impaired by alcohol. If current trends continue, more than one million Americans will die in alcohol-related crashes during the lifetime of today's high school seniors."

New programs to educate members of the black and Hispanic communities about the risks of acquiring AIDS are being planned. Blacks and Hispanics now make up nearly half of all new AIDS cases in Chicago. . . . "We have to get the information to these groups . . . we will be launching a larger effort directed to minority populations throughout the state," said Chet Kelly, AIDS section administrator for the Illinois Department of Public Health.[1]

The American Medical Association will spearhead a multimillion-dollar "Campaign Against Cholesterol." The campaign will blitz the public and physicians with ads, brochures, TV programming, and a cholesterol reduction book in an effort that will link concern over high cholesterol and heart disease. The AMA described its campaign as a "war on one of America's leading killers."

Project Match, housed at the Center for Urban Affairs and Policy Research at Northwestern University, helps welfare recipients at Chicago's Cabrini Green housing project get and keep jobs. Project Match offers a case-management approach to coordinate education, training, employment and support services to clients. Clients are taken through a hands-on, step-by-step approach to finding and keeping a job and utilizing support services, in contrast to short-term, isolated services provided by most programs. . . . "We stay with clients indefinitely. We meet with them. We call them. We don't wait for them to call us." Sixty-six percent of Project Match clients were placed in jobs, training, school or internships within six months of enrollment in the program. On their first job, 62 percent of clients relied on Project Match's job development assistance to obtain a job; on the second job, 53 percent utilized the program; and on the third job, only 33 percent sought help. The information indicates that clients are learning how to obtain jobs on their own.

Unfortunately, many social change campaigns accomplish little, and this fact can breed widespread cynicism among social reformers and citizens. Whether social change campaigns must inevitably fail is a hotly debated topic. Postmortems of them may reveal a number of deficiencies that could have been corrected. The campaigns may not have targeted the appropriate audience, the reform message may not have been sufficiently motivating, the individuals, and groups, or populations that were targeted (the target adopters) were not given a way to respond constructively, or a campaign may have been underfunded. All these problems, fortunately, are solvable once the correct approach to identifying objectives and methods is found. Later, we describe social change campaigns that were successful and that can serve as replicable models for social change planning in diverse situations.

HISTORY AND NATURE OF SOCIAL CHANGE CAMPAIGNS

Campaigns for social change are not a new phenomenon. They have been waged from time immemorial. In Ancient Greece and Rome, campaigns were launched to free the slaves. In England during the Industrial Revolution, campaigns were mounted to abolish debtor prisons, grant voting rights to women, and abolish child labor. Colonial America also was the scene of numerous campaigns. In 1721, Cotton Mather sought to convince the citizens of Boston, in what was then the Massachusetts Bay Colony, to accept inoculations to ward off a smallpox epidemic. James Madison, Alexander Hamilton, and others published the Federalist Papers after the 1787 Constitutional Convention to win public acceptance of the new U.S. Constitution. Notable social reform campaigns in nineteenth-century America included the abolition movement, the temperance and prohibition movements, the suffragette movement, and a movement to have the federal government regulate the quality of foods and drugs.

In recent times, social change campaigns have focused on health reforms (antismoking, the prevention of drug abuse, nutrition, and physical fitness), environmental reforms (safer water, clean air, the preservation of national parks and forests, and the protection of wildlife refuges), educational reforms (to increase adult literacy, to improve public schools, to raise students' test scores in science and mathematics, and to grant merit-pay increases to increase the morale of teachers), and economic reforms (to revitalize older, industrial cities; boost job skills and training; and attract foreign investors). Other countries, such as Sweden, Canada, and Australia, have launched vigorous campaigns to reduce smoking and alcoholic consumption, encourage safe driving, and protect the environment. In some cases, these countries have been more effective in their social change campaigns than has the United States. For example,

> Sweden has developed a program that aims to raise a nation of nonsmokers. The program includes intensive antismoking education in the schools and in maternity clinics, progressive restrictions on cigarette advertising and promotion, high cigarette taxes, bans on smoking in public places, and full-service clinics to assist people who want to stop smoking.

Developing countries, such as the Philippines, Indonesia, and China, conduct forceful social campaigns to inoculate children against viruses; to make widespread the use of oral rehydration therapies; and to promote family planning, literacy, and healthful diets.

But what do we mean by a social change campaign? A social change campaign is an organized effort conducted by one group (the change agent), which intends to persuade others (the target adopters) to accept, modify, or abandon certain ideas, attitudes, practices, and behavior.

In many cases, the change agent ultimately seeks to change the target adopters' behavior. Behavioral change may occur at the end of a series of intermediate stages, such as change in a population's information, knowledge, and attitudes. Most of the social campaigns that we examine are high-consensus campaigns—to foster brotherhood, prevent forest fires, and rehabilitate drug abusers—with which most citizens agree. Others may enjoy less-widespread public support (such as family planning) or face opposition (abortion). The technology of social campaigning also applies to political campaigns and fund-raising campaigns for candidates for public office, although we shall say little about them here.

HOW EFFECTIVE ARE SOCIAL CHANGE CAMPAIGNS?

American social scientists in the 1950s began to study social change systematically. Some reached the pessimistic conclusion that mass information and persuasion campaigns are largely ineffectual. For example, an evaluation of Cincinnati, Ohio's, effort to build citizen support for the newly formed United Nations in 1946 showed that after the campaign, many citizens still knew little about the United Nations, despite the outpouring of radio spots and newspaper articles.[2] The failure of other post–World War II campaigns to make a dent in the public's knowledge or attitudes led Hyman and Sheatsley to conclude that information campaigns often fail because

1. A hard core of "chronic know-nothings" exists who cannot be reached by information campaigns. In fact, "there is something about the uninformed that makes them harder to reach, no matter what the level or nature of the information."
2. The likelihood of an individual responding to new information increases with the audience's interest or involvement in the issue; if few people are interested, few will respond.
3. The likelihood of an individual being receptive to new information increases with the information's compatibility with the audience's prior attitudes. People tend to avoid disagreeable information.
4. People will read different things into the information they receive, depending on their beliefs and values. The bigot, for example, often does not recognize and process antiprejudice literature. People respond in different ways to the same body of material.[3]

Several information-oriented campaigns in subsequent years fared no better. In a campaign to get drivers to wear seatbelts in automobiles, frequent public service announcements were broadcast to one set of households but not to another matched set.

However, the drivers who heard these announcements did not use seatbelts at a significantly higher rate than did those who did not hear them.[4] Similarly, many of the antidrug campaigns of the 1970s failed to change young people's attitudes toward drug abuse.[5] In some cases, the antidrug commercials may even have increased the youths' interest in drugs.[6]

It is not surprising, then, that, over the years, social researchers have concluded that the use of mass communication to change public attitudes or behaviors was limited. Researchers cited several factors that dilute mass media impact:

1. Audience factors, such as apathy, defensiveness, and cognitive ineptness.

2. Message factors, such as messages that do not convey real motivating benefits to citizens in an attention-getting way.

3. Media factors, such as the failure to use appropriate media vehicles at the proper time or in effective ways or to reach target adopters with the type of media they are most receptive to.

4. Response-mechanism factors, such as a failure to provide receptive, motivated citizens with an easy and convenient way to respond positively to a campaign's objectives and to carry out the campaign's intentions.

Not all social change campaigns, however, have performed poorly. Quite a number have been successful when they were carefully crafted. These include campaigns on smoking,[7] drinking,[8] littering,[9] and mental retardation.[10] Two campaigns, were particularly well planned.

The Stanford Heart Disease Prevention Program

Maccoby and his colleagues at Stanford University sought to test the power of mass communications to inform and motivate people to change behaviors that lead to cardiovascular disease.[11] Their aim was to influence people to stop smoking, eat better foods, keep their weight down, exercise regularly, and avoid stress and high blood pressure. The researchers recognized that interpersonal interventions (such as lectures and visits to clinics) and personal communications are the most effective means of stimulating people to adopt healthy habits. However, they did not have enough funds to hire skilled trainers to conduct full-scale interpersonal interventions. Therefore, they decided to try a mass media approach.

They identified three comparable small-sized California communities with populations of 12,000 to 15,000—Tracy, Gilroy, and Watsonville. Tracy received no media treatment, and Gilroy was exposed to a variety of television and radio spots, newspaper advertisements and articles, billboards, direct mail, and so on. In Watsonville, messages were placed in newspapers, and a group of residents who were at high risk of developing cardiovascular disease also received face-to-face interpersonal interventions.

The experiments were carried out over a three-year period. The researchers were pleased to find that the mass media messages produced positive changes in dietary behavior and exercise. However, when these messages were supplemented by personal interventions, the combination led even more people to stop smoking and control their weight. The conclusion was that mass media appeals, when effectively planned, can inform, motivate, and lead to sustained healthful behaviors, even in the absence of supplementary interpersonal interventions.

Sweden's Campaign to Change Rules of the Road

On September 3, 1967, at 5 A.M., Sweden changed the rules of the road from driving on the left to driving on the right.[12] This new law meant that almost 8,000,000 Swedes would have to change an old, ingrained pattern of behavior. Two million automobiles and another million vehicles would have to be driven on the right instead of on the left, with drivers passing one another on the left instead of on the right. In addition, the Swedes had to learn new traffic patterns in large towns, many of whose streets were changed from two way to one way.

This massive change in driving habits depended on an information campaign about the new traffic patterns and driving rules. Over a two-week period, an information campaign of seldom-experienced proportions was put into effect. All conceivable media were used, including three or four television programs a day, two daily radio programs, and a 32-page brochure distributed to every household in Sweden. The brochure was translated into nine languages for use by resident aliens, and was issued in special editions for deaf, blind, and other handicapped people.

Communications were also distributed to specialized markets

like schoolchildren, who received study materials adapted to each educational level. The campaign utilized virtually every poster and billboard site in the nation; signs along highways were set up every three to five kilometers. Advertisements were carried in all the 130 daily and weekly newspapers and trade papers. Even comic books of the "Donald Duck" variety carried advertising. Films were shown in movie houses, and a sound track reminded audiences of the changes in driving before they left the theaters. Spectators heard advertisements at sports events. Information also was provided on milk cartons, soft drinks, plastic cups, coffee cans, and grocery bags. Private businesses furnished "right-hand" traffic games and men's underwear suitably marked with messages about the changes.

After the campaign was in effect, detailed analyses of accident statistics showed that in the initial stages, bicycle and moped accidents occurred at a high rate and head-on collisions were two to three times greater than normal. Therefore, supplementary information measures were adopted, which proved effective. Over time, the accident rate declined. The conclusion to be drawn from the Swedish campaign is that it is eminently possible to change behaviors if the social change campaign is planned and implemented effectively.

CONDITIONS ASSOCIATED WITH SUCCESSFUL CAMPAIGNS

Social scientists have analyzed the conditions that favor successful social change campaigns. Here we will look at some of their conclusions.

Lazarsfeld and Merton identified the following conditions for successful mass media-oriented information campaigns.[13]

1. *Monopolization.* An information campaign has to enjoy a monopoly in the media, so that there should be no messages that are contrary to a campaign's objectives. However, most campaigns in a free society face competition (several alternative campaigns that pursue a similar goal or other social causes that compete for attention) and are unable to monopolize the media.

2. *Canalization.* Mass- and information-oriented social campaigns depend on a favorable public attitude base. Commer-

cial advertising is effective because its task is not to instill basic new attitude or create new behavior patterns but to channel existing attitudes and behavior in one direction or another. For example, a toothpaste manufacturer does not have to convince people to brush their teeth but only to direct them to use a particular brand of toothpaste. Preexisting attitudes are easier to reinforce than to change.

3. *Supplementation.* Social campaigns work best when mass media–oriented communication is supplemented by face-to-face communication. To the extent that people are able to discuss what they hear with others, they will process information better and are more likely to accept changes.

Wiebe raised a pertinent question about social change campaigns: ''Why can't you sell brotherhood like you sell soap?''[14] Sellers of commodities, he noted, are generally effective, while ''sellers'' of social causes are generally ineffective. Wiebe examined four social change campaigns to determine the conditions of success. He concluded that the more a social change campaign resembles a commercial product campaign, the more successful it is likely to be. He identified five factors from the perspective of the target adopters:

1. *The Force.* The intensity of a person's motivation toward a goal that results from a predisposition before a message is received and the stimulation level of the message.
2. *The Direction.* Knowledge of how and where to respond positively to a campaign's objectives, namely, the presence of a means of carrying out the objectives.
3. *The Mechanism.* The existence of an agency, office, or retail outlet that enables an individual to translate motivation into action.
4. *Adequacy and Compatibility.* The ability and effectiveness of the agency in performing its task.
5. *Distance.* An individual's estimate of the energy and cost required to change an attitude or behavior in relation to the expected reward.

Wiebe analyzed the Kate Smith campaign to sell U.S. bonds during World War II. Kate Smith was a popular singer and entertainer. This campaign succeeded, according to Wiebe, because of the presence of force (patriotism), direction (bonds to buy), mechanism (banks, post offices, telephone orders), adequacy and compatibility (so many appropriate centers to purchase the bonds), and distance (ease of bond purchase). Extra telephone lines, installed on the night of the campaign at 134 radio and television stations, made it easy to respond to Kate Smith's appeal. According to one study, the effort to buy bonds

> was literally reduced to the distance between the listener and his telephone. Psychological distance was also minimized. The listener remained in his own home. There were no new people to meet, no unfamiliar procedures, no forms to fill out, no explanation, no waiting.[15]

Weibe examined three other social change campaigns that failed because they lacked one or more of these conditions. A campaign to recruit civil defense volunteers drew more volunteers than the mechanism (the recruitment offices) was prepared to handle, so many citizens turned away after waiting a long time to sign up. A campaign to encourage people to form neighborhood councils to fight juvenile delinquency failed because it put the burden of creating a mechanism on the people themselves. And a campaign to arouse citizens to call for better government failed because citizens are not directed to an appropriate mechanism.

Rothschild also sought to explain why social change objectives are harder to sell than are commercial products.[16] He studied the antilittering campaigns of American cities, most of which used a social advertising approach, exhorting people not to litter and to remove litter when they found it. This campaign was not successful because of the following factors:

1. *Situation Involvement.* Littering is not important or of much interest to most people.
2. *Enduring Involvement.* People generally had little previous involvement with the issue.
3. *Benefits/Reinforcers.* Antilittering behavior produces only slight personal benefits and satisfaction for most people and it does not lead to a sense of personal efficacy, since the cleanup of litter depends on the collective action of many people.

4. *Costs.* Antilittering behavior may incur personal cost and inconvenience.

5. *Benefit/Cost.* The benefit/cost ratio for the person who does not litter or who picks up litter is low.

6. *Preexisting Demand.* The demand for a clean environment is not strong or universal.

7. *Segmentation.* The message calling for antilitter behavior cannot be general. It must be tailored separately to each group of target adopters.

Rothschild applied this set of factors to other social campaigns, such as encouraging people to cooperate with the 55 mile-per-hour speed limit, attracting high school graduates to join the army, and so on. Generally speaking, the lower the target adopters' involvement in the issue and the lower the personal benefit/cost ratio, the lower the impact of the mass communications campaign.

A successful social change campaign depends on a society's readiness to adopt a particular objective, or change, and this readiness varies at different times. For example, Ralph Nader could not have "sold" consumerism if he had campaigned for it in the late 1950s, but he launched it successfully in the mid-1960s precisely because all the conditions for it were ripe. These conditions include structural conduciveness, structural strain, growth of a generalized belief, precipitating factors, mobilization for action, and social control.[17] They were applied by Kotler[18] to explain why the consumer movement was successfully launched in the mid-1960s (see Figure 1–1).

Structural conduciveness refers to developments in society that lead to heightened capabilities and expectations that, in turn, can engender frustration and discontent. Three developments in the United States were noteworthy in this regard:

1. As incomes and educational levels advanced, better-off and better-educated citizens were bound to be concerned with the quality of their lives.

2. Technology had become increasingly complex and led to consumer problems, such as unsafe products.

3. The natural environment was heavily exploited. An abundance of cars produced a shortage of clean air. Industry pol-

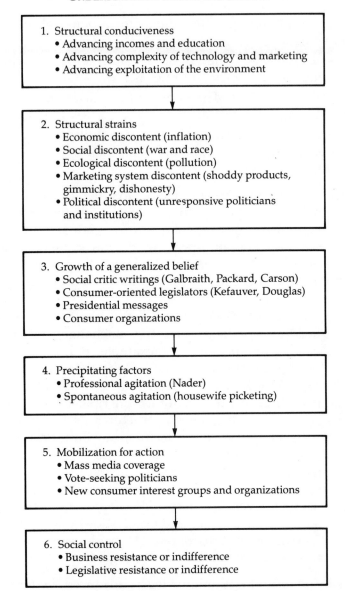

1. Structural conduciveness
   • Advancing incomes and education
   • Advancing complexity of technology and marketing
   • Advancing exploitation of the environment

2. Structural strains
   • Economic discontent (inflation)
   • Social discontent (war and race)
   • Ecological discontent (pollution)
   • Marketing system discontent (shoddy products, gimmickry, dishonesty)
   • Political discontent (unresponsive politicians and institutions)

3. Growth of a generalized belief
   • Social critic writings (Galbraith, Packard, Carson)
   • Consumer-oriented legislators (Kefauver, Douglas)
   • Presidential messages
   • Consumer organizations

4. Precipitating factors
   • Professional agitation (Nader)
   • Spontaneous agitation (housewife picketing)

5. Mobilization for action
   • Mass media coverage
   • Vote-seeking politicians
   • New consumer interest groups and organizations

6. Social control
   • Business resistance or indifference
   • Legislative resistance or indifference

FIGURE 1-1 Factors Contributing to the Rise of Consumerism in the 1960s

SOURCE: Philip Kotler, ''What Consumerism Means for Marketing,'' *Harvard Business Review,* 40 (1972), pp. 48–57. Copyright © 1972 by the President and Fellows of Harvard College; all rights reserved.

luted air and water. The Malthusian specter of scarce resources became a growing concern.

American society in the 1960s was characterized by structural
strains. Economic discontent was fueled by steady inflation and
deteriorating real incomes. Social discontent erupted over the
plight of the poor, racial conflict, and the Vietnam war. There was
new awareness of the overpopulation of the world and pollution.
Discontent deepened toward gimmicky products, safety hazards,
products that broke down, and commercial noise. Political discontent reflected widespread feelings that politicians and governmental institutions were failing to serve the people.

Discontent alone is not enough to produce social change. In
addition, a generalized belief has to develop about the main
causes of the social malaise and the effectiveness of collective social action to remedy it. In the 1960s, this generalized belief grew
stronger as a result of the writings of social critics, such as John
Kenneth Galbraith, Vance Packard, and Rachel Carson, who articulated social problems and their solutions; hearings conducted
in Congress that identified governmental and legislative reme-
dies; the proconsumer messages of President Kennedy in 1962
and President Johnson in 1966, which legitimated the interest in
consumerism; and the emergence of consumer education organizations that reinforced public interest.

Some precipitating factors in the environment were all that was
needed to ignite the highly combustible social mood. Two sparks
specifically fired the consumer movement of the 1960s. One was
the secret attempt by the General Motors Corporation to discredit
consumer advocate Ralph Nader, thereby elevating him to the
status of a hero. Nader's successful attack against General Motors
encouraged other reformers to undertake actions against other
sectors of the business system. Another factor was the emergence
of spontaneous and widespread consumer boycotts by housewives who picketed grocery stores in search of a better deal.

These precipitating conditions were then reinforced by the mobilization of other resources. Front-page coverage and editorial
support of consumer activities by the newspapers dramatized
consumers' concerns. Numerous politicians at all levels of government began to advocate consumerism because it was a
vote-getting issue. New organizations rose to the defense of
the consumer, including labor unions, consumer cooperatives,

credit unions, product-testing organizations, consumer education groups, senior citizens groups, and public-interest law firms.

The progress and direction of a fledgling social movement often depends on the reaction to it by those in power, who wield social control. A thoughtful co-opting response by leaders can sometimes succeed in draining a social campaign of its force. In the 1960s, however, the opposite occurred with regard to consumerism. The attacks on consumer advocates by many businesses strengthened the advocates' cause. Legislative bodies were slow to respond with positive public policies and programs, showing themselves to be unresponsive to the needs of consumers. Thus, all the requisite conditions for a successful social movement were met.

STAGES OF SOCIAL MOVEMENTS
AND SOCIAL CHANGE CAMPAIGNS

Social movements can succeed, but will they persist? A social movement or campaign is developmental; it goes through changing phases but, as Cameron noted, there are as many life-cycle patterns as there are social movements:

> There is no characteristic life cycle of social movements. . . . If we quantify the development of movement by counting members, amounts of income and expenditures, number of outside persons needed, number of pieces of literature, and so on, we find great variations. . . . Some movements grow very slowly . . . others seem blessed with the vitality and reproductiveness of a mushroom and accumulate personnel and property with great rapidity . . . some skyrocket into prominence and then almost as quickly decline.[19]

Despite the variations in the rates of growth and decline of social movements, many pass through well-defined stages. Each stage is characterized by a particular set of problems, strategic options, and leadership styles. One pattern, identified by Kotler, consists of four stages—crusading, popular cause, managerial, and bureaucratic.[20]

Numerous social movements start out as a crusade led by a few zealous individuals with the ability and charisma to dramatize a social ill. To the extent that their appeal is effective, new supporters are attracted, and the movement can reach the stage of a broad-based popular campaign for change. Still led by the original leaders, the movement is driven at this stage by zealous involvement and the leader's charisma.

As the ranks of the movement swell, new problems arise, such as the need to develop clearer notions of roles and responsibilities and the need to attract financial resources to keep it going. New types of leaders are favored, who have organizational skills. At this point, the movement passes into the managerial stage. The reins of leadership are tightened, and specific goal-setting, planning, and coordination functions are put into place. With luck, the new leaders may retain some of the original zeal.

Finally, the movement may pass into a bureaucratic stage in which the original zeal is lost and the cause for reform is placed in the hands of functionaries whose primary concern is organizational survival. In this late stage, the social movement is run like a business with a product to sell; it has a rigid hierarchy and established policies to maintain functional specialization and control. Even the task of maintaining a following and public support may pass from a charismatic leader to a media specialist.

These stages of a social change campaign are not inevitable or irreversible. Many variations in the pattern of development are possible, including the emergence of a new leader who revives a moribund social movement. The important thing is for social change agents to have the ability to optimize a campaign in each stage, counteracting debilitating influences in one stage and revitalizing the popular appeal in another. Their awareness of the special problems that accompany the various stages will allow them to make sound adaptations in the campaign.

THE MARKETING CHALLENGE OF SOCIAL CHANGE CAMPAIGNS

The preceding analysis of social change campaigns and the factors of success and failure now enables us to specify the core elements in a social change campaign:

- *Cause.* A social objective that change agents believe will provide a desirable answer to a social problem.
- *Change Agent.* An individual, organization, or alliance that

attempts to bring about a social change—that embodies the social change campaign.

- *Target Adopters.* Individuals, groups, or entire populations who are the target of appeals for change by the social marketer.
- *Channels.* Communication and distribution pathways through which influence and response are exchanged and transmitted back and forth between change agents and target adopters.
- *Change Strategy.* The direction and program adopted by a change agent to effect the change in target adopters' attitudes and behavior.

Types of Causes

There are unlimited social issues and causes that might attract social action. Some causes aim to ameliorate a social problem, such as drug abuse or environmental pollution; others attempt to establish rights for certain groups, such as women and minority groups; others try to reform social institutions or sectors, such as education or labor; still others want nothing less than to bring about a revolution in the way society is run. In this book, we emphasize social causes that enjoy widespread public support.

Every social cause has a social objective to achieve. This objective will involve achieving changes in people. In order of difficulty, these include cognitive change, change in action, behavioral change, and change in values.

Many social change campaigns have the limited objective of furnishing new information to people and raising their awareness of some desired goal by bringing about cognitive change in them. These public information or public education campaigns include those that explain the nutritional value of different foods and raise people's awareness of nutrition, inform people of how to avoid exposure to the AIDS virus and impress young people with the benefits of obtaining a higher education. They are relatively easy to carry out because they do not seek to change deep-rooted attitudes or behaviors. Nevertheless, many of these campaigns fall short of their goals because the target adopters and their needs were not researched, the media to communicate new information were poorly chosen, or budgets were inadequate to mount effective programs.

A second class of campaigns seeks to persuade a maximum number of individuals to perform a specific act or practice in a given time. Examples include campaigns to persuade people to be inoculated against a disease in a mass-immunization program; to donate blood; to vote in favor of a referendum for cleaning up the environment; or, in the case of women over age 40, to have an annual Pap test for the early detection of cancer.

Action-oriented campaigns require not only informing a target audience but getting it to commit a discrete act such as voting or immunization. They may involve a cost. Even if an individual's attitude toward an action is favorable, he or she may not carry it out because of time, expense, inconvenience, or plain inertia. For this reason, a change agent in such a campaign must arrange rewards or incentives that are perceived to override the costs.

The goal of yet another set of campaigns may be to induce people to change some behavior for their own well-being. Behavioral campaigns include efforts to get people to quit cigarette smoking, to limit their consumption of alcohol and to change their food habits to combat obesity.

Behavioral change may be harder to achieve than is cognitive or single-action change. People have to unlearn old habits, learn new habits, and maintain the new pattern of behavior. Mass-communication messages typically are insufficient to bring about such changes; they have to be supplemented by interpersonal interventions and personal communications.

The final class of changes involves altering deeply felt beliefs or values. Some examples are campaigns to alter people's ideas about abortion or birth control and to uproot bigotry and general prejudice.

Efforts to change deeply held values typically have a low success rate. A person's sense of identity and well-being is rooted in his or her basic values. Disturbing any one of these values creates stress. People usually try to avoid disturbing information, rationalize it away, or resist such assaults on their values in some other way. Therefore, social change agents prefer to use the law and legal sanctions to promote new behaviors and values that people would not adopt voluntarily. After a while, compliance with a new law can produce the desired changes in attitudes and values. It is possible to induce changes in values by first inducing changes in behavior, since new patterns of behavior can define new ways of looking at things.

Types of Social Change Strategies

Change agents have a variety of methods and tactics at their disposal for influencing target adopters, including lobbying, petitioning, publicity, advertising, and rewarding the desired behavioral change. Behind any set of tactics is a broader conception, or change strategy, of how to achieve social change.

Five major change strategies are technological, economic, political/legal, educational, and social marketing.[21] (A sixth strategy—coercive—is not discussed in this book.) Here we explore the first four strategies; the fifth—social marketing—is examined in Chapter 2. To differentiate the four strategic approaches, we use the example of combating cigarette smoking.

A technological breakthrough, such as air bags in automobiles and oral rehydration solution to combat dehydration in infants who have diarrhea, can lead to a socially desired behavior or practice. Technological solutions, in the case of cigarette smoking, might be of three types.

1. *Product-Modification Technology.* Altering certain features of cigarettes can attenuate the harmful effects of smoking. Examples include altering the genetic structure of tobacco to reduce the level of carcinogens, using filters to reduce the transmission of tar and other particles, or developing "smokeless" or "tobacco-free" cigarettes.

2. *Product-Substitution Technology.* An understanding of the nature of the smoking habit might suggest cigarette substitutes, including the ingestion of nicotine and the use of chewing gum, some forms of which contain nicotine. The smoker's claim that smoking is "something to do with my hands" also has inspired substitutes. Some smokers purchase "worry beads" to dangle and rattle when they are tense; others acquire Steuben Glass crystal "hand coolers" to nestle in the palms of their hands when the urge to smoke arises.

3. *Product-Innovation Technology.* A confirmed smoker may also hope for some product or procedure, such as a smoker's "morning-after pill," which would reduce or eliminate the dangers that accompany smoking. At present, the discovery of a technological approach that would eradicate the adverse effects of smoking is remote.

Economic strategies for social change campaigns seek to impose costs on undesirable behavior and reward desirable behavior. For example, the addition of a substantial "health tax" on each pack of cigarettes might accomplish this goal. Funds could then be allocated for the treatment of the victims of smoking-related diseases. Efforts to reduce smoking by raising the price of cigarettes have had a limited impact, although a high-enough price could be a deterrent. The imposition of a stiff cigarette tax might at least make smokers aware of the negative consequences of smoking, much as dramatically increased gasoline prices in the United States in 1979 impressed consumers with the folly of big cars.

Instead of imposing costs, it may be more effective to reward desired behavior. Some employers encourage nonsmoking by paying a bonus to employees who quit or by subsidizing employees' attendance at smoking withdrawal clinics. Employers figure that the cost of this reward system is rapidly recovered by reduced absenteeism and increased productivity among workers.[22] Some employers refuse to hire smokers or ban smoking in their offices.

An economic strategy for combating smoking can involve the supply side of the economic equation, as well as the demand side. For example, subsidies for tobacco cultivation (including in the United States subsidies for federal and state-supported agricultural research on tobacco cultivation) could be eliminated and farmers could be subsidized to replace tobacco with other crops. Requiring cigarette manufacturers to spend a fixed percentage of their advertising expenditures to research smoking-related diseases is a way of reducing the social costs of cigarette use.

Legal and political means present yet another approach to bring about the cessation of cigarette smoking. Political/legal interventions can take the form of restricting the production, sale, and use of cigarettes. Nonsmokers who are primarily concerned about the health hazard that smokers present have launched political campaigns to win the adoption of restrictive ordinances. Citizens' groups have successfully lobbied legislators to approve ordinances that limit smoking in public places, such as libraries, hospitals, theaters, and restaurants. Legislators can pass laws that restrict the quantity, availability, form, place of consumption, and promotional channels for cigarettes. Medicare, social security, and other benefits might be reduced (or contributions increased) to known smokers on the grounds that they are failing to take reasonable precautions to avoid illness and dependence. Cigarettes might be refused to patients in government-supported hospitals and to others whose medical care is, in any way, subsidized by the government. Currently, most states ban the sale of cigarettes to minors.

Educational approaches constitute the bulk of the antismoking movement in the United States. The belief that the decision to stop smoking can be influenced by information on its negative consequences has shaped the adoption of this approach. The initial response to the first U.S. Surgeon General's Report on Smoking and Health reinforced confidence in the power of information. Its January 1964 publication led millions of smokers to quit smoking or to reduce their cigarette consumption. However, three months later, cigarette consumption had returned to the prereport levels. Subsequent studies indicated that habitual smokers are generally aware of the health risks of smoking but continue to smoke.[23]

Some smokers seem to "blank out" information on the health hazards of smoking; in doing so, they reduce the dissonance between their knowledge and their smoking by dismissing the validity of the information or its applicability to themselves. In Roberto's survey of Filipino smokers, some smokers saw the risk of cancer as real only if one smoked excessively: "You'll only get cancer if you smoke too much." Others thought that changing one's brand often might be harmful: "My own doctor told me that smoking is safe if you stick to one brand." Still others cited their disbelief in the link between smoking and early death: "I know many who don't smoke but who are more sickly than those who smoke. Why is it that Mao Tse-Tung reached the age of 82 even though he was a chain smoker?"[24]

Public education efforts in the United States reflect a mandate for information strategies and assume that target adopters make rational decisions. Most states and school districts require schools to instruct children about the hazards of smoking. The American Cancer Society, the American Heart Association, and the Seventh-Day Adventists distribute antismoking literature. The U.S. government requires that health warnings be printed on cigarette packages and in cigarette advertising. However, the warning "Cigarette smoking is dangerous to your health," although unequivocal, is abstract in that the specific dangers are not cited, and repetition of the message probably diminishes the impact. Sweden requires the printing of a number of different types of specific health messages on cigarette packages.

These social change strategies can be viewed as potentially valuable elements in an antismoking campaign, rather than as a comprehensive social change approach. Their limitations as piecemeal programs can be rendered effective as components of an orchestrated social marketing approach.

2

The Social Marketing Approach to Social Change

Social marketing is a strategy for changing behavior. It combines the best elements of the traditional approaches to social change in an integrated planning and action framework and utilizes advances in communication technology and marketing skills.

THE NATURE AND TASKS OF SOCIAL MARKETING

The term "social marketing" was first introduced in 1971 to describe the use of marketing principles and techniques to advance a social cause, idea, or behavior.[1] Since then, the term has come to mean a social-change management technology involving the design, implementation, and control of programs aimed at increasing the acceptability of a social idea or practice in one or more groups of target adopters. It utilizes concepts of market segmentation, consumer research, product concept development and testing, directed communication, facilitation, incentives, and exchange theory to maximize the target adopters' response. The sponsoring agency pursues the change goals in the belief that they will contribute to the individual's or society's best interests.

What is meant by (1) a social idea or practice, (2) one or more groups of target adopters, and (3) a social-change management technology?

Social Product: Ideas and Practices

Change from an adverse idea or behavior or adoption of new ideas and behaviors is the goal of social marketing. Ideas and behaviors are the "product" to be marketed. Three types of social products are shown in Figure 2-1.

One type is a social idea that may take the form of a belief, attitude, or value. It may be a belief, as in the theme, "Cancer can be checked if detected early enough," which is used in cancer-detection campaigns, or in "Cigarette smoking is hazardous to one's health," which is in anti-cigarette-smoking campaigns. A belief is a perception that is held about a factual matter; it does not include evaluation.

The social idea to be marketed may be an attitude, as exemplified in the expression used in family planning programs, "Planned babies are better cared for than babies from accidental pregnancies." Attitudes are positive or negative evaluations of people, objects, ideas, or events.

The social idea also may be a value, such as "human rights," which is promoted by the many projects of Amnesty Interna-

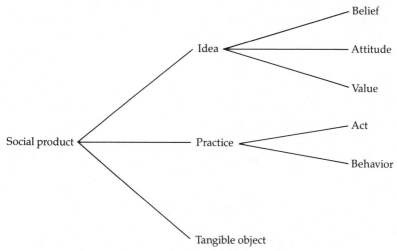

FIGURE 2-1 Social Marketing Products

tional. Values are overall ideas of what is right and wrong. Rokeach suggested that "a person has many beliefs, some attitudes, and few values."[2]

The second type of social product is a social practice. It may be the occurrence of a single act, such as showing up for a vaccination or turning out for a vote. Or it may be the establishment of an altered pattern of behavior, such as quitting smoking or using condoms for birth control.

The third type of social product is a tangible object, such as a contraceptive pill, condom, or foam that is distributed in family planning campaigns or the safety belt for marketing defensive-driving practices. But it should be understood that the main product is not the contraceptive pill, condom, foam, or safety belt; these are tools to accomplish a social practice, which in this case is the practice of family planning or the practice of defensive driving. The tangible-product base refers to physical products that may accompany a campaign.

Social marketers promote ideas as well as social practices; their ultimate aim is to change behavior. Thus, the purpose of a nutrition campaign is not simply to help consumers know about and desire better nutrition, but to change their eating habits. Social advertisers may be content to work at the informational or attitudinal level. Social marketers aim to bring about "purchase and use" and to "close the sale."

The claim was made earlier that social marketing represents an advance over traditional social change strategies. Many of these traditional strategies employed advertising exclusively, rather than probing the needs of clients and consumers to design campaigns that fit them. Social marketing is built around the knowledge gained from business practices: the setting of measurable objectives, research on human needs, targeting products to specialized groups of consumers, the technology of positioning products to fit human needs and wants and effectively communicating their benefits, the constant vigilance to changes in the environment, and the ability to adapt to change.

Target Adopters

Social marketing aims to target one or more groups of target adopters. Consider, for example, a family planning program that wants to distribute contraceptive devices. There are numerous groups that are definable in various ways, such as by age, socio-economic status, family size, or geographic location. Therefore, the social marketer must distinguish such segments of the market as black teenage girls who live in cities, married Hispanic women who do not want any more children, and single white women who want to practice birth control. Since each target-adopter group has a particular set of beliefs, attitudes, and values, social marketing programs are tailored and structured around the needs of each particular segment of a target population.

Social marketing requires knowledge of each target-adopter group, including its

1. sociodemographic characteristics (external attributes of social class, income, education, age, family size, and so forth),
2. psychological profile (internal attributes, such as attitudes, values, motivation, and personality), and
3. behavioral characteristics (patterns of behavior, buying habits, and decision-making characteristics).

To know the target adopters in these three related ways enables the social marketer to make more accurate predictions. Predictions, in turn, are prerequisites to the ability to influence outcomes.

In addition to differentiating among and selecting target-adopter groups, the social marketer will identify influence-holding groups, or influentials, who can affect a program's success. For instance, religious groups may oppose the program, physicians may have to be recruited, funding agencies may have to be solicited, and legislators may have to be apprised of the agency's activities. The aim is to neutralize the opposition and gain the support of influentials for the program. These groups can be classified as follows:

- Permission-granting groups, such as regulatory bodies whose permission or legal authorization may be required for the distribution program to get set up or started.
- Support groups, such as the physicians and other medical staff whose participation or active support is needed for the delivery of services in a clinical contraceptive-distribution program.
- Opposition groups, such as the religious community whose

nonopposition or tolerance of the distribution program may be called for.
- Evaluation groups, such as legislative committees whose postevaluation may have beneficial or adverse effects on the distribution program.

An effective social marketing program requires knowledge of the characteristics of each influence-holding group and addressing the needs of each group with an appropriate "megamarketing" strategy.[3]

Social-Change Management Technology

A social-change management technology must effectively answer the following four questions:

Question	The Task
1. "What is the fit between the idea, or social practice, and what the target-adopter group is looking for?"	Defining the fit
2. "What makes a good fit?"	Designing the fit
3. "How do I bring this fit to my target-adopter group?"	Delivering the fit
4. "How do I sustain or change the fit to defend it against a premature demise?"	Defending the fit

We illustrate these tasks under optimal circumstances in which budgets, time, and personnel are not constraining factors. Social marketers, of course, make adjustments when facing actual constraints in the marketplace.

Defining the Product-Market Fit

The first requirement of success in social marketing is either to create a new social product to meet a need that is not being satisfied or to design a better product than those that are available (see Figure 2–2). It is the very essence of what the marketing literature calls "the marketing concept." According to Kotler, "the marketing concept holds that the key to achieving organizational goals consists in determining the needs and wants of target markets and delivering the desired satisfactions more effectively and efficiently than competitors."[4]

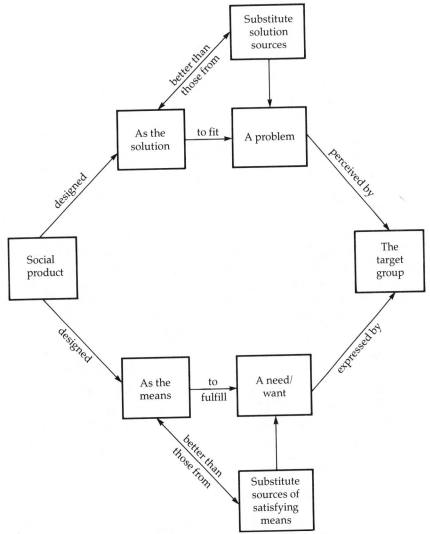

FIGURE 2-2 Defining the Product-Market Fit

It follows that the degree of product-market fit determines the value to the target adopters of what the social marketer is offering. Therefore, the fit affects the perception, attitude, and motivation of the target-adopter group. The wrong fit results in an inadequate or contrary response by target adopters.

How does the social marketer choose the right fit? By knowing the target group inside-out. Thus, the social marketer must research how and why a target-adopter group views a situation in which the social marketer wishes to intervene. Typically, the re-search will reveal that the target-adopter group either has a prob-lem it wants to solve or an objective (a need or a want) that it seeks to achieve. Case 2–1 shows how a social marketing cam-paign defined its problems and needs.

Many causes and social change campaigns fail because their target-adopter group does not perceive a problem, want, or need. Antismoking campaigns are a case in point.[5] Although smokers acknowledge that smoking is a health hazard, many do not see a problem or do not feel any want or need to do anything about the risk. Or in the case of economic-development campaigns in developing countries, particular groups may not want or need economic development. Economic problems cannot be solved, however, unless citizens first recognize that growth is desirable.[6] In these cases, the task of defining the product-market fit be-comes one of raising the salience of a cause or social need and inducing the target-adopter group to perceive its value as a solu-tion to a problem, as a satisfier of a need or want that was over-looked or avoided in the past.

The possibility of a better life through changes in social ideas and processes is not widely perceived in many parts of the world; rather, resignation to the existing order—a fatalistic attitude—pre-vails. For this reason, social change campaigns and social market-ing are not simply a set of tools to accomplish social change. They represent a new ideology, or mindset, the assimilation of which can prepare the ground for widespread and more effective social change.

Designing the Product-Market Fit

The social marketer's next task is to present the solution effec-tively to the target-adopter group. Three marketing inputs are needed for this purpose. The social marketer must (1) translate the fit into the corresponding positioning of the social idea or practice, then (2) dress it up to reinforce the chosen positioning, and then (3) develop a reinforcing image for the cause that is con-sistent with the nature of the cause. This process is illustrated in Figure 2–3 for a case in which a cause has no tangible-product base, and an example is presented in Case 2–2.

Marketing a cause with a tangible-product base requires the ad-ditional stages of positioning and dressing up. At the positioning

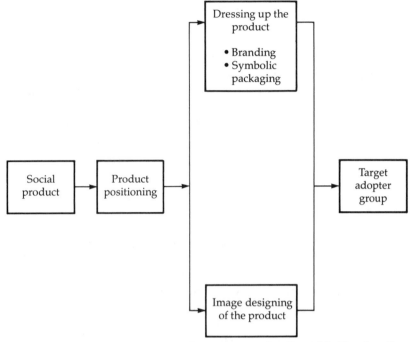

FIGURE 2-3 Designing Social Products that Lack a Tangible-Product Base

stage, the tangible-product base must also be positioned. Consider the example of oral rehydration therapy.

A major cause of infant mortality in the Third World is dehydration resulting from diarrhea. According to Meyers, Block, and Ferguson, "every year, 5 million children under the age of five die due to diarrheal dehydration."[7] Death occurs largely because of ignorance. Children in Third-World countries usually have diarrhea several times a year. When a case gets more severe than usual, a rural mother usually purges the suffering child and stops feeding because she believes this practice will relieve the child. She does not know that the problem is the dehydration that the diarrhea is causing. Soon the child loses appetite and the capacity to absorb liquids through the gut.

Rural mothers often are unable to bring their children to a nearby doctor or hospital for dehydration therapy. Within hours, the children die. Fortunately, there is a home-treatment solution, known as oral rehydration therapy, that the mother can administer directly to the child. This "breakthrough" product, in the form of sacheted oral rehydration powder, is being promoted by the U.S. Agency for International Development to the Third-World ministries of health.

Suppose the social marketer has positioned the therapy as something used by loving and caring mothers. The tangible product—the oral rehydration powder—should then be positioned to reinforce this theme. To position the powder as "a convenient homemade remedy against the Number One killer of infants in the country" may not be as effective as to position it as "a convenient easy-to-follow means that any responsible, loving mother can resort to when her baby has diarrhea."

Another stage involves dressing up the tangible product. The tangible product has to be given a brand name and symbolically packaged; it also has to be physically packaged in a consistent and reinforcing way. Figure 2-4 summarizes the design process for a social change campaign with a tangible-product base.

Delivering the Product-Market Fit

The social marketer now is ready to deliver the desired social practice to the target-adopter group. The required steps are a function of two factors: (1) whether there is a tangible-product base and (2) whether the start and maintenance of the target adopter's acceptance of the social idea or practice requires personal service. Let us trace the effects of each factor on the delivery process.

In the case of a tangible product, the social marketer will arrange with outlets to store, display, and distribute the tangible product. The tangible product may also require a personal presentation and demonstration. In the case of contraceptives, for example, condoms do not require a personal presentation, whereas the intrauterine device (IUD) and the diaphragm do. A personal presentation/demonstration also may be required even when a tangible product is not involved. For example, trainers are necessary to teach literacy skills to a target-adopter group.

There is one further step in the delivery process, namely adoption triggering, or getting the target-adopter group to try or adopt the product. The social marketer will initiate activities that motivate the target-adopter population to act now, rather than later.

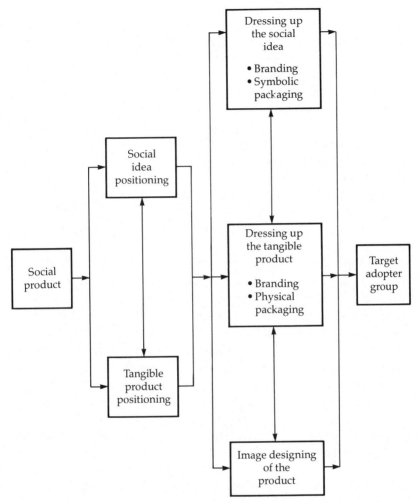

FIGURE 2–4 Designing Social Products with a Tangible-Product Base

In sales parlance, this is called "closing the sale." Such activities include special events, incentives, gatherings, rallies, and other efforts that pull the target adopter into the delivery outlet to try the product.

When a campaign requires a presentation/demonstration, three "P" elements must be managed:

1. the delivery personnel
2. the delivery presentation
3. the delivery process

The presentation/demonstration step must be correctly performed if the target adopter is to be satisfied and motivated to accept the product and advertise it to others. Let us consider an actual case.

An IUD-insertion campaign was conducted by public health and family planning centers in a group of low-income communities in metropolitan Manila, capital of the Philippines. Most of the centers were successful. One center that reported a low acceptance rate explained it by citing women's natural fear of the IUD and its reported side effects. The campaign team found it difficult to accept the center's explanation. Therefore, the director of the campaign team decided to spot check the center by having his wife act as a prospective IUD adopter.

The wife described the activities inside the operating room, where she observed other adopters being "processed" for the IUD insertion. She reported that there were two delivery personnel, a nurse and a doctor, both of whom were uninspiring. The presentation occurred in the operating room of a health center that was crowded, sparsely furnished with only one operating table, had no air conditioning, and was unsanitary in appearance. The process of performing the IUD insertion was quick, abrupt, noncommunicative, and traumatizing. It is small wonder, then, that the rate of acceptance at this clinic was low. In fact, it is a wonder that the clinic had any adopters.

Figure 2–5 summarizes the four possible delivery situations. They are:

- The campaign has a tangible-product base, such as IUDs, that requires a personal presentation or demonstration.
- The campaign has a tangible-product base, such as seat belts, whose delivery does not require a personal presentation or demonstration.
- The campaign (of a literacy program, for instance) has no tangible-product base but its delivery requires a personal presentation or demonstration.
- The campaign (for human rights campaign or against jaywalking, for example) has no tangible-product base and its

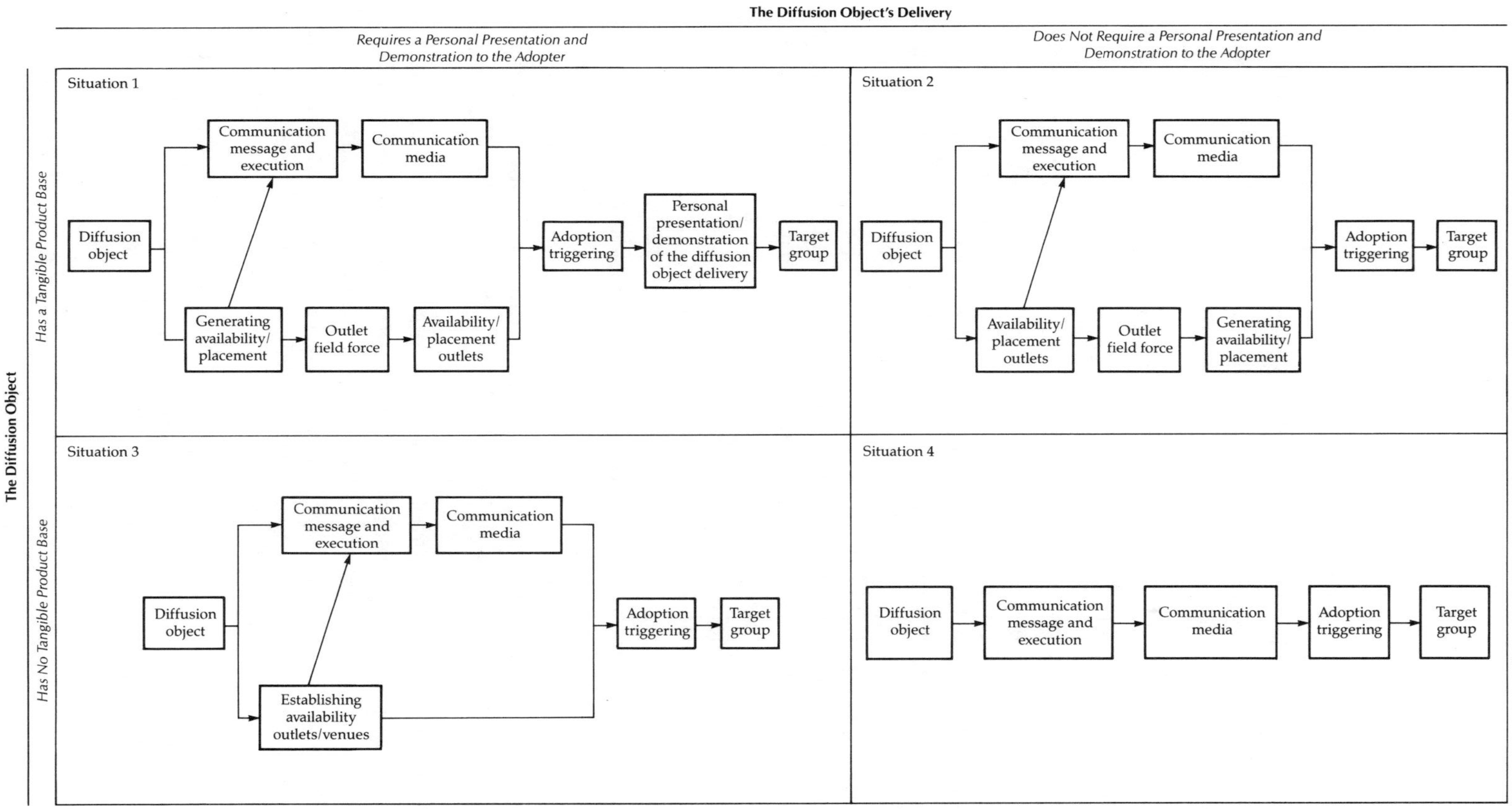

FIGURE 2-5 Four Possible Delivery Situations

delivery does not require a personal presentation/demonstration.

Defending the Product-Market Fit

The final task is to sustain or change the product-market fit to respond to relevant changes in the environment and in the target-adopter population. There are three steps in this stage of a marketing campaign.

First, the target group's condition must be researched and monitored, as in the following example.

> The ministry of health in a Central American country wanted to improve nutrition in the country. The campaign was directed to lower-class mothers in urban and rural areas and involved the marketing of an inexpensive yet nutritionally rich biscuit for children. The biscuit was positioned as a meal product, not as a snack. The product was inexpensive because it was manufactured from two raw materials (wheat and sorghum) donated by two large international agencies and other local ingredients that were cheap sources of protein and vitamin A and B complex. Distribution was through an existing distribution network.
>
> After four months of "encouraging heavy sales," the demand leveled off. A postevaluation survey indicated that most mothers served the product as a snack rather than as a meal, despite the clear statement on the package and in communications that the product should be served for lunch and dinner. Less of the product was consumed as a snack than if it were used as a meal. Also many other snacks for children competed with the product.
>
> The survey revealed that the product's biscuit form, size, shape, packaging, and taste communicated its usage as a snack more strongly than the written messages communicated its usage as a meal. The cause of the leveling off of sales was uncovered, and the product was redesigned to fit better as a meal item.

The second step is the utilization of research. With regard to the nutritional biscuit, for example, here are some possible conclusions that the ministry of health could have drawn:

1. Do not do anything to change the product. Instead, intensify persuasive communication to get mothers to serve the biscuits at mealtime.
2. There is no need to modify the biscuit form. Just increase the protein, vitamin A, and B complex content per biscuit.
3. Modify the form of the product and its packaging to resemble bread, which the target-adopter mothers are used to serving for lunch and dinner.
4. Change the product from a solid to a liquid, such as canned soup, or to powder, as in instant packaged soup, or to a semiliquid, such as porridge.

The issue raised at this stage is, "Which alternative will be most effective?" Further research may be needed to shed light on the alternatives.

In the third step, the social marketer makes the needed adjustments and changes in the marketing plan. Social marketing requires continuous tinkering, or adjustment of fit, as circumstances change. For this reason social marketing can be viewed as a management process that requires vigilant, active management as well as planning.

THE SOCIAL-MARKETING MANAGEMENT PROCESS

Organizations that are engaged in social marketing often do not concentrate their marketing personnel or efforts in one place but usually scatters them throughout several departments. This was the case with the John F. Kennedy Family Service Center, a community social service agency in Charlestown, a section of Boston, which served families who had been dislocated by urban renewal programs. The center operated five departments: (1) Program Development, (2) Day Care Services, (3) Counseling Services, (4) Elderly Service, and (5) Employment Services. Social marketing was conducted in all five departments with little coordination.[8]

Kotler proposed that the following relationship should exist between the program departments and a strategic planning department (see Figure 2-6).[9] Each program department should submit goals and requests for resources to the strategic planning department (Step 1) which would analyze and evaluate them (Step 2).

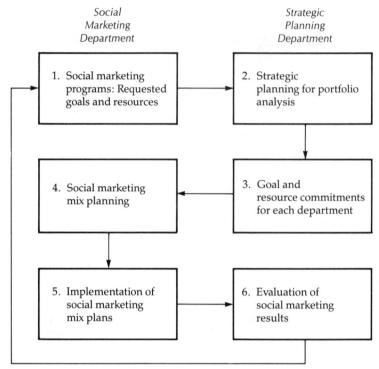

FIGURE 2–6 The Relationship Between Social Marketing and Strategic
Planning
SOURCE: Philip Kotler, *Marketing Management: Analysis, Planning, Implementation and Control*, 6th ed., ©1988, p. 717. Adapted by permission of Prentice-Hall, Inc., Englewood Cliffs, N.J.

The planning department would then negotiate goals and allot resources to each department (Step 3). Each department would formulate marketing-mix plans (Step 4) and implement them (Step 5). The planning department would subsequently evaluate the results (Step 6) and the process would start again. The role of administration, finance, procurement, operations, human resources, and other departments is to support the marketing goals and strategies with the needed four Ms: money, materials, machines, and manpower.

The social-marketing management process consists of analyzing the social marketing environment; researching the target-adopter population; defining the social marketing problem or opportunity; designing social marketing strategies; planning the social marketing-mix programs; and organizing, implementing, controlling, and evaluating the social marketing effort. The remainder of this chapter presents an overview of the entire process. Figure 2–7 and Cases 2–3 and 2–4 illustrate the steps in the process; the reader is advised to read these cases before going on.

Analyzing the Social Marketing Environment

The first step in the social-marketing management process is to analyze the environment immediately surrounding the particular social campaign. In the case of the Condom Social Marketing Program (CSMP) in the Philippines, the management first looked into the target-adopter population's situation with regard to contraceptives.[10] This review indicated many couples wanted to plan their family and practice contraception. The problem, however,

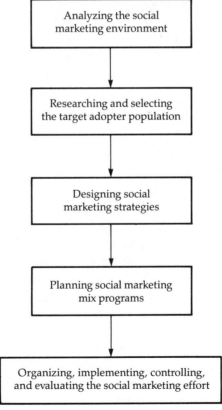

FIGURE 2-7 Steps in the Social-Marketing Management Process

was their lack of access to available and inexpensive contraceptive methods. The next step was to review the sponsoring organization's ability to distribute contraceptives. This review concluded that (1) the sponsoring organization's distribution capability was extremely inadequate and (2) the private sector had superior size and reach but was suitable only for the distribution of contraceptives that do not require clinical treatment, for example, condoms and spermicides, rather than pills and IUDs.

This analysis led to the following conclusion: the best way to reach the target-adopter group was a campaign restricted to nonclinical contraceptives using the distribution capabilities of the private sector.

In the case of the Canadian Action on Drug Abuse campaign, the management team reviewed the drug programs in Canada, as well as pertinent past research studies.[11] They concluded that the long-term solution to the drug abuse problem in Canada rests with the segment of the population for which abuse is most serious—young people, aged 11–17—together with their parents. This conclusion defined the appropriate target-adopter segment and therefore helped shape the next step in the management process: researching the target-adopter group.

Researching the Target-Adopter Population

Social marketers need to achieve a thorough understanding of the target-adopter group and its needs. Adopter segmentation is the task of breaking the total target-adopter population into segments that have common characteristics in responding to a social campaign. Social marketers can perform this task in a number of ways.

The CSMP management team, for example, could segment the "favorably predisposed population of couples" by (1) the nonclinical contraceptive methods they want or prefer and by (2) their socioeconomic status. The available nonclinical methods include the condom and spermicides, such as jellies, creams, and foams. Available measures of socioeconomic status were Class AB (the upper class), Class C (the middle class), and Class DE (the lower class). Crossing these two broad variables yields the target-adopter segmentation grid shown in Figure 2–8. The CSMP management could then estimate which of the six segments has the most need for contraception and is the most reachable by the program.

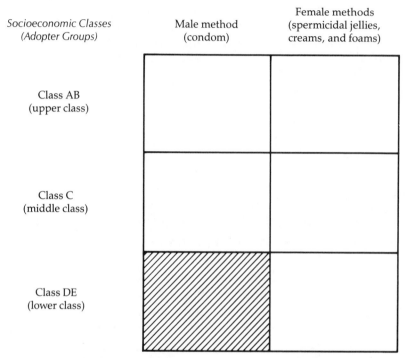

FIGURE 2–8 A Target-Adopter Segmentation Grid for Nonclinical Contraceptives

Suppose the most needy and reachable segment is the "condom-predisposed lower-class" segment, the shaded cell in Figure 2–8. Since even this segment may be larger than what the program organization can serve, the CSMP management might need to divide up the group further by, say, geographic areas. CSMP might find that the best target-adopter segment is the condom-predisposed lower-class segment in metropolitan Manila.

The program would then need to develop a positioning strategy for this segment. The aim of positioning is to satisfy the target-adopter segment's need and to do so better than others.

The key task is to identify the competition. The competition, however, is not other brands of condoms and other nonclinical contraceptives. The CSMP social marketers are committed to encouraging the practice of contraception, whatever the form. Thus, the competition is the nonpractice of contraceptive behavior. The same conclusion applies to the Canadian Action on Drug Abuse campaign. The competition is not other antidrug programs; it is the practice of drug abuse.

The question of the needs of the target adopters now becomes more specific and strategic. What, for example, does drug use satisfy? Only when the social marketers find a satisfactory answer can they find a satisfactory "positioning" of their program.

Designing Social Marketing Objectives and Strategies

The social marketing strategy specifies the game plan for achieving the objectives of the social marketing campaign. It defines the broad principles by which the social organization expects to attain its objectives in a target-adopter segment. It consists of basic decisions on the total marketing expenditures, marketing mix, and marketing allocation.

Social marketers must first set specific, measurable, and attainable social marketing objectives. This may sound easy to do, but it is not. Consider the criteria of "specific" and "measurable" objectives. Social organizations tend to state their program objectives in broad terms like "raising the quality of life," "raising children's social competence," "empowering people," "conserving energy," "preventing crimes," and so on. Because these objectives are nonspecific, they are also nonmeasurable.

Some social scientists, however, take issue with the notion that program objectives should be measurable. For example, Corwin believes that this idea is based on a mistaken simplistic model of change in social organizations:

> These assumptions are unreasonable in most cases, because in practice [social] organizations constantly elaborate new goals and shift priorities as a condition of their existence; they are faced with constraints beyond their control; and seldom is power sufficiently concentrated . . . to permit the kind of internal control necessary to implement a program as planned.[12]

But the argument could apply just as well to business organizations that face a constantly changing environment but establish specific and measurable objectives. The fact is that business organizations have decided to stand up on their own and attempt to master the forces of change.

How can social marketers designate specific and measurable objectives? Samuels suggested that they can start with broadly stated objectives but then identify the specific behavior and actions of target adopters that manifest the broadly stated objectives.[13] Several clarifying examples are presented in Table 2–1.

The measurement of the more specific actions of target adopters will typically require the collection of primary data. For this, social marketers must undertake social marketing research. Program objectives may be called "goals."

What about the criterion of attainability? This criterion considers the motivational and control aspects of objectives. Objectives should not be set so high that they cannot be attained with the available resources or so low as to be unchallenging. When the objectives are too high, the people in the organization lose the motivation to achieve them.

Having set the objectives of the program, social marketers must now decide what level of social marketing expenditures is needed to attain them. This step calls for some budgeting effort. The conventional budgeting approach is by "target setting," using some acceptable expenditure-to-goal ratio. For example, suppose a similar program a few years ago cost $10 per target adopter reached.

TABLE 2–1 Designating Specific Measurable Objectives from Broadly Stated Ones

Broad Objectives	Related Adopter Behavior/Actions or Manifestations
1. Prevention of accidents & their related social & economic costs	a. Wearing seat belts. b. Maintaining safe following distances. c. Reducing drinking before driving. d. "Correct" pedestrian behavior.
2. Energy conservation	a. Promoting energy consciousness. b. Installing energy-saving devices (e.g., loft insulation, etc.).
3. Crime prevention	a. Locking car doors. b. Keeping valuables out of sight.
4. Fire prevention	a. Keeping matches out of chidren's reach. b. Education in how to cope with chip-pan fires.

SOURCE: John Samuels, "Evaluating Social Persuasion Advertising Campaigns—An Overview of Recent C.O.I. Experience." Paper presented at a seminar on communication and social research organized by ESOMAR (European Society for Marketing and Opinion Research), London, 1977.

Assume that the cost per target adopter has risen 10 percent, to $11. If the current target is 1,000 adopters, the marketing expenditure is $11,000 ($11 x 1,000).

As social marketers gain budgeting experience, they find that it makes better sense to analyze the marketing expenditures required to reach various numbers of target adopters. To do so, they must predict how many adopters would respond to alternative levels of marketing expenditure—the adoption-response function.

Social marketers must next decide how to allocate the budget to the several tools in the social-marketing mix that the social organization will use to pursue its objectives in the target-adopter segment or segments. These tools, known as the four Ps, are the

- product: the offer made to the target adopters (including services, quality, features, options, style, brand name, packaging, sizes, warranties, and returns).
- price: the costs that target adopters have to bear (including the list price, discounts, allowances, payment period, and credit terms, as well as the nonmonetary costs of time, effort, and stress).
- place: the means by which the social product is delivered to the target adopters (including distribution outlets and channels for delivering services, both governmental and in the private sector; location, inventory, and transport).
- promotion: the means by which the social product is promoted to the target adopters (including advertising, personal selling, sales promotion, and public relations).

Social marketers have suggested adding three additional Ps to the 4-P classification, especially in connection with the delivery of services:

- personnel: those who sell and deliver the social product to the target adopters.
- presentation: the visible sensory elements of the setting in which the target adopters acquire or use the social product.
- process: the steps through which target adopters go to acquire the social product.

The important point is that the social-marketing mix consists of many specific tools, regardless of their overall classification. The considerable number of tools gives rise to many possible marketing strategies.

The social agency must formulate a social-marketing mix not only for the target adopters but for the distribution outlets. Figure 2–9 shows a social agency preparing an offer mix of social products and services and their prices and using a promotion mix of mass communication, direct nonpersonal communication, direct personal communication, and promotion incentives to reach the distribution outlets and the target adopters. In the example of CSMP, the distribution outlets included neighborhood shops, stalls at public markets, groceries, drugstores, bazaars, department stores, and supermarkets. The distribution outlets for the social marketing of an idea are the media. The social marketers of an antidrug campaign must reach out to the operators of television, radio, print, and direct media and treat them as an intermediate target-adopter segment.

Social marketing tools vary in their degree of adjustability. Social marketers can quickly adjust the prices, assignment of sales-

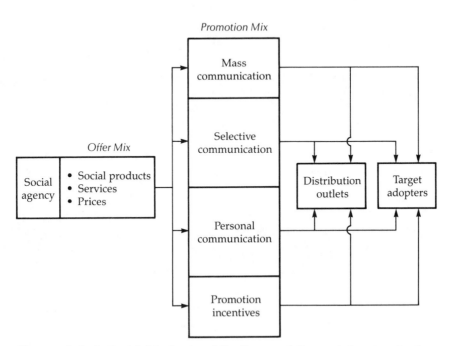

FIGURE 2–9 A Social Marketing Mix Targeted Toward Service Outlets and Target Adopters

people, and frequency and reach of communication. However, many other tools take longer to adjust, such as the number of trained salespeople, the number of distribution outlets, and the physical products.

An added complexity is that social marketing tools are interdependent, rather than independent, in their impact on the target market. Some tools may turn out to be incompatible even when previous work has established that they are effective. This problem is illustrated in Case 2–3. Although CSMP offered high-quality condoms, the CSMP management team chose a low price. This price was best from the standpoint of making condoms affordable to the target segment, but it might convey the image that CSMP was offering a low-quality product.

The next step is to allocate the budget to the various elements of the social-marketing mix. How much should go to direct non-personal versus direct personal communication? To promotion incentives versus better service delivery? If social marketers knew how adoption of the product would be affected by each possible allocation, then the answers would be readily apparent. If social marketers could anticipate the acceptance levels of the target-adopter groups, then the allocation problem would be rationally solvable.

Planning Social Marketing Programs

After the broad strategy is formulated the management of more detailed social-marketing-mix programs must be prepared. Consider the CSMP's marketing project once again. The first element of the social-marketing mix to be formulated is the social product. The tactical program for the social product included determining the following:

1. How condoms were to be positioned on the basis of research into target adopters' perceptions, attitudes, and motivations about the use of contraceptives and condoms.
2. The suitable "brand" name that would reinforce the product's positioning.
3. Suitable packaging, including the material, size, shape, label, color, and wording on the package.

Then the marketing-mix elements of mass and selective communication must be turned into tactical programs. For CSMP this step encompassed these actions:

1. carefully choosing the advertising agency,
2. designing and presenting the advertisements,
3. selecting the right media and timing.

Tactical programs must also be developed for distribution and direct personal communication. In CSMP's case, careful tactical programming for these two revealed serious problems. Although the commercial sector's distribution capabilities were far superior to the government's, they were not geared toward marketing social products. Selling social products demands different skills and attitudes than the marketing sales force of a business normally exhibits. These problems were not evident at the higher level of strategy formulation.

Pricing is another marketing tool that requires its own tactical program. It must also take other target-adopter costs into consideration.

The target-adopter promotion program aims to present target adopters with inducements to act now. The appropriate tactical measures to accomplish this vary from one social product to another.

Finally, social marketers must work out the tactical program for delivering services. The social product determines the appropriate type of delivery. For example, the type of service delivery system needed by the CSMP, a tangible-product-based campaign dealing with the distribution of condoms, would be different from that needed by the Action on Drug Abuse campaign, a heavily service-based campaign.

Organizing, Implementing, Controlling and Evaluating the Social Marketing Effort

In the social marketing management process, the final step is to organize the marketing resources, implement the social-marketing-mix programs, control the performance of the programs, and evaluate the results (the social and ethical impact) of that implementation. A well-known management principle stresses that even the best and most carefully drawn plan gets nowhere until it is effectively implemented and controlled. Effective control and evaluation require data about the target-adopter group's responses to the implemented social program, which are generated by social marketing research.

CASE 2–1
Defining Problems and Needs: An Example

A government survey of residents in a South American city illustrates how a target group perceived a distinction among a problem, a need, and a want. The survey first asked the city residents what problems they saw in regard to various city services such as potable water, garbage disposal, flood control, traffic regulation, peace and order, and so on. Specifically, three questions were asked for each city problem:

To what extent do you feel [city problem] is a concern to you and to the rest of the residents of this city? Would you say it is a concern: 4 = to a very great extent, 3 = to quite an extent, 2 = to some extent, or 1 = not really a concern?

How often would you say that you and the people here consider [city problem] that kind of concern when thinking or talking about city problems? Would you say: 4 = practically all of the time when you talk about city problems, 3 = many of the times . . . , 2 = a few of the times . . . , or 1 = almost none of those times . . . ?

How serious a concern for the city is [city problem]? Would you say it is: 4 = very serious, 3 = quite serious, 2 = somewhat serious, or 1 = not really serious?

For each problem, the scores of each respondent on the three questions were multiplied to obtain an index of problem importance. Each problem's problem importance index was then used to rank the problems. The rank ordering made it possible to identify the city's major problem.

Next, the survey asked the respondents to react to the city's current services by answering the following two questions:

To what extent would you say that you expect each city service? Would you say that you look for this: 4 = a whole lot, 3 = pretty much, 2 = somewhat, or 1 = not really?

How do you feel about each of these city services? Would you say that: 4 = you most likely cannot do without this one, 3 = you probably cannot do without this one, 2 = you probably can do without this one, or 1 = you most likely can do without this one?

The first question measured city services that people wanted and the second, those that people needed.

The city mayor who commissioned the survey expected that the citizens would rank the city services the same whether the focus was on problems, wants, or needs. However, the results of the survey did not bear this out. The major problem was identified as garbage collection, the greatest need was for potable water, and the strongest want was for flood control.

Once the major problem, need, and want are identified, the task then is to design the social product as a superior solution to the problem or means of fulfilling the target-adopter group's want or need. Figure 2–2 highlights these points (see p. 29).

The search for a superior solution or want satisfier is not easy. For example, in one of its antismoking brochures, the American Cancer Society suggested to smokers "Twelve Things to Do instead of Smoking Cigarettes." Although each suggestion would satisfy the smoker's need "to relax or fill his time," none appeared to the target-adopter group as superior to smoking as a means of relaxing and filling one's time.

CASE 2–2
Amnesty International

Amnesty International has pioneered in the "international protection of human rights" of prisoners.[14] The goal of one of its major continuing projects is to "arouse world opinion [for] the release of men and women detained anywhere for their beliefs, color, sex, ethnic origin, language or religion." The social product here is the social idea the "people of all walks of life should work impartially and peacefully for the release of . . . men and women imprisoned . . . for their political and religious beliefs." The target-adopter group is the "more than 350,000 [Amnesty International] members, subscribers and supporters in over 150 countries and territories."

The designing process involved positioning Amnesty International as an organization that does something for world peace. The positioning statement uses the words of Albert Schweitzer: "World peace can only be achieved when there is freedom for people of all politics, religion and races to exchange their views in a continuing dialogue."

To implement this positioning, the social product was dressed up with the brand name of "freeing prisoners of conscience" and with the symbolic packaging, which represents the movement as "a lighted candle surrounded by barbed wire." Another support came from positioning the source, Amnesty International, as "an impartial independent worldwide movement . . . concerned solely with the protection of human rights . . . regardless of either the ideology of the government or the beliefs of the victims."

CASE 2-3
Getting Contraception Through Condom Usage Accepted and Practiced in the Philippines

Social Marketing Environment

In a 1973 Philippine National Demographic Survey, close to 80 percent of the eligible population—married women of reproductive age, 14–45 years—expressed the desire to practice contraception. Demographers concluded that by concentrating on this predisposed segment, the country's population program could achieve the 10-year demographic objective of reducing population growth from a 3.1 percent annual rate to 2.0 percent.

Decreasing this rate depended, however, on making available to target adopters everywhere in the country the contraceptive products they preferred. At the time the population program's distribution capability was limited to 2,400 government-sponsored family planning clinics. According to a subsequent survey, these clinics could reach only 38 percent of the target-adopter population.

The Philippine Population Commission, the national agency responsible for family planning, recognized the need to build alternative systems for delivering contraceptive products to those who wanted them. An alternative system was found in the private sector. The private business sector already had a vast distribution network, numbering some 200,000 stores throughout the coun-

SOURCE: Eduardo L. Roberto; "Social Marketing and Its Applications: A State of the Art Review." Research paper prepared for the World Bank, Washington, D.C., 1987.

try. The vast majority of these outlets were small *sari-sari* neighborhood stores that supplied the daily needs of a community and served as gathering places for social activities. Although fewer in number, other types of outlets, such as groceries, supermarkets, drugstores, bazaars, and stalls in public markets served a large volume of customers daily. These business outlets, together, were far more numerous than were the family planning clinics.

This business network was not only vast but efficient. Wholesalers supplied retail outlets with their goods. In turn, a number of national and regional distributors supplied the wholesalers. According to industry sources, an average-sized distributor, by employing only two salespeople, could reach as many business outlets in a month as could the total number of family planning clinics. The business outlets also reached a large number of customers, according to a 1973 study.[15] Retail outlets typically were clustered in urban neighborhoods. For example, in one neighborhood, there were 6 drug outlets within a five-minute walk of each other and 16 retail stores. Retail outlets carried contraceptives and served far more customers per store than did a family planning clinic: an average of 80 contraceptive customers a day compared to 23 per month at the clinics.

The Social Marketing Strategy

In 1975 the staff of the population program determined that the target-adopter population consisted of 1.1 million couples. However, since the business outlets could provide only nonclinical contraceptive products, the program would have to build acceptance among the target-adopter group for the use of such products as condoms. Furthermore, only the U.S. Agency for International Development (AID), the source of supply, could offer condoms in the volume required. This became the basis of CSMP. The strategy for reaching target adopters was distribution-led. The objective was to reach eligible couples who preferred to practice contraception with the use of condoms and who had access to retail outlets. Studies showed that in this target-adopter segment, the easy availability of condoms at convenient locations was the key to closing the gap between the inclination and actual adoption of family planning.

A distribution-led social marketing strategy first had to be tested in a pilot area to assess its strengths and weaknesses. Because the retail outlets were more widespread in urban areas, the pilot area chosen was urban, the Metro Manila area. CSMP, at least initially, could not reach rural groups on a similar scale. For that purpose, the Philippine Population Commission's rural facilities constituted the best delivery channels.

Social-Marketing-Mix Programs: Product Positioning

CSMP planned its social marketing mix to include product positioning, branding and packaging, advertising, selling and distribution, pricing, promotion, and point-of-purchase service delivery.

In designing a positioning program, CSMP assessed the target-adopter segment's contraceptive needs, particularly its acceptance of the condom. Qualitative research was gained through six focus-group interviews with condom-using couples. These interviews generated a comprehensive list of the target-adopters' felt "needs" for contraception in general and the condom in particular. The major findings were as follows:

1. A critical factor in triggering the husband's trial, retrial, and continued use of condoms was the wife. The wife's perception that condoms cause pain would immediately terminate its use. A wife's approval led to her husband's continued use.

2. Perceptions of the negative aspects of condoms were more imagined than real. They included the lessening of sexual pleasure, the suitability of condoms only for prostitutes, and nondurability.

3. Sustained use of condoms removed from the user's mind many but not all the negative perceptions of them.

4. Condom users appreciated the many positive features, such as the absence of side effects, the need to use condoms only when required (unlike the pill), and the inexpensiveness and convenience of condoms.

5. Continuous condom use, however, did not guarantee awareness of its positive characteristics; misperceptions in users' minds still had to be allayed.

CSMP used these findings in the second phase of product positioning, which modeled the target-adopter group's need for condoms by means of additional quantitative research. CSMP concluded from the research that the attitudes and practices of wives were the most significant marketing factors in motivating men to use condoms. These findings were translated into a positioning concept: "The use of condoms is what wives expect of husbands, and husbands owe it to their wives to use them."

The Branding and Packaging Program

With the adoption of a positioning concept, CSMP moved to a decision on an effective brand name that would reinforce product positioning. The AID-supplied condoms already carried the name Conform on the individual pieces. Should the testing of target adopters find that another brand name was desirable, CSMP would use the new brand name on the packages placed in store outlets. The project team tested 48 different brand names; the name finally chosen was Family Planning Condom. The product packaging for the condoms could not be modified; however, the store display could be designed. CSMP then asked an advertising agency for packaging "studies." These studies tested target adopters' reactions regarding material, label, size, color, shape, and copy. A package design was chosen for its recognizability and reinforcement of product positioning.

The Advertising Program

To develop its advertising program, CSMP first searched for an advertising agency. Three criteria were employed in the search: (1) experience and track record in the successful advertising of a personal, intimate product, (2) an advertising manager who was familiar with family planning and population control; and (3) willingness to follow closely the CSMP marketing schedule. No single agency satisfied all three criteria, but the agency that proposed "a demand-creating campaign plan" was chosen.

Close supervision began with the first advertising decision: what to say (the ad message) and how to say the message (the ad execution). The ad message already was determined by the choice of a positioning concept. The advertising agency presented two alternative proposals: one conveying the husband's viewpoint and one conveying the wife's. Each proposal was pretested with a sample of target adopters. The pretest asked respondents about their (1) feelings and thoughts about what they saw and read, (2) perceptions of the pretest ad, (3) perceptions of the advertised product, and (4) interest in using the product on a trial basis. The pretest results showed similar ratings of effectiveness for each ad execution, and CSMP decided to use them both.

The next decision was which of the media to use. The major challenge was to replace a condom's negative image with an appealing one; therefore, condoms needed a "respectable" image. The campaign needed a primary medium that was credible to target adopters, and the print media were found to be the most credible. Because readers perceived the editorial page of a newspaper as the most credible, condom ads would then be placed on the page opposite the editorials.

Budget constraints also narrowed the choice of media. Electronic media were too costly. Moreover, on television, ads for cigarettes and liquor would overwhelm an ad for condoms. Radio was rejected because of the large number of stations and the incompleteness of data on radio's advertising reach.

The Distribution and Selling Program

In the Metro Manila pilot-test area, CSMP had to make condoms available to a large number of retail outlets, as follows:

Type of Outlet	Number	Percentage of Total
Neighborhood stores	32,632	89.9
Public market stalls	2,182	6.0
Drugstores	929	2.6
Groceries	355	1.0
Bazaars	133	0.3
Supermarkets	29	0.1
Department stores	29	0.1
Total	36,289	100.0

To reach a majority of these outlets effectively, CSMP had to find a distributor that was organized to distribute directly to retail outlets through a sales force; indirect sales through intermediaries, such as wholesalers, were too inefficient. Once a distributor was found, a large-enough base of cooperative retail outlets would be established that later would interest wholesalers.

The CSMP team approached seven large distributors, offering the following terms: (1) a liberal 30 percent distribution fee versus the prevailing 20 percent, (2) advertising support, (3) merchandising support consisting of posters, dispensers, sales organizers, shelf talkers, signboards, and shelf strips, (4) sales training and incentives, and (5) trade-promotion support. Only four distributors expressed interest, and after two months of negotiation, only one remained, and it proved unsatisfactory. This distributor made excessive demands, including a minimum guaranteed payment for services, regardless of whether targets were met, and a 30 percent commission if targets were exceeded.

The experience taught CSMP a lesson. CSMP concluded that although the retail distribution network was far superior to the 2,400 family planning clinics in making contraceptives available, it was not set up to "handle" a social product, even on liberal terms. Ultimately, CSMP found a high-volume distributor that operated through wholesalers and jobbers.

The Pricing Program

The pricing program required a sensitive decision. Part of the Philippine Population Commission argued that condoms should be distributed free to reach the greatest number of people. This approach, however, would not have offered incentives to attract commercial distributors and was rejected. CSMP surveyed family planning clinics. The survey indicated that the so-called free condoms were not actually free. Family planning clinics asked their clients to "donate" from 25 to 50 centavos for each condom. CSMP then decided on the high end of the donation rates, namely, 50 centavos—still a low price relative to commercially available condoms. At this retail price, it was determined, the program had the best chance of becoming self-sustaining and would later attract many other distributors and outlets.

The Adoption-Promotion Program

The adoption-promotion program ingeniously pursued two trial purchase-and-use plans for target-adopter groups. The first attempted to stimulate the movement of the product down the distribution pipeline to create an image that the product was "taking off." To accomplish this goal, CSMP intervened in the "natural" flow of the product from distributor to wholesaler to retail outlet. A task force of "distribution sweepers" was organized to go store to store to sell the condom. Selected retail outlets were persuaded to carry the line of condoms by guaranteeing sales of 80 to 100 percent of the inventory within two weeks. A second task force of "promotional buyers" was organized to buy the condoms. The funds for the promotional buyers were chargeable to product promotion. Buyers visited retail outlets that sweepers had covered, acting like ordinary consumers, and purchased the condoms that were then returned to CSMP's inventory. When retail outlets experienced the 80–100 percent "movement" of condoms from the shelves, most contacted their wholesalers for additional stocks. This plan involved, of course, artificial movement. The true purchasers, target adopters, had yet to be enlisted. To complement this product-movement plan in the retail outlets, a product-sampling campaign to motivate real buyers was organized.

A product-sampling task force of three people was hired to distribute samples of condoms at the two gates of a basketball coliseum with a seating capacity of 30,000. Spectators were handed a sample condom in a folder pack that carried advertising copy. The samplers estimated that 30 percent of those offered the samples refused them and that the 70 percent who took the sample would try it. If they liked the condom they would use it again. Thus began the real movement of condoms among customers, who then purchased them in stores.

The Point-of-Purchase Service Delivery Program

CSMP recognized that the program required a point-of-purchase service delivery program in non-drugstore outlets, since this was the first time that stores carried condoms on their shelves. There was no certainty that condoms would sell in these novel retail environments.

To design this service program, CSMP researched the in-store behavior of shoppers, first in the supermarkets. This study found the following:

1. Of the shoppers who passed the shelf where condoms were displayed, 83 percent stopped to look.
2. Of those who stopped to look, 19 percent picked up a piece and inspected it; many of the rest moved to the other side of the shelf and returned later to check out the product pack.
3. Of the 72 percent who went around the shelf and then re-

turned, 91 percent did so because someone else was in the aisle where the condom packs were displayed.

4. Of those who inspected the condom package, 88 percent put some in their shopping cart (most of them placed the pack underneath other grocery items).

5. Near or at the check-out counter, 70 percent of those with condoms in their cart returned them to a nearby shelf or display rack.

A second study of neighborhood shops uncovered similar embarrassed behavior. CSMP concluded that the service delivery program had to find a way to spare the buyer embarrassment. Less-conspicuous product-and-shelf locations and point-of-purchase arrangements were sought in supermarkets. It was discovered that two sections in a typical supermarket had their own cashiers—hardware and cosmetics. CSMP persuaded supermarket operators to reposition the condoms from the drug section to the cosmetics section. Shoppers then were able to purchase condoms without being seen by many people.

Implementation, Control, and Evaluation

CSMP relied on private-sector organizations for implementation. These organizations became subcontractors who syndicated their services to distribution agencies, advertising agencies, merchandising and trade-position agencies, selling agencies, and consumer-promotion agencies to achieve an integrated social marketing effort.

For the purposes of control, CSMP utilized "operational evaluation" methods, to determine the "cause-effect" impact of the program. However, this plan was never implemented. A number of ethical issues were raised in a number of quarters about CSMP. A Catholic Church group called the Catholic Women's League (CWL) challenged the program on the "morality of its focus on one contraceptive method." The group also had a legal basis for their opposition. The National Population Program had, at the start, committed itself to a "cafeteria policy" with respect to contraceptive methods. The policy meant that the Philippine Population Commission would not favor any single method in its efforts to deliver family planing services. The CWL interpreted CSMP as a violation of this policy. Addressing the ethical side of CSMP was never part of its evaluation plans.

CASE 2–4
Getting Action on Drug Abuse
among the Youths in Canada

Social Marketing Environment

Canada's Ministry of Health identified drug abuse as a leading cause of highway accidents and fatalities, the loss of productivity in the workplace, and the mounting inpatient and outpatient caseloads in hospitals. Its Health Services and Promotion Branch (HSPB) identified both legal and illegal drugs, such as alcohol, prescription drugs, over-the-counter drugs, and solvents. The most abused drugs were alcohol, tranquilizers, and sedatives.

HSPB estimated that over 600,000 Canadians, out of a population of 25 million, were dependent on alcohol. Many more were drinking their way to dependence, even though, it was acknowledged, Canadians tend to minimize alcohol's potential harm and many do not consider it a drug. Canadians also ranked among the world's biggest users per capita of legal psychoactive drugs, such as tranquilizers and sedatives. A 1985 survey indicated that 1.1 million Canadians had used cannabis (marijuana) in the previous year.[16]

The Target-Adopter Population

In 1987 the government of Canada mounted a five-year National Drug Strategy to confront the country's drug abuse problem. This initiative aimed to decrease the "harm to individuals, families and communities from the abuse of drugs through a balanced approach." Six elements constituted this balanced approach: (1) education and prevention, (2) treatment and rehabilitation, (3) enforcement and control, (4) information and research, (5) international cooperation, and (6) national focus. Of these six ele-

SOURCE: James H. Mintz and Colin May, "Action on Drug Abuse: 'Really Me,' Canada's Program in Alcohol and Other Drugs." Paper presented at the 38th International Congress on Alcoholism and Drug Dependence, Oslo, 1988.

ments, the first (education and prevention) absorbed close to 75 percent of the program's allocated $210 million budget. Anti-drug-abuse planners justified this priority by stating that it struck at "the root cause of the problem"—the demand for drugs and the need to reduce that demand. The program's second element, although addressing the source of the demand, did so after the harm had already taken place. Other elements attacked the "supply" side of the drug problem.

In the education and prevention program, HSPB identified youths and their parents as the most important target-adopter group. Parents were critical because they exerted considerable influence on the youths. HSPB research revealed the following:

1. Alcohol and drug use had become widespread and was increasing among youths.
2. Parents were poorly informed about drugs.
3. A wide gap in information and perceptions about drugs separated the parents and the youths, and their lack of communication was itself a problem.

The Social Marketing Strategy

To reach the target youths and their parents, HSPB decided on a public awareness, information, and persuasion strategy. The planners determined that education and prevention would be effectuated in the initial year by accomplishing three objectives:

1. Making the youths and their parents aware of the drug problem.
2. Informing the youths and their parents about the damage of drugs to the body and the mind.
3. Persuading the youths about the benefits of a lifestyle free of alcohol and other drugs and persuading the parents of the need to discuss drug use openly with their children.

Social-Marketing-Mix Programs

A communication campaign was launched to translate the objectives into a positioning concept. The choice was to focus on the factual nature of the harmfulness of drugs (its believability) or on the evaluative response to drugs—the attitude toward its positive or negative characteristics. Another choice involved a focus on youths versus parents. HSPB chose attitude and youth and adopted the branding "Really Me?"

Distribution

To expose the "Really Me?" idea to youths and their parents, HSPB had to find a message distributor and selected an advertising agency. For the primary distribution channels, selected television and radio stations were chosen as an assured way of reaching young people and their parents. Supplementary channels to reinforce the primary media were bus and subway media, magazines, and booklets.

Adoption Promotion

To raise awareness of the "Really Me?" concept, HSPB programmed some special events:

1. It sponsored a two-day National Forum on Drug Awareness in Winnipeg to assist community volunteers, drug addiction specialists, and other health and social service professionals to acquire information and skills for developing community awareness programs.
2. It declared a National Drug Awareness Week across the country, with planned and widely publicized provincial and territorial drug-awareness activities.
3. It gained private-sector participation through *Really Me* booklets and messages tied to the product line of Canada's largest manufacturer of school supplies and a sweatshirt promotion campaign launched by the ministers of health and welfare and of youth and a corporate leader.
4. It aired a one-hour prime-time special on the "Really Me" campaign on English and French language radio and television stations.
5. It disseminated a *Really Me* calendar/magazine in 1.3 million school binders, called Note Totes, which were distributed through retail stores and provincial drug addiction and prevention agencies.

Implementation and Control

HSPB implemented the "Really Me?" campaign through a project office, Health and Welfare Canada (HWC), which cooperated with other governmental agencies, including the Royal Canadian Mounted Police, Correctional Service of Canada, the Ministry of Justice, the Ministry of Revenue (Customs and Excise Offices), the External Affairs Ministry, and the Ministry of State for Youth. HWC collaborated with the provincial and territorial governments in developing and implementing a community-level "Really Me" awareness program. Private-sector cooperation was achieved through the participation of many prominent companies, including owners of supermarkets and shopping malls, that promised to reach a large number of youths.

To evaluate the campaign's impact on the target-adopter groups, HWC hired a national public opinion organization to survey behavioral changes among young people and their parents. The surveys were timed to coincide with the campaign's major placements in the media. The survey design sought data on the target-adopter groups' awareness and reactions to the antidrug campaign and on their attitudes and behavior.

3

Social Marketing Research

Sound research is the basis of social marketing. Research is what differentiates the marketing approach to social change from earlier impressionistic efforts to influence changes in social ideas and practices. Only by researching and understanding the specific needs, desires, beliefs, and attitudes of target adopters and the specific characteristics of the social products that are being marketed can social marketers move toward the successful implementation of social change campaigns.

In designing a social marketing program, the planner makes decisions that seek to influence the behavior of target adopters. These decisions are made on the basis of personal logic and intuition, personal experience, what one hears from others, or what research data suggest.

The design of research and the collection of data represent the scientific approach. This superior basis for making social marketing decisions is examined here.

SOCIAL MARKETING RESEARCH TECHNIQUES

The social marketer can draw on a varied set of research techniques that are appropriate for different decisions that may be made. Consider, for example, the marketing of a specific tangible product—contraceptive devices—by the Condom Social Marketing Program (CSMP) in the Philippines. The findings in that program can be applied to the marketing of other social products—

literacy, the prevention of disease, community development, environmental protection, and so on.

Figure 3-1 shows the normal flow of events in planning this type of research. The three groups involved are research-and-development (R & D) personnel, social marketers, and communication specialists. After the marketing program is approved, social planners will research attitudes, behaviors, and needs and develop concepts that are translatable into a rough product base. If a product passes the product test, then the social marketers work closely with the communication specialists to develop a brand name, packaging, and various communication materials. These materials are tested in the marketplace to launch an effective campaign.

The decisions shown in Figure 3-1 are listed in the first column of Table 3-1. The second column identifies the characteristics to measure once a decision is made. The third column identifies appropriate research techniques for measuring a given characteristic. Table 3-1 is illustrated by examining the research techniques used in two different campaigns, namely, one that marketed contraceptives (CSMP) and one that marketed oral rehydration.

Research on Consumers' Use of Contraceptives

CSMP planners recognized two critical problems, namely, that condoms were not available in many parts of the country and that many target-adopter groups were ignorant of their convenience, effectiveness, and proper use.[1] The campaign eliminated the first problem by researching product-distribution channels. Condoms could be efficiently distributed, it was found, not only in traditional outlets, such as drugstores and community health centers, but in neighborhood retail stores, groceries, supermarkets, and bazaars. To tackle the second problem, planners used advertising in the mass media to communicate information about condoms and their use. Both problems were probed and resolved by means of substantial research. Planners decided that the research should begin with a study of usage, attitudes, and image. House-to-house interviews were conducted to generate the information identified in Table 3-2.

The gathered data proved highly useful: for example, the data sets 6b, 6c, 6e, and 6f were analyzed to predict data set 6d. It was found that the husband's behavioral intention to use condoms

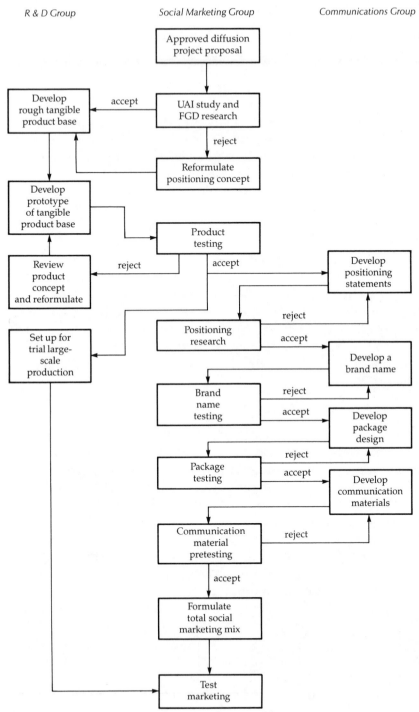

FIGURE 3-1 A Research Program for the Development of a Social Product

TABLE 3-1 Marketing Research Techniques

Social Marketing Decisions	Target-Adopter Response/ Characteristics	Appropriate Technique
Target-adopter groups	Sociodemographic, psychological, psychographic, and behavioral characteristics of the adopter segments	Adopter segmentation research
Positioning of the social product	Perception of superiority or distinctiveness	Positioning research
Features of the tangible-product base	Perception of the superiority or parity of the physical/sensory product	Product testing
Selection of the brand name	Recognition and impression of a meaning	Brand-name testing
Packaging of the tangible-product base	Recognition and impression of a meaning	Package testing
Image of the product/campaign agency	Perception of superiority or distinctiveness	Positioning research
Message of the mass-communication material and its execution	Perceptions, image, and motivation of the communication	Communication material pretest
Maintenance of the mass-communication campaign	Awareness, recall, image, and motivation of the communication	Postcommunication effectiveness research
Pricing of the tangible-product base	Acceptability of the intended price	Price-sensitivity research
Adoption-promotion and movement-generation campaigns	Adoption behavior and diffusion	Test marketing
Presentation and delivery of the product or service	Adoption behavior and satisfaction	Test marketing
Direct-communication campaign	Adoption behavior and diffusion	Test marketing
Distribution channels	Delivery of the product to the target-adopters	Distribution-channel research

TABLE 3-2 Study of Usage, Attitudes, and the Image of Condoms

1. Awareness of family planning methods
2. Past practice of family planning
3. Current practice of family planning
4. Methods ever tried and currently used
5. For current users of condoms
   a. What brand was used?
   b. Where were the condoms bought or otherwise obtained?
   c. How many were bought or gotten the last time?
   d. How long did the supply last?
   e. How much was paid?
6. For nonusers of condoms
   a. Attitude toward using condoms (23 evaluative rating scales)
   b. Beliefs about the consequences of using condoms (10 belief rating items)
   c. Evaluations of the importance of each of the 10 expected consequences
   d. Behavioral intention to use condoms (2 5-point scale measurements)
   e. Beliefs about what one's "significant others" (6 of them) expect one to do about using condoms
   f. Motivation to comply with each of the 6 expectations of significant others
7. Sociodemographics
   a. Age
   b. Number of children
   c. Total monthly household income
   d. Facilities in the house
   e. Schooling
   f. Occupation
   g. Vehicle ownership
   h. Home ownership

was influenced more by the wife's attitude than by any perceived beneficial consequences. The team decided, therefore, to construct an appeal with the message, "The wife expects the man to use condoms for their family planning and consequently the man owes it to the wife to use condoms."

As planning progressed, further questions surfaced about target adopters: If the husband's concern for the wife is key, what specific concerns does the husband have about the wife? Are those concerns valid? What kind of condom product knowledge do the husband and wife have anyway? To answer these questions, the project team decided to run focus-group discussions involving six groups: two groups of condom users, two groups of nonusers, one group of housewives whose husbands used or had used condoms, and one mixed group of condom-using and nonusing husbands and wives. There were eight to ten respondents in each group. The discussion was led by a professional psychologist with marketing experience. A discussion guide covered all the questions that had to be answered.

When the verbatim responses of the focus-group respondents were content analyzed, the following answers emerged:

The Husbands' Concerns for Their Wives. It became clear that husbands wanted to satisfy their wives sexually. Some men stopped using a condom because they thought it hurt their wives ("The condom used to irritate my wife; she would get sore from it"). Others discontinued using it because they saw it as a "barrier" to giving the wife complete sexual satisfaction. One wife said she told her husband: "I can't feel you coming inside me anymore. It doesn't seem complete." And so she quickly persuaded him to drop its use.

The implication was clear: if the campaign were to be successful, the wives had to become as educated as their husbands about the use of condoms.

Knowledge of Condoms. To some extent knowledge of condoms seemed to depend on experience with their use. Consider these two observations, the first from a nonuser and the second from a user: "The cervix of one of my friends was abraded by the condom her partner used." "The condoms we use now are of thin material, unlike the Gold Coin brand that was thick and painful to use." (In the past condoms lacked lubrication.)

What is apparent is that nonusers tend to emphasize the negative aspects of condoms while the users tend to stress the favorable aspects. This finding suggested that condoms should be distributed free to nonusers in the hope that their use would generate a favorable experience. However, a trial does not necessarily guarantee that the user will use the condom properly. An extreme case was a man who used the condom by unrolling it to cover both his penis and testicles! Small wonder he criticized the condom as a "painful" contraceptive method.

To both the user and the nonuser, the condom was a deceptively simple device whose use was often taken for granted. A sampling of pertinent comments by users will bear this out:

If the condom will be used again, it's better to lubricate it with Johnson's baby oil.

You should test the condom by blowing into it and tying the open end to check for air leaks in the rest of its length.

Sometimes a condom can be left inside the woman.

Few people use the condom because it reduces satisfaction, definitely for the man and for the woman as well.

These comments came from people who have been using condoms for years. Clearly, both users and nonusers needed better knowledge of the product, such as a list of dos and don'ts.

Research on the Oral Rehydration Campaign

The campaign to introduce oral rehydration therapy in the Philippines sought to control a major cause of infant mortality and morbidity, namely, diarrhea. Diarrhea is second to pneumonia as a leading cause of infant mortality and one of the major causes of infant morbidity. Oral rehydration therapy has proved "the most effective and efficient clinical management intervention for diarrheal diseases."[2] Other approaches, such as intravenous solutions, antibiotics, and antidiarrheal medications, are expensive, less effective, and medically contraindicated at times. They also may call for access to hospital facilities that are usually unavailable to people in rural areas.

In oral rehydration therapy, a mother dissolves a packet of oral rehydration powder (containing separate amounts of sodium and glucose) in a liter of water and administers the solution to her sick infant. In its five-year plan (1983–87), the government of the Philippines declared oral rehydration therapy to be a national health priority and employed it as prime entry point for developing primary health care services.

The social marketing team decided to run focus-group discussions with mothers to find out what mothers knew about infant diarrhea and dehydration, what they typically thought of doing in these cases, and what their reactions would be to using the oral rehydration product. The plan called for holding two focus-group discussions with mothers in each of four provinces.

The focus-group discussions yielded some eye-opening revelations. Here are two such findings:

1. Some rural mothers said that it was impractical to mix a one-liter solution. As one mother explained, "the baby can't drink all that amount in a day." She was responding to the fact that the solution, once mixed, had to be consumed within 12 hours because beyond that period, it was no longer potable. Also, the mothers typically did not own a one-liter household container.

2. A few mothers who had used the oral rehydration packets said they only dissolved the sodium, saving the glucose to serve to house guests for their coffee "because it's quality sugar." Other mothers said they tasted the solution after mixing it and found it "too salty," so they added table sugar "so the baby will be able to take it."

Having gained insight on the target adopters from these focus groups, the survey team decided it needed to quantify the following questions through a study of the target adopters:

1. How many rural mothers really know the difference between diarrhea and dehydration?
2. How many try to do something about each condition, and what do they do?
3. How many resort to using medications, and what medications do they use? Are these the right ones? Where do they get them?
4. How many realize the true risk of diarrhea and dehydration? Where did they learn about it?
5. What kind of expectations would they have from a home-made oral rehydration solution?
6. How many would use the solution properly? How many would mix the powder with the water correctly and properly?
7. What do mothers prefer with regard to the size of the pack, the mix of powders, the form of the package, and why?

Product Testing

The team decided to answer these questions by conducting a product test at this stage. The R & D personnel now had to develop one or more actual products to test with the mothers. If the mothers responded poorly to the test product, then it would have to be redesigned. If they responded well, then the team would recommend larger production for test marketing and for developing the product's positioning.

In preparing products for a test, the marketer would aim either for physical or sensory superiority, or at least parity with other products. For this product, the physical and sensory attributes included (1) taste, (2) feel, (3) appearance, and (4) scent.

To test a product, the marketer chooses either an on-the-spot test or a home-placement test. In the former, the respondent tries, uses, or inspects the product when approached. In the latter, the product is left with the respondent to try at home. After an agreed-on time, the respondent reports his or her reactions to the product.

Generally, a home-placement test reveals more than does an on-the-spot test. However, the on-the-spot test is quicker to implement and easier to control for extraneous factors. The home-placement test revealed the impracticality of the instructions for mixing a liter of the solution and ignorance of the proper mixing of the sodium and glucose powders.

Research on Positioning

At this point, research on positioning is needed to develop the right fit between the needs of the target-adopter group and the social product. In the oral-rehydration-therapy campaign, the product was positioned as the quickest and most effective way to help infants who are suffering from diarrhea. Since there are many possible positionings for social products, the role of research is to suggest and to test different positionings.

Testing the Brand Name and the Packaging

At this stage the social marketing team knows (1) the adopter group it is targeting, (2) the target group's needs and wants, (3) the fit of the product with the needs of the target group, and (4) whether the tangible product has physical or sensory superiority or at least parity with available substitutes. The team must now dress up the tangible product with a brand name and packaging.

The function of naming and packaging is to make the tangible product easily identifiable and recognizable, to convey an image that reinforces the product's positioning, and to win the target group's acceptance. The task of choosing a name involves generating a set of alternatives and testing the responses of the target-adopter population with respect to the evoked images, memorability, and motivational quality of each of the alternatives. Packaging requires making a number of decisions on the shape, color, size, weight, material, label, and copy. Various tests can be used to research brand names and types of packaging (see Chapter 7).

Pretesting the Communication Materials

Now, the planner will prepare communication materials to inform and persuade the target-adopter group to try the product. It is essential that the communication materials be pretested before being distributed. Otherwise, the materials may miscommunicate, as the following example shows.

> The Philippine Population Commission distributed a brochure to motivate prospective candidates for vasectomy. The brochure illustrated the vasectomy procedure with a sideview drawing of the male sex organ where the two vas deferens are each shown to have an incision. The communicators were surprised to find out later that some prospective adopters formed the opinion that this was a castration operation. Rural men who were surveyed said: ''The drawing of the operation showed that you are cutting the veins that connect and hold the scrotum to the penis. So what else is that but castration even if you call it vasectomy?''

A routine pretesting of that brochure would have caught this fundamental communication error.

Pretesting not only can prevent errors, but it can also provide insights into superior ways of executing messages. Here is an example from the East Java Family Planning Program, one of the most successful family planning programs in the Third World.

> The East Java Family Planning Program sought to increase acceptance of the intrauterine device (IUD). A communications team created a comic book to show how the IUD worked and where the IUD is placed, followed by a series of

frames showing a woman being freed of accidental pregnancy. When asked how effective they thought the IUD was as a contraceptive, after viewing the comics pages, women answered by drawing an analogy of the IUD to the metal rings that East Javans attached to parts of the body to symbolize personal prowess or skill. Thus, an East Javan would attach a brass ring through the skin and around the Achilles tendon if she were a good runner or at the tip of her tongue if she were a good singer. The research showed that the IUD was perceived positively; they thought of it as a ring that is attached to the place where the woman conceives—a symbol of her skill in controlling unplanned conception.

Test Marketing

Once the communication material is approved, the marketing team can develop the remaining components of the program, such as pricing, services, placement and delivery, and so on and then test market the whole social marketing mix in the marketplace. Test marketing is designed to answer two sets of questions: (1) What is the effectiveness of alternative marketing mixes? and (2) What can go wrong with a chosen marketing mix when it is carried out in the field?

With the CSMP campaign in the Philippines, the goal of test marketing was to test alternative social marketing mixes that varied in three ways:

- Retail price (25 centavos versus 10 centavos).
- House-to-house distribution (five rounds of house-to-house sampling and selling, two rounds of house-to-house sampling only, and sampling at public markets).
- Radio advertising (with and without radio spots).[3]

Researchers call this a 2 x 3 x 2 design. The numbers refer to the variations in the number of alternative levels of each marketing mix element. This example required at least 12 test areas for its execution. In each area, the test involved retail outlets for the monthly monitoring of condom sales and at least 2 surveys to measure those who purchased the condoms. The test marketing extended over ten months and entailed a considerable expenditure. In practice, such an exhaustive design is rarely implemented.

DESIGNING THE SOCIAL MARKETING RESEARCH PROGRAM

To implement marketing research techniques, the following questions have to be answered:

1. Who should be surveyed?
2. How many should be surveyed?
3. How should the respondents be selected?
4. How should their responses be gathered?
5. How should their responses be interpreted?

Who Should Be Surveyed? Surveys probe the types of individuals and groups whose behavior is being targeted for change. Once the types have been determined, the survey seeks to find specific individuals whose responses will indicate the most about the likely behavior of the target adopters.

With the CSMP social marketing campaign, the target adopters were men who were willing to use condoms for family planning but had not been using them. But nonusers are not necessarily the best group from which to draw insightful information. Other types of men to interview are users and ex-users of condoms. The latter group includes those who have switched to other methods (switchers) and those who no longer use contraception (dropouts). Current users are a good respondent group because they embody the behavior the survey seeks to understand. So are the switchers and the dropouts because they throw light on post-adoption behavior.

How Many Should Be Surveyed? The answer to this question depends on the variability of the data and the confidence level that is acceptable. The more variable the data and the more confidence that is sought, the larger the sample must be. A standard text on marketing research, such as Churchill's, provides formulas for setting the size of the sample.[4]

How Should the Respondents Be Selected? The sampling design determines the representativeness of the results of the marketing survey. For example, a survey estimate from 100 respondents is representative and projectable (within a ± 10 percent margin of error and a 95 percent confidence level) to the total population provided that the sampling design is random. In random sampling, a sample of the population is chosen so that each member of the population has an equal chance of being selected. This requires a list of all members of the population and the selection of respondents at random.

How Should the Responses Be Gathered? The next task is to determine the instrument to use for collecting the data. Among the most commonly used instruments are questionnaires and projective tests (such as word-association and sentence-completion tests). Each instrument must be constructed carefully and pretested on a small sample before being administered to the full sample. Thus, a questionnaire must be pretested for the wording of questions, their relevance in measuring characteristics, their completeness, and their ordering.

Another task is to decide whether the information should be gathered in person, on the telephone, or by mail. Each method has its own costs, time factors, and issues of validity.

Telephone interviewing is the best method of gathering information quickly, and the interviewer is able to clarify questions if they are not understood. The two main drawbacks are that only people with telephones can be interviewed and that only short, not-too-personal interviews can be carried out.

The mail questionnaire may be the best method of reaching persons who will not give personal interviews or who may be biased against interviewers. However, mail questionnaires require simple and clearly worded questions, and the return rate is usually low or slow or both.

Personal interviewing is the most versatile of the three methods. The interviewer can ask more questions and can supplement the interview with personal observations. However, personal interviewing is the most expensive of the three methods and requires more administrative planning and supervision.

Personal interviewing takes two forms, individual and group interviewing. Individual interviewing involves calling on people in their homes or offices or on the street. The interviewer must gain their cooperation, and the time involved can range from a few minutes to several hours. Sometimes a small payment or incentive is presented to the person in appreciation of his or her time.

In focus-group interviewing six to ten persons are invited to meet with a trained interviewer for a few hours to discuss a social marketing product or organization. The participants may be paid a small sum for attending. The interviewer usually starts with a broad question and then moves successively to more focused questions. The interviewer encourages free and easy discussion among the participants, hoping that the group dynamics will bring out actual feelings and thoughts. The comments are recorded through note taking or tape recording and are subsequently studied to understand the participants' patterns of thought. Focus-group interviewing has become one of marketing's major research tools for gaining insight into the thoughts of target adopters.

How Should the Responses Be Interpreted? Once gathered, the data have to be analyzed, interpreted, and presented in a way that answers the survey's specific objectives. The presentation usually takes the form of descriptive statistics and analyses of relationships among variables or characteristics. Descriptive statistics have many forms: frequency distributions and measures of averages, skewness, and dispersion. The relationship among variables can be explored through simple cross tabulations or through more advanced statistical methods.[5]

MANAGING SOCIAL MARKETING RESEARCH

There are alternatives to doing surveys. The social agency can use available official statistics or obtain someone else's survey data and then do secondary analysis on them. For example, social programs in the health sector typically conduct large-scale annual health surveys and make them available.

When secondary sources will not provide the needed information, the issue is whether to hire a marketing research agency to do the survey or to do it oneself. The former alternative will cost more, but the results will probably be more reliable.

The cheapest way to get survey information is to buy space on an omnibus survey—a syndicated survey that is usually offered by a large research agency. Those who subscribe to it share in the same pool of survey respondents. Survey agencies offer the service every quarter. They charge on a per-question-asked basis. For example, for ten "chargeable questions," the price may range from $5,000 to $10,000.

ANALYZING THE
SOCIAL MARKETING
ENVIRONMENT

4

Mapping the Social Marketing Environment

Although social marketers work to effect social change in their target adopters, their programs are subject to the forces of change arising from the environment. To be effective, social marketers must understand the marketing environment, the changes it is undergoing, the impact of those changes on their organization's capabilities and on their target-adopter segments, and the adaptations they need to make to sustain their program.

What is the social marketing environment? It is the set of forces that are external to the social change campaign and that impinge on its ability to develop and maintain successful influence on its target adopters. Kotler referred to six forces: demographic, economic, physical, technological, political/legal, and sociocultural forces.

Mapping the social marketing environment makes it possible for social marketers to predict and anticipate changes in it and hence to make a timely and orderly adaptation to change in the life cycle of a social marketing program. For this reason, social marketers must have access to information about the sources of change and the underlying causes of these changes.

Social marketers need a framework for mapping the environment to understand what forces to map and how to map and read the results. Mapping is directed both at the current environment and the likely future environment.

WHAT ENVIRONMENTAL FORCES TO MAP

Mapping the Current Environment

To understand the strategic role of environmental mapping, consider the mapping of changes and adaptations in New York City's drug-addiction rehabilitation programs from 1972 to 1982[1]. Let us assume what the demographic, economic, physical, technological, political/legal, and sociocultural environments were in 1972 that affected the program in the base year.

The most important demographic conditions were the age, socioeconomic status, and racial distribution of New York City's drug addicts. Most of the addicts were young, poor, and black or Hispanic. These demographic segments were growing faster than other segments in society.

A critical factor in the economic environment was the cost of rehabilitating each addict and the availability of funding. In 1972, the cost of caring for and treating drug addicts ranged "anywhere from $2,000 per addict per year for an outpatient drug substitution program to $30,000 per addict per year for an extensive inpatient withdrawal and rehabilitation program."[2] Yet, New York City's annual budget for narcotics rehabilitation was $6 million, which could serve about 3,000 addicts in outpatient treatment (at $2,000 each) or only 200 addicts in inpatient treatment (at $30,000 each). New York City's population of heroin addicts at that time was estimated to be 225,000, the largest group of narcotics addicts in the city. Therefore, available funds could help only between 0.08 percent and 1.30 percent of that population.

As a physical environment, New York City was a city of high stress and high pollution, which, according to therapists, are conditions that facilitate the use and abuse of drugs.[3] The technological environment of drug addiction consists of the inventory of addicting drugs and the addiction therapies. In 1972, the addicting drugs included marijuana, cough medicine containing codeine and opium, heroin, morphine, codeine, glues for sniffing, barbiturates, amphetamines, methamphetamines, LSD, DMT, and STP. Ten years earlier, this list was shorter; the newcomers were LSD, DMT, and STP. The development of new drugs was accelerating addiction.

In 1972 there were four major methods for treating drug addiction:

Long-term Institutionalization. In this approach, recovery rates are low because addicts are generally hospitalized forcibly by court order. Furthermore, readdiction rates are high.

Therapeutic Community. In this approach, the addict is admitted to a small, controlled therapeutic community and commits himself or herself to lead a nonaddictive life, earn the community's support, and participate in therapeutic-group encounter sessions. The length of stay varies from 36 months to 5 years.

Methadone Treatment. In this form of treatment, methadone is substituted for heroin. The addict's heroin intake is decreased until detoxification is complete. At the same time, the dosage of methadone, an addicting drug that counteracts the heroin's euphoric effects, is increased. The addict is maintained on methadone for the rest of his or her life.

The 'British System.' Basically a drug maintenance program, this approach assumes that withdrawal from heroin is risky to the addict's mental and physical health. Therefore, the physician prescribes maintenance doses of heroin.

Table 4-1 compares these four treatments. In 1962, methadone treatment was not available; by 1972, it had become the cheapest and most effective form of treatment.

What about the political/legal environment? In 1972, this environment consisted of drug addiction laws and enforcement, as well as pressure, public-interest, and self-help groups concerned with drug addiction. According to a directory of 130 self-help groups published by the National Self-Help Clearinghouse, drug addiction programs ranked at the top of self-help efforts in the 1970s, reaching more addicts than were admitted to inpatient or controlled therapeutic communities.[4] With regard to legal enforcement, the Controlled Dangerous Substances Act of 1970 had reduced the penalty for the possession of marijuana from a felony to a misdemeanor. This law differentiated marijuana from other illegal but riskier drugs, but may have led more people into drug abuse and later into harder drugs.

The most pertinent factors to map in the sociocultural environment were the values and attitudes that the citizens of New York City held about addicting drugs, their use, and addicts. One major study found that citizens regarded addiction as a criminal problem rather than as a social/medical one. As a result, the study

TABLE 4-1 Summary of Four Addiction Treatment Approaches

Alternative Approaches	Average Length of Stay	Rate of Success (percentage)	Direct Cost per Addict per Year	Legal Status in United States
Long-term in-stitutionaliza-tion	3.5 years	10	$30,000	Legal
Therapeutic community	4 years	65	4,400	Legal
British system	Remainder of the addict's life	not known	not known	Legal
Methadone treatment	Remainder of the addict's life	87	1,000	Legal

SOURCE: S. T. Maidlow and H. Berman, "The Economics of Heroin Treatment," *American Journal of Public Health,* 62 (1972), p. 1399.

noted, the public vigorously opposed efforts to establish community treatment programs "out of fear that the programs will merely concentrate dangerous sociopaths in the area with little benefit to the community itself."[5] Another study noted that in New York, "the popularity of living the 'high' life was spreading, for heroin had become respectable. . . . There is a growing use of heroin among white middle-class people because they tend to value the respect of peers above everything else. Taking the most dangerous drug is a way of gaining their respect."[6]

Mapping Future Changes

Social marketers can count on the marketing environment to change. Mapping the current environment reveals existing problems and opportunities, whereas mapping likely future changes can reveal how marketing programs have to be changed to remain effective.

Here are the major issues in the mapping of future changes in the social marketing environment:

- *Extent of Controllability.* Is there any aspect of a given or anticipated change that the social marketer can influence?

- *Probability of Occurrence.* How probable is it that the change will take place, and when will the change occur?
- *Locus, Magnitude, and Intensity of Impact.* What and how much will the change affect other social marketing environmental forces, the target-adopter segments, the marketing program's product or tangible-product base, the program's distribution capability?
- *Priority.* What changes should a social marketer assign priority to?

The mapping of future change can be illustrated by an analysis of the technological changes affecting New York City's drug addiction rehabilitation program. This example focuses on the controllability/occurrence probability issues. On the basis of this case study, a planning approach typology is developed as summarized in Table 4-2. Commitment planning is appropriate to environmental change that is both certain to occur and controllable in key respects. If a change is uncertain but controllable or certain but uncontrollable, the suitable planning approach is contingency planning. Responsive planning is appropriate when the change is both uncertain and uncontrollable.

The technological environment of addicting drugs in 1972 was largely uncertain and uncontrollable. In hindsight, we know that technology produced a plethora of new, potent drugs to add to the preexisting ones. All were uncontrollable in their development and introduction in the marketplace. The situation left the social marketer with no other way of managing change except by responding to the changes as they took place, namely, by responsive planning. Nevertheless, the technological change in addiction therapies that the social marketer confronted in 1972 was

TABLE 4-2 Alternative Planning Approaches

Extent of Controllability	*Probability of Future Occurrence*	
	Certain	*Uncertain*
Controllable	Commitment planning	Contingency planning
Uncontrollable	Contingency planning	Responsive planning

SOURCE: Constructed from C. D. Basil and C. W. Cook, *The Management of Change* (London: McGraw-Hill Publishing Company U.K. Limited, 1974).

controllable although uncertain. It was uncertain because no one knew what new therapies would emerge, yet these therapies were likely to be controllable. The situation, therefore, favored contingency planning.

The introduction of new, more potent addicting drugs and their declining cost and easier accessibility affected virtually all the other environmental forces. The demographic environment changed as more white middle-class people became users. This change, in turn, increased the per-person costs of treatment because the newer users could afford more expensive treatment. As a consequence, politicians and pressure groups demanded more punitive antidrug laws and stronger law enforcement. These changes alerted the social marketers that they would need increased budgets to discourage drug use and improve drug treatment. Unfortunately, a great gap existed between the rate at which new addicting drugs were being developed and the rate at which rehabilitation technologies were being improved. Addicting drugs multiplied, but rehabilitation technologies changed slowly.

Given the multiple, interacting environmental changes, which ones deserved the most attention? Priority should be based on the magnitude and speed of each change. This consideration leads to the following four classes of changes, as shown in Table 4–3.[7]

1. Turbulent: fast and vast changes in the environment for which the shortest planning horizon (for example, 1–2 years) is appropriate.
2. Unstable: fast but small changes that may be handled under a 2–3 year planning horizon.
3. Transitional: slow but vast changes in the environment for which a planning horizon of 3–5 years is appropriate.

TABLE 4–3 Characterizing Change in the Environment by Its Magnitude and Speed

Speed of Change	Magnitude of Change	
	Large	Small
Slow	Transitional change	Stable change
Fast	Turbulent change	Unstable change

SOURCE: Constructed from C. D. Basil and C. W. Cook, *The Management of Change* (London: McGraw-Hill Publishing Company U.K. Limited, 1974).

4. Stable: slow and small changes that argue for a 5–20-year planning horizon.

This classification suggests that the social marketer should assign priority to environmental changes in the following order: (1) turbulent changes, (2) transitional changes, (3) unstable changes, and (4) stable changes.

The qualitative results of assigning priorities to approaches to the New York City drug abuse program are summarized in Table 4-4. The analysis assigned as the Number 1 priority the likely changes in the technological environment because of the widening gap between availability of drugs and effective treatments. These asymmetrical changes in the technological environment forecast a highly turbulent environment for the drug problem.

The political/legal environment received the Number 2 priority because the needed outcomes for its two components, as indicated in Table 4-4, are precisely the opposite of their basic characteristics. Given the turbulent changes in the technological environment, the social marketer does not want a political setting that

TABLE 4-4 Priority Setting for Changes in the
Drug Addiction Environment

Environmental Changes	Change Classification	Priority
Demographics of addict population:		5
Age distribution	Stable	
Racial distribution	Stable	
Sociodemographics	Unstable	
Economics:		3
Cost of addiction rehabilitation	Turbulent	
Subsidy availability	Transitional	
Natural: pollution and stress	Stable	6
Technology:		1
Technology of addicting drugs	Turbulent	
Technology of rehabilitation	Stable	
Political/legal:		2
Laws on the use and possession of drugs	Stable	
Enforcement	Stable	
Sociocultural (public attitudes):		4
Toward addicting drugs and their use	Transitional	
Toward the addicts	Transitional	

is slow moving and incremental. Given these priorities, the social planner then has to develop and implement an action program that is directed at each major area.

HOW TO MAP THE ENVIRONMENT AND READ THE RESULTS

Having examined the environments to be mapped, the task is to do the mapping. Mapping consists of determining sources of information and analyzing the information received.

Environmental Mapping Research

Chase proposed four research methods for generating environmental data.[8] They are as follows:

1. *Opinion Leader Surveys.* Such surveys are useful for gathering estimates, expectations, and forecasts of environmental changes, their controllability, probability of occurrence, interactive effects, and priorities. The Delphi Method is the most effective method for gathering and processing the judgments of experts.[9]

2. *Media Content Analysis.* This technique involves the continuous content analysis of news topics that are featured in the mass media.[10] Topics that receive increasing coverage indicate the issues that will emerge on the public agenda in future years.

3. *Public Opinion Surveys.* Changes and trends in public opinion and consumer opinion can be measured in public opinion polls. Three organizations that are known for their public opinion polls are the Institute of Social Research of the University of Michigan, The Gallup Poll, and Yankelovich, Skelley, and White in New York.

4. *Analysis of Legislative Trends.* Here the data come from a survey procedure used with politicians and public figures. This method helps to determine "the predisposition of elected officials to vote one way or another on a particular issue."[11]

Since three of these methods involve surveys, can social marketers afford them? Surveys can be expensive, yet they actually need not be. Miller suggested ways to obtain cheap survey data: use someone else's survey data and reanalyze them, and select inexpensive survey designs and methods.[12] Survey data for re-analysis can be derived from census statistics and other aggregate data available in official publications; previous surveys undertaken by governmental organizations, political parties, and pressure groups; and surveys sponsored by the mass media (print, radio, and television). Inexpensive survey designs can be found by using the commercial pollsters' omnibus survey, subscribing to omnibus panels or a subset of them for some special purpose, utilizing mail questionnaire surveys, doing quota sampling rather than random sampling, and conducting telephone interviews rather than face-to-face interviews.

Social marketers can readily use these methods in industrialized countries. Roberto[13] pointed out the modifications necessary for social marketers working in developing countries:

1. Omnibus survey services are cheap and available in most Third World countries. However, they sample primarily urban populations and therefore must be supplemented by other means to reach rural respondents. A group of social agencies can join to co-sponsor a "syndicated survey" that targets a more representative population.

2. Telephone surveys must be used carefully in developing countries because they tend to be extremely biased toward upper-income urbanized populations.

3. The number of subsamples for a minimum necessary set has to be limited: as the number of subsamples is arithmetically increased, the required sample size increases geometrically, and so will the cost.

4. Trimming down the number of items in the questionnaire is helpful. Get rid of "nice to know" questions in favor of "necessary to know" questions. Open-ended items can be converted into checklist items, which will cut down on interviewing time, a factor of cost.

5. Perform only the tabulations needed. Design an analysis plan right from the start and stick to it.

6. If an outside research agency is used, eliminate the requirement of a submitted report. Doing so can save the project as much as 25 percent to 35 percent of the research cost. The percentage is high because reports are usually prepared by an agency's top managers, whose professional services are costly.

Analyzing the Mapping Data

There are three commonly used methods for analyzing environmental data: (1) the scenarios construction method, (2) the SWOT (strength, weakness, opportunity, threat) analysis method, and (3) the issue-identification and analysis method.

Scenarios Construction Method. This method calls for building up multiple plausible scenarios from the data. The commonly accepted procedures for constructing scenarios raise the following questions:

- What are some plausible or possible future conditions that are identifiable and definable by critical issues or factors?
- What is the sequence of events, conditions, or changes that can describe the evolution of each plausible future condition?
- What is the probability of occurrence of each future condition? What is the opportunity or level of threat in each case? What is each condition's major source (for example, technology driven, economically constrained, politically and legally driven)?

SWOT Analysis Method. The SWOT analysis method seeks to take advantage of an organization's opportunities by employing its strengths, while warding off threats by means of avoiding, correcting, or compensating for its weaknesses.[14] The method is guided by the following key questions:

- What trends, changes, or overlooked needs in a program's social marketing environment offer a chance for the program to attain its objectives more effectively?
- What situations, barriers, or constraints in the social marketing environment and changes in it appear to be potentially damaging or problematic to the program's attainment of its objectives?
- What resources or capabilities of the social marketing program can take advantage of identified opportunities in the environment or can be used effectively to achieve the social marketing objectives?
- What aspects of a marketing program or organization's weaknesses or limitations make it particularly vulnerable to the identified environmental threats or keep it from achieving the social marketing objectives?

TABLE 4-5 Issue Identification and Analysis Applied to the Addiction Rehabilitation Program

Priorities for Environmental Changes	Significant Trend	Major Issue	Influential Segments For or Against the Major Issue
1: Technological	The development of new addicting drugs will occur, while the development of new efficient rehabilitation techniques will lag.	Should the rehabilitation program's services be changed or expanded to take in new severer cases of addiction?	For a change in the program: legislators and medical groups For the expansion of the program: community leaders, religious/missionary groups, and groups of volunteers
2: Political/legal	Legal sanctions and law enforcement will lag.	Should the program for getting more legal and political support be increased?	For: reform groups Against: criminal syndicates/groups
3: Economic	The costs of addiction rehabilitation will continue to increase.	Should the program start charging participants or increase the current charges?	For: funding or donor agencies Against: social workers, and groups of volunteers
4: Sociocultural	Public opinion will even more regard addiction as a crime, rather than as a social problem.	Should the program shift to more educational and communication efforts rather than rehabilitation activities?	For: educators and media groups Against: community leaders, and groups of volunteers
5: Demographic	Drug addiction will spread to more whites and middle-class people.	Should the rehabilitation program change from treating predominantly blacks and Hispanics to white middle-class people?	For: groups of middle-class white volunteers Against: groups of non-white lower-class volunteers

Most applications of SWOT analysis will yield numerous SWOT items. The task is to sort them into major and minor items and to focus on the former.

Issue-Identification and Analysis Method. This method calls for identifying trends as precursors of issues. Chase defined an issue as any "unsettled matter which is ready for decision."[15] For our purposes, an issue is a debatable point affecting a social marketing program that has identifiable influence groups for and against it.

Let us apply this analytical framework to the drug abuse program discussed earlier. If the program planners accepted the environmental priorities indicated in Table 4-4, then they would confront the issues shown in Table 4-5. What social marketers should do about an issue involves questions of what to do about the views of advocating and opposing influence groups. This is essentially a "market segmentation" problem. Its resolution lies in developing and implementing separate programs addressed to each group. Having mapped the social marketing environment, we are now ready to analyze the target adopters.

5

Analyzing the Behavior of Target Adopters

At the core of any social marketing campaign are the individuals, groups, and populations who are intended to be the consumers of the campaign's products. They are called target adopters because they are the specific people whose acceptance and adoption of a social product will fulfill the objectives of the campaign. This is the case whether the social product is ideas, practices, or ongoing services that sustain the product's adoption or whether the social product is accompanied by a tangible item that is instrumental for adoption behavior.

To succeed in marketing social ideas or practices—the products that social change campaigners seek to market—requires being able to predict how the target adopters will behave. Prediction, in turn, requires knowing the processes that guide and determine the behavior of target adopters. Once this behavior is understood, social marketers can perform the task of segmenting groups of target adopters.

ADOPTING IDEAS AND PRACTICES

Social marketers seek to influence and effect changes in the ideas and practices of particular groups of people. Adopting a new idea means adopting or modifying either a belief, an attitude, or a value. The example of an antismoking program will illustrate what is meant by the adoption of beliefs, attitudes, and values.

A target adopter has adopted a belief when he or she says, "I believe smoking is hazardous to my health." This belief is converted into an attitude when the target adopter says, "I believe smoking is hazardous to my health and I would like to quit smoking." This attitude, in turn, becomes a value when the smoker says, "I believe smoking is hazardous to everyone's health and all smokers ought to quit smoking."

All these statements follow Rokeach's definitions:

> [A belief is] any proposition, conscious or unconscious, inferred from what a person says or does, capable of being preceded by the phrase, "I believe that." [An attitude, on the other hand, is] a relatively enduring organization of beliefs around an object or situation predisposing one to respond in some preferential manner. [A value is] a type of belief, centrally located in one's total belief system, about how one ought or ought not to behave, or about some end-state of existence worth or not worth attaining.[1]

Thus social marketers can think of their task as converting a nonbelief into a belief, a belief into an attitude, or an attitude into a value.

Adopting a new practice, either performing a single act such as having a vasectomy or donating blood or adopting a new pattern of behavior, is another type of social product. Adopting a new pattern of behavior may involve rejecting an existing practice, such a smoking; accepting a new practice, such as doing aerobic exercises three times a week; or using a tangible product, such as strapping on a safety belt when preparing to drive.

Different Kinds of Adoption

Adopters may accept a particular idea or practice for different reasons. After the first major oil crisis in the 1970s, for example, some people joined car pools because their company requested them to comply or gave them an incentive to comply (compliance adoption). (In some cases, the government will pass laws to secure compliance.)

Other people joined car pools because people who they admired and with whom the identified had joined car pools (identification adoption). Still others joined car pools because this action seemed to be a reasonable adjustment under the new circumstances (knowledge-based adoption). Yet other people joined car pools because they believed that it was the right thing to do. It was not just personally sensible, it made sense for everyone. They internalized a new norm, or standard, or behavior (internalization adoption).[2]

The four adoption behaviors can be classified according to their speed (slow versus quick) and the time horizon (for the immediate versus for the longer term). Figure 5–1 illustrates these classifications and suggests there is a hierarchy of adoption, from compliance to identification to knowledge and finally to internalization. If social marketers want quick results, compliance adoption will suit their objective. Subsequent efforts may be directed toward achieving identification or knowledge adoption. Social marketers ultimately will work toward achieving internalization adoption, the most sustained source of behavior by target adopters. Figure 5–2 shows the ease of effecting each behavior and the social marketer's preferences for each behavior.

ADOPTION PROCESSES

Social marketers have identified four different models of how target adopters can be moved to the final decision to adopt an idea, behavior, or tangible product, or "closing the sale." These models are (1) "learn-feel-do" adoption, (2) "do-feel-learn" adoption, (3) "learn-do-feel" adoption, and (4) "multipath" adoption.[3]

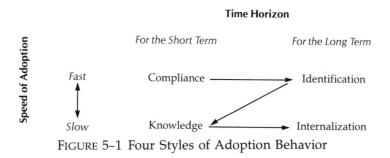

FIGURE 5–1 Four Styles of Adoption Behavior

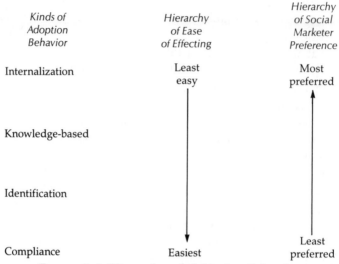

FIGURE 5-2 Hierarchy of Adoption Behavior

'Learn-Feel-Do'

In this sequence of behaviors, adoption will not take place unless the target adopters first learn about and then develop an attitude toward the social product. This "learning model" is the most widely used and researched model for influencing the behavior of target adopters.[4] Energy-conservation behavior, for example, is viewed as proceeding in this way.[5] However, focusing on awareness and belief to influence conservation behavior has not been completely successful; one study reported that "belief in the energy problem did not have the impact in actual reduction of energy consumption expected."[6]

This model gets the best results when two conditions are present: potential target adopters are highly involved in the adoption objective and they perceive clear differences between adoption and its alternative.[7] Figure 5–3 links models to conditions for success; the learn-feel-do model is shown in the second quadrant of Figure 5–3.

Innovations, perhaps healthier and more productive lifestyles, fit readily into this model's conditions. Target adopters tend to get involved with an innovation if only because of its novelty. Innovation also presents a clear alternative to existing ways of doing things, which may be unpleasant or unproductive. In the

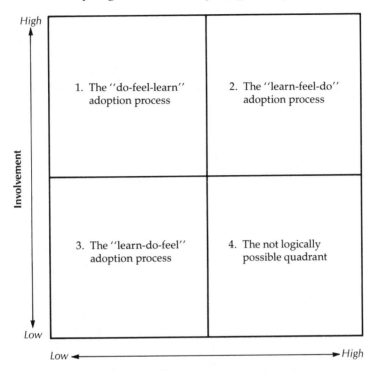

FIGURE 5-3 Conditions for Selecting Adoption Process Models
SOURCE: Constructed from M. L. Ray, *Advertising and Communications Management* (Englewood Cliffs, N.J.: Prentice-Hall, 1982)

learn-feel-do process, target adopters first are made aware, then are led to take an interest in and to like the innovation, and then are moved to try it and adopt it. Information to heighten their awareness of and attraction to the social product needs to be communicated effectively.

'Do-Feel-Learn'

In this process, target adopters proceed along the reverse of the normal learning sequence. First, they adopt an idea or practice on a tentative basis; next, they change their attitudes as a result of a trial-adoption experience; and then, they push their attitude toward a final step of better learning.

This model has two theoretical bases: cognitive dissonance theory and attribution theory. According to cognitive dissonance theory, when target adopters are in a situation of forced choice between closely similar alternatives, their choice will be followed by an improved attitude toward the idea or practice. Thus, target adopters will gather information that is favorable to the choice they made and unfavorable to the choice they avoided. According to attribution theory, however, target adopters behave like "self-perceiving" actors. They attribute their attitude toward an idea or practice to their behavior toward the idea or practice. Hence, if they have not adopted an idea or practice, they attribute this choice to the absence of a positive attitude. But if they have adopted it, they conclude that they must have had a positive attitude. Following the decision to adopt an idea or practice, target adopters then select information that reinforces their attitude. So again, the resulting sequence is do-feel-learn.

The two conditions in which social marketers may expect this process to take place are when adopters feel involved with an idea or practice and when the choices are practically the same. For instance, when a man enters a drugstore to buy condoms but cannot distinguish among the brands, he decides to buy the brand that is on sale. Later, he sees a positive ad about this brand, and this "learning" reinforces the likelihood that he will buy the same brand again. Thus, the marketer triggered the "do" step with a sale price and then moved the buyer through a "feeling-learning" sequence with a positive ad.

'Learn-Do-Feel'

In the third type of process, target adopters select an idea or practice only on the basis of familiarity with it, usually from heavy repetitive media communications. They have not yet formed any attitude toward it. If they are in a situation in which they have to make a choice, they select the social product even when they have little involvement with it. Afterwards they may change their attitude if their experience has been satisfying. This sequence is learn-do-feel.

This process is illustrated in attempts to deal with malnutrition and eating habits in the Third World. The social campaign objective is to find a way to enrich the diet of malnourished people with protein. At least four approaches have been tried in developing countries with various rates of success:

1. To enrich the existing staple foods, usually cereals.
2. To produce nutritious substitutes for such staples as milk and meat.
3. To introduce new products that require radical changes in people's eating habits.
4. To introduce nutritious products in the form of snack and fun foods, such as soft drinks, candy, or biscuits, rather than as meal foods.

The fourth approach has been the most successful. Sheth and Sudman reasoned that this approach was successful because "the new [meal] foods cannot be distinguished from currently used foods." The other approaches failed because of "their lack of compatibility with people's habits and norms although these failures have been rationalized as due to higher unit or absolute prices."[8]

This example provides insight into an important shift in the perspective of target adopters. Although the social product, high-protein/low-cost food, is generally a high-involvement product, this does not mean that it has to be presented as such. Beverages and snacks have the advantage of being promoted as low-involvement products, as shown in Figure 5–3. This fact has strategic implications for social marketers. It indicates that sometimes social marketers can transform the adoption objective or process into one that they can more easily manage.

Multipath Process

The multipath adoption model synthesizes the other models. It draws on important conceptual distinctions among belief or cognition (the "learn" effect), affect (the "feel" effect), and volition (the "do" effect). A target adopter may respond with a lower-order or a higher-order belief or other effect.

A target adopter acquires a lower-order belief when he or she is uncertain about the association between a desired attribute and the social product to be adopted and finds the information on the product to be acceptable only at low levels. This lower-order belief results in a low affect, "too weak to register in commonly used attitude scales" in social marketing surveys.[9]

A target adopter gains a higher-order belief when he or she

experiences an adoption objective either directly through trial adoption or indirectly through a vicarious experience, such as a person visiting or observing a session of Alcoholics Anonymous. This experience provides a higher certainty of association and more acceptable information and forms a much stronger belief base since it is processed directly through the senses. Higher-order beliefs generate higher-order affects "possessing sufficient strength to control" adoption or other relevant behaviors.[10] Because target adopters may directly or vicariously "try" an idea or practice to find out more about it before committing themselves to it, trial adoption is important.

These concepts allow us to differentiate among three sequences of target adopters' responses to a social product. In Figure 5–4,

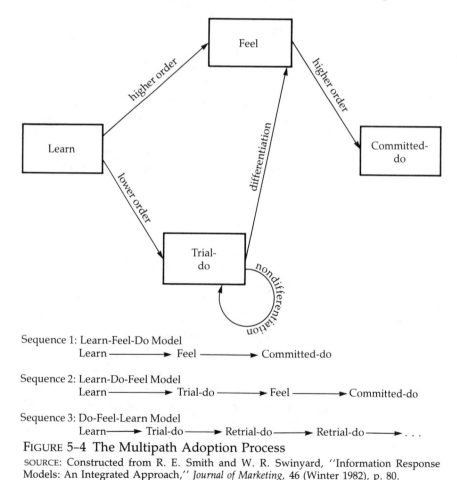

Sequence 1: Learn-Feel-Do Model
Learn ⟶ Feel ⟶ Committed-do

Sequence 2: Learn-Do-Feel Model
Learn ⟶ Trial-do ⟶ Feel ⟶ Committed-do

Sequence 3: Do-Feel-Learn Model
Learn ⟶ Trial-do ⟶ Retrial-do ⟶ Retrial-do ⟶ . . .

FIGURE 5–4 The Multipath Adoption Process

SOURCE: Constructed from R. E. Smith and W. R. Swinyard, "Information Response Models: An Integrated Approach," *Journal of Marketing*, 46 (Winter 1982), p. 80.

Sequence 1 is the classic learn-feel-do model. The distinctions among a higher-order and a lower-order belief and affect and between trial adoption and committed adoption make it easier to understand why this learning process is effective in "fewer situations than originally suspected."[11] The typical sources of information on a social product are low-credibility sources and therefore do not generate higher-order beliefs. Consequently, the learning model applies to situations in which the target adopter gets information predominantly from interpersonal sources.

Sequence 2 (the low-involvement, or learn-do-feel, model) is more frequent. Most of today's current social programs rely on mass media communications. Even though target adopters regard these media as biased and self-serving, mass media messages, if repeated often enough, can lead to trial adoption. The trial experience serves the target adopter's need for a credible source of information of a higher-order belief. The trouble is that the belief may be of two kinds: (1) the kind that appreciates the distinctiveness of the adoption product, which then leads to committed adoption, and (2) the kind that concludes that the adoption product is no different from its alternatives and, therefore, leads to another trial (Sequence 3). The multipath adoption model is useful in clarifying the behavioral distinctions that advance the understanding and prediction of specific adoption processes.

DETERMINANTS OF ADOPTING BEHAVIOR

Some elements, or determinants, trigger learning, feeling, and doing—the three components of adopting behavior. Social marketers can use to great advantage their knowledge of these determinants to refine their social marketing strategy. Appendix 5–1 illustrates how social marketers may measure them.

Determinants of the 'Learn' Effect

The sources of learning. To learn, target adopters must have access to information about the idea or practice to be adopted. Their learning, then, is a function of the kind of sources that provide the data that adopters use to make decisions. There are three important sources of information (1) personal sources, (2) nonpersonal sources, and (3) the adoption experience itself.

Information that is obtained through personal communication often is more effective in influencing people than is information obtained through the mass media.[12] Although social change programs use both sources, personal communications usually take the lead role.

Most social marketing products cannot be appreciated and valued until a target adopter tries them. Nevertheless, before adoption by trial use, social marketers can offer target adopters vicarious experiences of the product, the major source of which is personal information. Ideas and practices that are characterized by high involvement, visibility, testability, complexity, and perceived risk are most amenable to personal influence and communication for their adoption.[13] Furthermore, personal sources become more significant to target adopters as they move from the awareness stage of the adoption process into the succeeding stages.[14] The practical question for social marketers is, How can they trigger personal communication and influence to work on potential target adopters? One preferred way is to use opinion leaders.[15] However, opinion leadership is not person specific, but situation specific.[16] That is, no one is an opinion leader on all matters but may be an opinion leader in some areas and with some groups, depending on the situation.

The important consideration for social marketers, then, is not so much to reach so-called opinion leaders but to get people to talk about the social marketing product without regard to who is leading or following whose opinions. This form of personal influence is called word-of-mouth communication. Word-of-mouth communication may be stimulated by identifying influential individuals and organizations who can act as opinion leaders, including club presidents, local disc jockeys, wives of government officials, and the like; featuring influential people in testimonial advertising; and developing advertising that has high "conversation value."[17]

Robertson, Zielinski, and Ward[18] summarized the research findings on learning as follows:

- The target adopters' search for information is typically limited both in the number of alternative products to consider and in the amount of information actually used to make the decision. Thus, social marketers must carefully consider the type and amount of information they provide to target adopters.

- The greater the number of alternative social products, the greater the amount of information that target adopters search for. Alternative products trigger in the adopters' minds a perception that these products have different benefits and thus the perception that they will not gain satisfaction if they pick the wrong product. Hence, social marketers must, at a minimum, highlight information on their product's distinctiveness from the alternatives.

The timing of learning. Another issue is what kind of learning should target adopters be exposed to at each stage of the adoption process. Earlier we indicated that learning that comes after trial adoption, for example, often leads to commitment by target adopters. In general, knowing the type of learning process enables the social marketer to "time" different information flows at different stages in the adoption process.

The adopters' evaluation. When social marketers present their social products to target adopters, the target adopters will evaluate, on some basis, how satisfying the social product may be. The evaluation criteria and process, therefore, are important for social marketers to understand. Major aspects of the evaluation process can be illustrated with regard to the adoption of a weight-loss program.

- The potential set of attributes surrounding any social product is usually large. In choosing among weight-loss programs, a person may consider such attribute as the duration of the programs, their cost, the amount of weight they say can be lost, the type of foods they permit, the risk to health, the exercise component, and so on.
- The average target adopter considers only a small subset of total attributes to be important. A particular target adopter, for example, may consider only the cost of a program and the risk to health.
- The target adopter makes a subjective judgment of each attribute, using various measures. A target adopter may judge the cost of a weight-loss program on the basis of the fee or the fee plus the cost of the food or the time it takes to travel to and weigh in at the program. The adopter may judge the risk to health on the basis of either reported statistics or hearsay.

- The target adopter places different weights on the evaluation criteria. A target adopter who has a small income may place most weight on the cost of the program and less weight on its risk to health.

- The target adopter processes evaluation criteria in a specific way. A target adopter may multiply the attributes by their weights to reach a decision or may set minimum levels for each attribute and reject weight-loss programs that do not satisfy these minimum levels.

Typically, the end result of evaluation is an overall subjective impression of the social product that often transcends the information that was gathered. Therefore, in planning product development, communication, and promotion, social marketers have to understand the full range of information and evaluation criteria that their target adopters have used to form an impression of the social product.

Motivating adopters to learn. Social marketers can use a variety of motivators to induce learning. For example, a social marketing campaign to change people's perceptions of conserving electric energy used television and newspaper advertising to convey a fear message: ''It is good to have electricity. Save, so you will not lack it.'' The campaign took place right after a popular television show in Israel in 1980 that dramatized Israel's overuse of electricity. The show's host asked the audience to turn off all the extra lights in their homes. The viewers then saw the effect of their actions on their screen: a camera focused on the Israeli Electric Company's electricity-consumption gauges. Within a few seconds, the gauges dropped sharply.

The vividness of the means-end relationship that this campaign demonstrated convinced viewers to use electricity more carefully. Deutsch and Liebermann estimated that the collective behavior saved Israel 6 percent in aggregate electricity consumption during the 8 months of the campaign.[19]

The Israeli campaign appealed to people's need to plan to save energy. Two other energy-conservation campaigns appealed to people's need for a sense of autonomy. These campaigns, launched by the U.S. Department of Energy (DOE), occurred in the late 1970s. The first campaign, known as Project Payback, took place in six U.S. cities. It sought to motivate consumers to purchase energy-using products on the basis of the "life-cycle" costs of the products. Life-cycle costing leads consumers to consider not only the initial cost of an appliance but cost of operating it over its lifetime. For instance, although gas ranges containing electronic pilot lights have a high initial cost, they have a lower operating cost over their lifetime.

A second DOE campaign, known as the Low Cost/No Cost (LC/NC) Program, was implemented in six New England states in spring 1979 when New England was facing a heating oil shortage. The campaign informed homeowners about 11 specific actions they could take to save up to 25 percent on their utility bills.

Evaluation research indicated that Project Payback produced little discernible energy saving. Pilgrim and Shoemaker hypothesized that the project's life-cycle-costing concept was "too complex and too abstract for widespread public and retail business excitement."[20] In contrast, the LC/NC campaign convinced a significant proportion of households to complete at least 3 of the 11 recommended conservation practices: installing flow-control devices in their showers, checking for gaps around fireplace dampers and making improvements, and increasing the efficiency of their furnaces. DOE estimated that approximately $67 million were saved from just these three practices; the savings in oil was some 2.6 million barrels each year.

What made LC/NC more effective than Project Payback? Pilgrim and Shoemaker concluded that LC/NC was "simpler, more focused, and encouraged individual action to counteract feelings of helplessness in the face of an energy crisis and rising fuel costs."[21] In other words, LC/NC effectively tapped a consumer's need for autonomy and control, which was the trigger that induced target adopters to learn about energy conservation.

Determinants of the 'Feel' Effect

People are drawn to adopt a social product on the basis of feelings, which trigger attitudes. What are the influences on "feeling" states?

Target adopter's beliefs about outcomes. The adopter's beliefs about the outcomes or consequences of adopting a new idea or practice can determine his or her attitudes toward a practice yet to be accomplished.[22] For example, in thinking about quitting smoking, smokers consider what the outcome would be and how significant those consequences are to them. These two considerations influence an adopter's attitude, which will differ from the attitude toward smoking itself or toward the cigarette.

If social marketers know what specific feelings and beliefs exert the most influence on the attitude they wish to shape, they can target communications more precisely. In Roberto and Valbuena's study of men's attitudes toward using condoms, the dominant belief was the conviction that "using a condom is being a responsible husband."[23] The social marketing program then launched a condom-communication campaign that stressed "the image and sense of responsibility which accrue to the person using condoms for family planning."

The influence of trial adoption. Sternthal and Craig suggested that "in situations where people are uncertain about their attitudes . . . they may engage in [adoption] behavior to determine their beliefs [attitude]."[24] The adoption involved here is trial adoption. Target adopters resort to experience-based information that would help them ascertain their true feeling (attitude) toward the social product. Their attitude will be shaped, in part, by the situational characteristics in which the trial adoption occurred. According to Belk,[25] there are at least five situational characteristics:

1. Physical surroundings in which the trial-adoption behavior occurred.
2. Social surroundings (the other people present in the situation).
3. The time of day, season, and length of time since the last related behavior.
4. The way the target adopter perceives the task at hand.
5. The antecedent states, such as the target adopter's mood.

All these situational characteristics should be checked when formulating a social marketing campaign.

Motivational forces that shape feelings. Social marketers can tap several motivational forces to influence the feeling effect. The main ones are the need for excitement and novelty, the need to be accepted and loved, the need for catharsis and acting out, and the need to imitate and match. Each will be illustrated in turn.

When target adopters are placed in a situation that feeds on their desire for excitement and novelty, this triggers sensory and emotional experiences. In the three-community program in California whose goal was to help people change their behavior to reduce risk of coronary heart disease, the participants in one community received personal instruction that generated real involvement.[26]

To encourage diet behavior, the program provided the participants with weekly menu plans on which they planned and reported on the food they ate. Each person's weight loss was recorded and reported back. A point system on a giant sheet tracked the group's progress. Group instruction was given on shopping, planning menus, and preparing food.

To encourage people to stop smoking, the program asked smokers to record, for several days, the time, place, and importance of smoking at that time, along a 5-point scale. Instructors encouraged smokers to break up their habitual smoking patterns by changing brands weekly or by buying only one pack at a time. Then the smokers were asked to substitute sugar-free lozenges. Afterwards, the target adopters were asked to review whether they really wanted to quit, then to set a specific date, and then to announce it to their fellow group members.

To encourage exercising behavior, a physical therapist presented target adopters with new or increased exercise activities from which each adopter could decide to join. Each person's exercise progress was recorded.

The reinforcement of behaviors was provided through encouragement from instructors and spouses, group support, weekly weigh-ins, and progress/feedback reports. Because these programs met the target adopters' need for novely and excitement, they have been successful.

The need to be accepted and loved is another powerful motivator of adoption behavior. For example, a study of safety belt users found that it was the fear of being disabled or disfigured, rather than the fear of death in a crash, that strongly motivated people to use safety belts; the need to be attractive was a stronger motivator than the need to survive.[27] Similarly, Philliber and Philliber found that the desire for "better marital relations" was the strongest motivator for voluntary sterilization.[28]

Still another motivator is the need for catharsis and acting out. Geen and Quanty, using the old Aristotelian concept of cathartic value in tragedy, argued that television violence should be allowed to go on because programs provide a vicarious acting-out channel for viewers' feelings and emotions that they might otherwise express destructively in real-life situations.[29] Feingold and Knapp found evidence of a "boomerang" effect of negative reinforcement with certain messages.[30] Repeated exposure to messages that were designed to engender or reinforce negative attitudes toward amphetamines/barbiturates led respondents to shift from negative attitudes to significantly less negative attitudes. As McGuire put it, "drug-taking by teen-age males may be attractive, not in spite of its dangerousness but rather because of its dangerousness."[31]

Another source for motivating adopters' behavior is the human inclination to imitate and match. Adopters often express a positive feeling toward a product because some respected or significant others feel that way. For example, Stevens, Greene, and Primavera found that the most significant predictor of successful smoking cessation for male smokers was "the absence of other smokers in the household."[32] Similarly, Philliber and Philliber's review of studies of voluntary-sterilization behavior revealed "significant others" as the adopters' major source of motivation for seeking the operation.[33]

Determinants of the 'Do' Effect

We distinguish here between two forms of adoption by doing: trial adoption versus committed adoption.

Determinants of trial adoption. Adopters may undertake trial adoption because of a need to manage a perceived risk, or their low involvement with a social marketing product predisposes them to adopt it tentatively after an overwhelming repetition of the adoption message. Many social marketing campaigns seek to change ideas and practices without accompanying tangible products. As a result, potential adopters have to rely on experience (direct or vicarious) to convince themselves of the social product's performance in the absence of tangible products. Furthermore, many social marketing products, such as intrauterine contraceptive devices, drug-addiction rehabilitation, and alcoholism therapy are highly technical in nature; potential target adopters are less likely to have the knowledge or the experience to evaluate them properly. The less information one has about a social product, the greater the perceived risk. Even after adoption, target adopters may not be sure about a social product's level of risk. Unlike a tangible product, adopted ideas or practices cannot be returned if they prove to be unsatisfactory. Nor can the target adopter be sure that when a service is rendered the next time, it will be satisfactory. Social products are harder to standardize than are tangible commercial products.

Target adopters are most satisfied when they can allay their concerns about the potential risks of adopting a social product by means of trial adoption.[34] Gemunden[35] identified five types of perceived risks:

1. Social risk: "Is this socially acceptable to people whose opinions I care about?"
2. Psychological risk: "Will this yield its promised benefit?"
3. Physical risk: "Does this have any side effects? Could it be harmful?"
4. Functional risk: "Will this do what it is said to do?"
5. Financial risk: "Will this be worth what I spent for it?"

One other consideration is important. In a low-involvement setting, target adopters may move to trial adoption as a result of receiving many messages. Social marketers who seek to generate trial adoption quickly can use the repetition of messages to prod

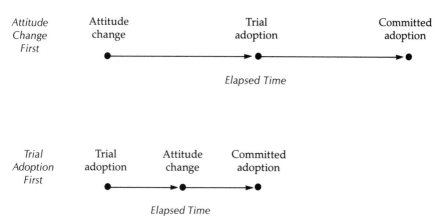

FIGURE 5–5 Starting with Attitude Change versus Starting with Trial Adoption

target adopters, even though excessive repetition can turn off some people.

Determinants of committed adoption. When adopters continue "doing" a new social practice or believing in a new idea, committed adoption has been attained. Committed adoption takes place because adopters believe in and like the social product, after being satisfied with their initial trial experience (see Figure 5–5).

According to current theory, target adopters are satisfied with a social product when its performance is at least equal to their expectations. When the performance exceeds their expectations, then they move to being delighted. They are likely not only to repeat the behavior, but also to advertise it to others.

APPENDIX 5-1
Ways to Measure Adopter Characteristics

Social marketers face the practical problem of measuring the several characteristics of adopters that were discussed in this chapter so they can evaluate a campaign. These measures are illustrated here with reference to the oral rehydration solution product (Oresol). (The characteristics are listed alphabetically.)

AFFECT

Higher-order Affect
I like Oresol because it stops my sick baby's loss of body water.

    5 = completely agree,
    4 = generally agree,
    3 = neither agree nor disagree,
    2 = generally disagree,
    1 = completely disagree.

Lower-order Affect
Oresol strikes me like it's a nice therapy.

    4 = definitely what I feel about Oresol,
    3 = generally what I feel about Oresol,
    2 = generally not what I feel about Oresol,
    1 = definitely not what I feel about Oresol.

ATTITUDE

Because of Oresol's ability to stop my sick baby's loss of body water, I think Oresol is good and I like it.

    5 = completely agree,
    4 = generally agree,
    3 = neither agree nor disagree,
    2 = generally disagree,
    1 = completely disagree.

BELIEF

Higher-order Belief

I believe in Oresol's ability to stop my sick baby's loss of body water and because of this, I think Oresol is good.

5 = completely agree,
4 = generally agree,
3 = neither agree nor disagree,
2 = generally disagree,
1 = completely disagree.

Lower-order Belief

I believe I've heard about Oresol before and I think I know what it is.

4 = definitely true of my case,
3 = generally true of my case,
2 = not that true of my case,
1 = definitely not true of my case.

COMMITTED ADOPTION

I've used Oresol before and will continue using it if my baby gets dehydration with diarrhea again.

2 = true,
1 = not true.

COMPLEXITY OF THE ADOPTION PRODUCT

Do you find Oresol to be

4 = very easy to understand or use,
3 = generally easy to understand or use,
2 = generally hard to understand or use, or
1 = very hard to understand or use?

COMPLIANCE ADOPTION

I've used Oresol because pressure has been put on me to use it.

2 = true,
1 = false.

DIFFERENTIATION OF ALTERNATIVES

Think of all the other things you can do for your sick baby in place of Oresol. Including Oresol, how different are all these treatment methods from one another on [therapy attribute]? Would you say that they are

4 = very different,
3 = quite different,
2 = a little different,
1 = practically the same?

DISCONFIRMATION OF EXPECTATIONS

Attribute-specific Expectations
My expectation of the ease of following this therapy was

5 = too low (it was much harder than I thought),
4 = somewhat low,
3 = accurate (it was just as I expected),
2 = somewhat high.
1 = too high (it was much easier than I thought).

Global
   My expectation about what Oresol will overall do was

5 = too low (it did much better than I thought),
4 = somewhat low,
3 = accurate (it was just as I expected),
2 = somewhat high,
1 = too high (it was much worse than I thought).

EXPECTATIONS

Attribute-specific Expectations
   I expect this therapy to be

5 = very easy to follow,
4 = generally easy to follow,
3 = neither easy nor hard to follow,
2 = generally hard to follow, or
1 = very hard to follow.

Global

Overall, I probably will rate this therapy:

5 = very high,
4 = generally high,
3 = neither high nor low,
2 = generally low,
1 = very low.

FEELING MOTIVATORS

The following are statements to each one of which the respondent will be asked to express his or her agreement or disagreement along a 5-point scale:

Need to Imitate/Match Motivator

"I'd like Oresol for my sick baby if I know that my close friends also use it for their babies."

Catharsis/Acting-out Motivator

"Every time my baby gets diarrhea, I'm reminded of my childhood when I used to get that sick, too."

"If I had gotten over this kind of illness when I was a baby, my own baby should also be able to."

Need to Be Accepted/Loved Motivator

"Giving Oresol to my sick baby is a part of being a caring mother."

Excitement/Novelty Motivator

"If the baby's loss of body water during diarrhea can be stopped quickly, then the days of anxiety and sleepless nights for us mothers are over."

IDENTIFICATION ADOPTION

I was led to use Oresol because I found out that Mrs. X [a respected community leader] also uses it for her sick babies.

2 = true,
1 = not true.

INFORMATION USAGE

Suppose you were to decide whether to use Oresol for your sick baby. Which of the following information will you ask from me first? (Give information.)

1. Do you think you now know enough for you to make a decision?
2. If not, which information will you want next? (Give information asked for.)
3. Do you now think you can reach a decision?

INSTRUMENTALITY BELIEFS

Will you tell me to what extent you agree or disagree with each of the following. Would you say that you

5 = completely agree,
4 = generally agree,
3 = neither agree nor disagree,
2 = generally disagree, or
1 = completely disagree with the statement that

1. Your baby would not like the taste of Oresol.
2. Oresol will not stop your baby's diarrhea [and so on to other belief statements].

INTERNALIZATION ADOPTION

I've used Oresol on my sick baby because it is the right thing to do and not to use it is unfair to the baby.

5 = definitely agree,
4 = generally agree,
3 = neither agree nor disagree,
2 = generally disagree,
1 = definitely disagree.

INVOLVEMENT LEVEL

As far as I am concerned, I would

5 = completely agree,
4 = generally agree,

3 = neither agree nor disagree,
2 = generally disagree,
1 = completely disagree that

1. My use of Oresol on my baby is a costly idea [the "cost" dimension].
2. Giving Oresol to my dehydrating baby will say something about myself as a mother [the self-presentation interest dimension].
3. I would like to give Oresol to my dehydrating baby because I'm one of those mothers who care enough to know what to do with their babies on such occasions [the social-acceptance interest dimension].
4. There's a lot for me to lose if I am wrong about Oresol [the perceived risk/consequences dimension].
5. It may be likely that I would lose a lot if I am wrong about Oresol [the perceived risk/likelihood-of-consequences dimension].
6. Oresol is for serious cases of diarrhea [the situational dimension].
7. When/if I use Oresol on my dehydrating baby, I can't help thinking of what other people would say if they knew that I was doing so [the social visibility dimension].
8. I found that I liked knowing more about Oresol after I used it on my sick baby [the cognitive dissonance dimension].

KNOWLEDGE-BASED ADOPTION

I've used Oresol because it is the correct treatment for dehydration:

5 = definitely agree,
4 = generally agree,
3 = neither agree nor disagree,
2 = generally disagree,
1 = definitely disagree.

LEARNING MOTIVATORS

The respondent will be asked to express his or her agreement or disagreement, along a 5-point scale, with each of the following statements:

Planning Need Motivator

"I want to see exactly how Oresol works."

"I want to understand what Oresol does to my sick baby."

Sense-of-Autonomy Need Motivator:

"When my baby is sick, I want to know what is really going on."

"When my baby is sick, I like knowing what to do to help him or her."

MOTIVATION TO COMPLY WITH SIGNIFICANT OTHER'S EXPECTATION

Will you tell me to what extent you feel you want to do what each of the following thinks you should or expect you to do? Would you say that you would

   5 = definitely want to,
   4 = probably want to,
   3 = not know if you want to,
   2 = probably not want to or,
   1 = definitely not want to

do what each of these people expect you to do?

  1. your husband?
  2. your mother? [and so on]

PERCEIVED SIGNIFICANCE OF CONSEQUENCES

To what extent would you say that each of the following would be important for you to know about the use of Oresol? Would you say that for you it would be

   4 = extremely important,
   3 = quite important,
   2 = somewhat important, or
   1 = not that important to know that

  1. your baby would not like the taste of Oresol?
  2. Oresol will not stop your baby's diarrhea?

PERFORMANCE OF THE SOCIAL MARKETING PRODUCT

Attribute-specific Performance

My baby_____the taste of Oresol.

> 5 = definitely liked,
> 4 = liked,
> 3 = neither liked nor disliked,
> 2 = did not like, or
> 1 = definitely did not like.

Global

Overall and considering everything, Oresol was

> 5 = very good,
> 4 = good,
> 3 = neither good nor bad,
> 2 = bad, or
> 1 = very bad.

PERSONAL/NONPERSONAL INFORMATION SOURCES

From which one of the following sources did you first learn about Oresol?

Personal Sources	Nonpersonal Sources
( ) neighbor	( ) radio
( ) health center doctor	( ) television
( ) health center nurse/mid-wife	( ) posters
	( ) newspapers/magazines
( ) friends	( ) handouts/brochures
( ) relatives	( ) billboards
( ) other_____	( ) other_____

PHYSICAL/SENSORY CUES FOR PRODUCT ATTRIBUTE INFERENCE

Suppose that you have these two Oresols. Oresol A is more effective than Oresol B. From off the top of your head, which would be

	A	B
1. lighter in color	( )	( )
2. heavier in weight	( )	( )

	A	B
3. fresher smelling	( )	( )
4. granulated	( )	( )
5. packaged in singles	( )	( )

RESPONSE TO OUTCOME

Will you please tell me the extent to which each of the following would affect your decision to give Oresol to your sick baby. Would you say that you

1 = would definitely not give Oresol,
2 = would probably not give Oresol,
3 = are not sure,
4 = would probably still give Oresol, or
5 = would definitely give Oresol?

1. If you thought your baby would not like the taste of Oresol.
2. If you found that Oresol would not stop your baby's diarrhea [and so on to the other "conditional" items.]

SATISFACTION

Attribute-specific Beliefs
Oresol saved my baby from dehydration:

5 = completely agree,
4 = generally agree,
3 = neither agree nor disagree,
2 = generally disagree,
1 = completely disagree.

Attribute-specific Affect
I liked what Oresol was able to do.

5 = definitely agree,
4 = generally agree,
3 = neither agree nor disagree,
2 = generally disagree,
1 = definitely disagree.

TESTABILITY OF THE ADOPTION OBJECT

Do you believe that Oresol can

    4 = very easily be,
    3 = generally be,
    2 = probably not be, or
    1 = definitely not be

physically tested or tried?

TRIAL ADOPTION

I'm using Oresol for my sick baby because I just want to try it.

    2 = true,
    1 = not true.

VALUE

I believe in Oresol's ability to stop a sick baby's loss of body water, and because a baby's health is worth everything to a mother, Oresol ought to be used by all mothers for their dehydrating babies.

    5 = strongly agree,
    4 = generally agree,
    3 = neither agree nor disagree,
    2 = generally disagree,
    1 = strongly disagree.

VISIBILITY OF THE ADOPTION OBJECTIVE

Do you think that your using Oresol will

    4 = immediately be obvious/evident to others,
    3 = probably be obvious/evident to others,
    2 = not likely be obvious/evident to others,
    1 = not at all be obvious/evident to others?

CHAPTER

6

Analyzing the Diffusion of Social Products

The aim of social change campaigns is the adoption of an idea or practice by all the members of a target-adopter group or population. In this chapter we expand the analysis to the spread or diffusion of a new social idea or practice from individuals to a whole population of target adopters, focusing on collective or mass behavior. For example, a series of individual target adopters or mass media messages can persuade others to adopt a particular behavior or both can be done simultaneously.

The ability of social marketers to plan and manage the diffusion or spread of adoptions to the largest possible target-adopter population requires an understanding of both individual behavior and the mechanisms by which new ideas and practices spread to the larger group or population of target adopters. Social marketers are concerned about whether new ideas or practices are diffused among many, some, or a few members of a target-adopter population.

PREDICTING SOCIAL DIFFUSION AND CHANGE

Marketing scientists have developed prediction models that successfully forecast the spread of adoptions. Kotler classified these models into three types: (1) rapid penetration diffusion, (2) grad-

119

ual penetration diffusion, and (3) contagionlike diffusion.[1] Case 6-1 illustrates the reality and usefulness of these models.

Rapid-Penetration Diffusion Model

Social marketers who use the rapid-penetration diffusion model are dealing with a diffusion process as shown in Figure 6-1. To use this model, social marketers must estimate two items. The first is the total number or percentage of potential adopters. In Figure 6-1, this proportion is 40 percent; that is, it is unlikely that more than 40 percent of the population will ever adopt the social product. This "ceiling" can be estimated by conducting a survey to determine the percentage of persons who express a strong desire for the product. The next step is to estimate the constant rate at which the remaining potential target adopters will be penetrated. For example, a rate of 30 percent would mean that in each period, 30 percent of the remaining potential target adopters would be converted. The higher the penetration rate, the faster the curve in Figure 6-1 approaches the ceiling.[2]

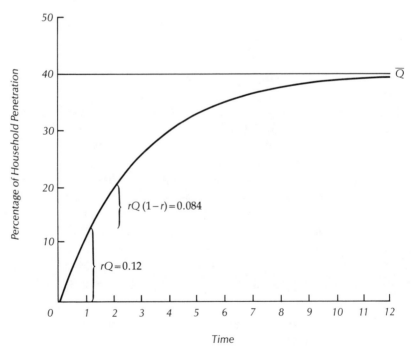

FIGURE 6-1 The Rapid-Penetration Diffusion Model

This model will provide accurate estimates as long as none of the characteristics of the diffusion program are changed and no superior alternative to the social product is introduced. The developer of this model has reported successful applications of it.[3]

Gradual-Penetration Diffusion Model

Social marketers who forecast diffusion on the basis of this model can refer to the diffusion (S) curve, as shown in Figure 6–2. Here, the diffusion starts slowly. Beyond some point, diffusion accelerates at an increasing rate and subsequently decelerates until it stops at a plateau.[4]

To use this prediction model, social marketers must estimate the S-curve's parameters. A pilot test of the diffusion program can provide initial rough estimates. If the social product is launched differently in several pilot areas, the social marketer

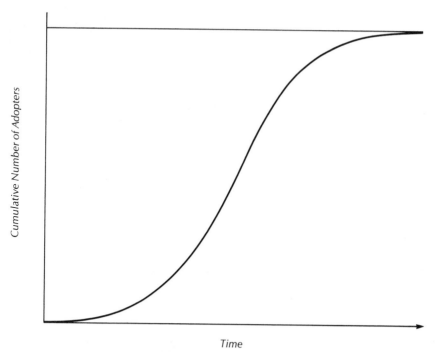

Time

FIGURE 6–2 The Gradual-Penetration Diffusion Model

must estimate the parameters for each area separately and choose the most efficient diffusion program for each.

Contagionlike Diffusion Model

When the diffusion process resembles the spread of a contagious disease, its pattern is like the curve shown in Figure 6–3.[5] In application, the use of the contagionlike diffusion model calls for the estimates of the total possible number of potential target adopt-

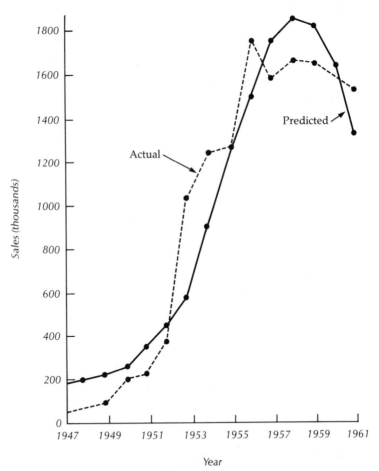

FIGURE 6–3 The Contagionlike Diffusion Model: Actual versus Predicted Diffusion Curves

SOURCE: Reprinted by permission from F. M. Bass, "A New Product Growth Model for Consumer Durables," *Management Science*, 15 (January 1969), p. 219. Copyright 1969 The Institute of Management Sciences.

ers, the rate by which target adopters influence nonadopters, and the rate by which nonpersonal media influence nonadopters.

According to Bass, there are two major influences on the total possible number of potential adopters: the price or cost of acquiring the social product and the effectiveness of the social marketing program in establishing multiple uses or consistent users of the adoption product.[6] (These influences would apply to the two previous models as well.) The major determinant of the rate of influence of target adopters on nonadopters is the social product's capacity to stimulate favorable word-of-mouth communication. The rate of influence of nonpersonal media on nonadopters is mainly a function of the size and effectiveness of the mass media communication.

Bass used this model to forecast the diffusion of eleven major appliance products, such as room air conditioners, electric refrigerators, home freezers, black and white and color television, power lawn mowers, and so on. The forecasts matched the patterns of the actual diffusion extraordinarily well, considering that the predictions were based only on the first three years of data, not the whole time series. Figure 6–3 reproduces Bass's forecasts for the diffusion of room air conditioners versus the actual pattern of diffusion. The forecasts of the diffusion of these commercial products apply to social products and social marketing campaigns as well.

Selecting a Prediction Model

The diffusion models should fit the specific social products to be marketed. Each has a set of conditions that it meets best, so one can determine which model is most appropriate for a particular purpose. The rapid-penetration model is best for forecasting social products that are expected to have a penetration level of only a fraction of the target-adopter population, to penetrate the target-adopter population rapidly, and to penetrate the remaining nonadopters at a constant rate.

The gradual-penetration model is more suited to social products with the following expectations for adoption: earliest adoption by a small fraction of target adopters, known as innovators; further adoptions by another relatively small number of the targeted population, known as early adopters, who, in turn, will influence an early majority to adopt; further adoption by a late majority; and further adoption by laggards who are finally converted to adoption.

The contagionlike model is most predictive if these conditions are met: adoption is expected to reach the total target population, as determined by the social marketing program's pricing characteristics, multiple-use, and persuasion characteristics; product penetration by two rates of penetration (the rate of influence exerted by target adopters on nonadopters and the rate of nonpersonal media influence on nonadopters).

EXPLAINING THE DIFFUSION OF SOCIAL PRODUCTS

Why Is the Initial Diffusion Phase Rapid or Slow?

There are several alternative explanations for why the initial diffusion phase may be rapid or slow. In looking at the adoption of contraceptives, Roberto suggested that the social marketers' choice of target-adopter segments may provide the answer. If the target segments are highly predisposed, then initial diffusion will be rapid.[7] Robertson, Zielinski, and Ward noted the rate of initial diffusion is influenced by the aggressiveness of retailers who introduce the product.[8] Brown identified innovation as the source of rapid initial penetration—the product's "continual technological improvement and adaptation to the market."[9] Rogers determined that rapid diffusion occurs when a social product is characterized by simplicity, communicability, relative advantage, compatibility, and divisibility.[10]

So what value do these alternative explanations have for social marketers? Each raises the social marketer's confidence in the manageability and controllability of the diffusion process. For example, we can conclude that the initial diffusion rate is manageable by the marketer's choice of target-adopter segments and by the choice of retailers. Other characteristics of the product, such as technical improvements and communicability, are similarly manageable.

How Do Adoptions Aggregate into Diffusion?

The contributions of several disciplines will be examined to explain how adoptions spread across a larger group.

Marketing Simulation

Marketing scientists have built several simulation models to understand the diffusion process. Consider, for example, Alba's simulation model of the adoption diffusion of the "touch-tone" telephone in Deerfield, Illinois.[11] Alba wanted to forecast the number of new target adopters in each period, as well as the order in which they would adopt the touch-tone telephone. He gathered data on seven traits of target adopters (including venturesomeness, cosmopoliteness, social integration, social mobility, privilegedness, and status concern); information sources about the new telephone, such as personal or mass media; and adoption dates.

Alba developed the probabilities that each resident in a sample would be exposed to a touch-tone telephone and word-of-mouth communications about it and, in turn, expose others to touch-tone telephones. These probabilities were made a function of the target-adopters' traits. Then to determine if the target adopter saw a persuasive communication during a given period of time, a random number of target adopters were surveyed. Of the ones who saw a message, another random number were surveyed to determine whether a change in their attitude had led to an adoption. The probability of a respondent's change in attitude was a function of the message's persuasiveness, which, in turn, depended on the message, source, transmitter, and content.

The resident who did not yet adopt the touch-tone telephone could be exposed to a neighbor who might talk about it. The model generated a probability about the likelihood of any two Deerfield residents discussing the touch-tone phone. This probability was a function of the degree to which the two residents shared the same traits.

The simulation covered eight periods of approximately two months each. Fifty replications were done, and their mean, or average, results were compared with the actual diffusion curve. Although the overall prediction of diffusion was unsatisfactory, the predictions for the early and later target adopters were impressive. The model also accurately discriminated between the individuals who changed attitudes because of mass media influence and others who changed because of personal influence. It tested, in addition, the relative impact of high- and low-level advertising on adoption, finding that higher advertising levels did not significantly increase the rate of adoption.

Innovation Diffusion Research

Innovation diffusion research suggests that different types of adopters accept an innovation at different points in time.[12] Table 6-1 summarizes the size, timing of adoption, and motivations for adoption of each target-adopter segment. The diffusion process begins with a small (2.5 percent) segment of innovative-minded adopters. These adopters are drawn to novelty and have a need to be different. They are followed by an early segment of target adopters (13.5 percent), who are drawn by the social product's intrinsic value. A third early majority segment (34 percent) perceive the spread of a product and decide to go along with it, out of their need to match and imitate. The late majority (34 percent) jump on the bandwagon, and the remaining segment, the laggards (16 percent), follow suit as the product attains popularity and broad acceptance.

TABLE 6-1 Elements of the Innovation Diffusion Model That Are Useful for Diffusion Planning

Target-Adopter Segments	Size[a]	Timing Sequence of Adoption	Motivation for Adoption
Innovator segment	2.5	First	Need for novelty and need to be different
Early adopter segment	13.5	Second	Recognition of adoption object's intrinsic/convenience value from contact with innovators
Early majority segment	34.0	Third	Need to imitate/match and deliberateness trait
Late majority segment	34.0	Fourth	Need to join the bandwagon triggered by the majority opinion legitimating the adoption object
Laggard segment	16.0	Last	Need to respect tradition

[a]Percentage of the total population of target adopters.

SOURCE: Adapted with permission of The Free Press, a Division of Macmillan, Inc., from *Communication of Innovations: A Cross-Cultural Approach,* second edition, by Everett R. Rogers with F. Floyd Shoemaker. Copyright © 1971 by The Free Press.

The five segments of target adopters, it should be noted, are somewhat overstated in terms of their size and even motivational differences. The scheme basically assumes a learn-feel-do sequence. Figure 6–4 depicts Rogers and Shoemaker's conceptualization of the entire diffusion process.

All stages of the adoption process, shown in Figure 6–4, are potentially manageable by social change agents. For example, the "knowledge" stage, while under the influence of the characteristics of target adopters and the social system, also is affected by the marketing campaign's communications and the social product's perceived characteristics. The "persuasion" stage is influenced by a product's characteristics as well as the communications. Table 6–2 identifies appropriate marketing tools for each stage in the Rogers-Shoemaker paradigm of social change.

Social Geography

Social geography is a method for explaining the spatial pattern and the timing exhibited in the adoption diffusion of innovative products. According to Brown, the Rogers-Shoemaker model unrealistically assumes that target adopters have an equal opportunity to adopt a product. A "market and infrastructure perspective" must be incorporated in any theory of diffusion. Unless a social marketing campaign is established that ensures that information about the product and the product itself is available in each location where target adopters are found, adoption will not take place.

TABLE 6–2 Influencing Adoption Diffusion

Target Adopters' Responses	Appropriate Marketing Tools
Knowledge	Communication: personal and nonpersonal
Persuasion	Communication, product positioning, and price
Decision	The whole social marketing mix
Adoption	The whole social marketing mix
Confirmation	Communication and the performance of the product
Continue	Service delivery, product positioning, and performance of the product

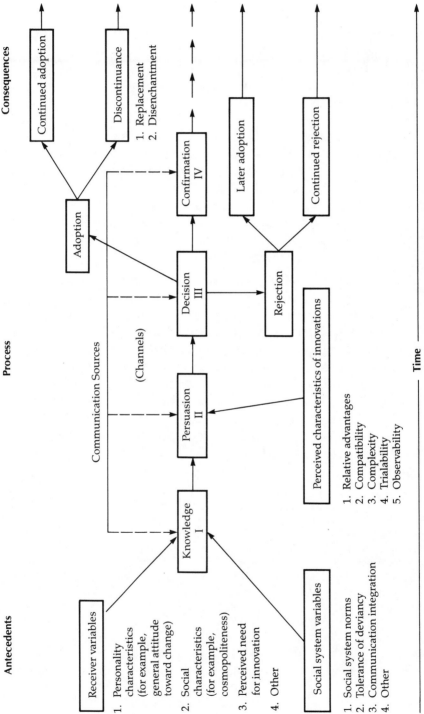

FIGURE 6-4 The Rogers-Shoemaker Adoption Diffusion 'Paradigm'

SOURCE: Reprinted with permission from The Free Press, a Division of Macmillan, Inc., from *Communication of Innovations: A Cross-Cultural Approach*, second edition, by Everett R. Rogers with F. Floyd Shoemaker. Copyright© 1971 by The Free Press.

Social Change Theory and Research

Social change theory is useful in alerting social marketers to the conditions that facilitate the adoption of new social products and social changes by individuals, groups, and entire populations, as well as the key determinants of adoption to consider in adoption and diffusion planning.

From the perspective of social change theory, diffusion occurs as an accumulation of individual adopters' "selective acceptance" of a new idea or practice.[13] What are the influences on selective acceptance? At least five can be identified.

The first is an individual adopter's specific attitudes and values toward a new idea or practice. Apodaca described the process whereby Spanish-American farmers in New Mexico's Rio Grande Valley adopted a hybrid corn introduced by government extension workers.[14] The farmers were receptive because they were convinced of the new variety's superior yield. However, within three years, practically all the target adopters returned to the old corn because the hybrid did not make as good a tortilla as the old corn. In this case, the change in products did not fit the community's attitudes and preferences.

A second factor is a new social product's compatibility with the existing culture. For example, in the American culture, cattle are basically utilitarian—a source of income. Therefore, new profitable ways of breeding, culling, and slaughtering cattle will be readily accepted. However, the Nilotic African cattle raiser perceives the animal as having intrinsic value. Slaughtering cattle is tantamount to a crime; therefore, new ways of improving cattle-raising practices that run counter to the traditional culture's view of cattle will find slow or no acceptance.[15]

A third factor is a social product's demonstrability, or the extent to which adoption of a new social product can be shown to be desirable or have value for the target adopter. Unfortunately, some social marketing products are not readily demonstrable. For example, the personal usefulness of the cessation of drug use to a person who is enrolled in a drug-addiction rehabilitation program or the value to consumers of energy conservation is not easily demonstrated in the short run and requires, in some cases, protracted trial-and-adoption behavior. This situation poses a dilemma: target adopters will hesitate to adopt what cannot be shown to be tangibly and immediately useful, but this usefulness can be demonstrated only if the new social idea or practice is first adopted and experienced.

A fourth factor is the felt costs of social change or of adopting a new social product. There are two kinds of felt cost: one is the technical cost or difficulty of adopting something new; the other is the perceived potential loss from changing the status quo. Wertheim illustrated the first by way of the "Green Revolution" in Asia.[16] This social change campaign involved disseminating to farmers new higher-yielding varieties of rice, along with more advanced planting methods and technologies. However, adoption required farmers to use fertilizers and insecticides, and the new rice varieties required abundant irrigation. These technical requirements proved too costly for the target-adopter farmers in Indonesia and the Philippines to undertake.

The second kind of felt cost is experienced by target adopters who have a vested interest in the status quo. For example, in the industrialized states of the North, the National Labor Relations Act fortified the political power of organized American labor because the labor unions were prepared "to make use of the formal authority created by the legal change."[17] However, in the less-industrialized and less-unionized southern states, organized labor did not grow as fast. Those to whom the lack of unions was profitable dominated public life and opposed the changes that the Labor Relations Act sought to bring about.

A fifth factor is the change agent or the social marketing campaign itself. The Indonesian East Java family planning program became the most successful birth control program in the Third World precisely because the then Indonesian head of state, President Suharto, personally spearheaded its development. In every annual state-of-the-nation address, Suharto emphasized that overpopulation was the country's most critical problem. He also made the head of national family planning a member of the cabinet.

MANAGING SOCIAL DIFFUSION

Robertson, Zielinski, and Ward identified an ideal pattern of adoption diffusion:

1. Rapid takeoff: initial adoptions achieved with speed.
2. Rapid acceleration: cumulative adoptions secured along a steep diffusion curve.

3. Maximum penetration: the greatest number of adoptions achieved within the targeted adopter segment.
4. No dropouts: stable, committed adoptions over the long term.[18]

Achieving Rapid Takeoff

The factors affecting the rate of takeoff are summarized as follows:

1. The more the social marketing program is focused on market segments that are highly predisposed to the social product, the more rapid the takeoff.
2. The more the program focuses on the innovators and early adopters in the target segments, the more rapid the takeoff.
3. The more the social product fits the attitudes and values of the culture, the more rapid the takeoff.
4. The more the social product embodies the characteristics of simplicity, communicability, relative advantage, compatibility, and divisibility, the more rapid the takeoff.
5. The greater the accessibility of the social product by means of aggressive retail or service outlets, the more rapid the takeoff.

Achieving Rapid Acceleration

The factors affecting a rapid acceleration of adoption diffusion are these:

1. The greater the social interactions among members of the target adopter population, the more rapid the acceleration.
2. The greater the exposure of nonadopting segments of the target population through personal and nonpersonal communicatioins, the more rapid the acceleration.
3. The more manageable the technical difficulties and the costs of adoption, the more rapid the acceleration.
4. The greater the frequency with which respected leaders or other public figures promote the social product, the more rapid the acceleration.

Achieving Maximum Penetration

Kotler identified two factors that affect maximum penetration of social change campaigns that are accompanied by tangible, concrete products (such as the diffusion of contraceptives in family planning campaigns).[19] One is the social product's price or cost; the other is the social marketing program's effectiveness in establishing multiple uses or consistent users of the product.

Let us now examine maximum penetration in connection with social campaigns that do not involve tangible products. For example, Amnesty International manages a human rights campaign that seeks to abolish torture and other forms of inhumane punishment. The social change campaign has the objective of "rousing public opinion and mobilizing people internationally against torture."[20] The antitorture campaign has proceeded in two stages. In the first stage, Amnesty International obtained more than a million signatures from prominent political leaders, government ministers, religious and labor leaders, police and prison officers, scientists, physicians, educators, artists, and writers in some 90 countries. In the second stage, it submitted the signed appeal with a million signatures to the president of the United Nations (UN) General Assembly.

The question then arises, Was maximum penetration achieved in mobilizing the world's peoples against the political uses of torture? The answer depends on which target-adopter segments were being targeted. Amnesty International aimed for adoption behavior from the following three segments:

The Segment	The Sought-After Adoption Behavior
Prominent citizens of member-countries of Amnesty International	Acceptance of the need for an appeal to the UN and signing the appeal.
Members of the UN General Assembly	Adoption of a formal resolution outlawing torture.
All citizens of all UN-member countries	Public awareness that torture violates cherished human rights.

In this example, maximum penetration was brought about by the social marketer's determination of the diffusion objective for each target-adopter segment and the achievement of adoptions by the greatest number of members in each segment.

Achieving Diffusion by Committed Target Adopters

Social change campaigns succeed if they achieve committed adoption, not just trial adoption. Ideally, there should not be any target-adopter "dropouts." According to Rogers and Shoemaker, continued adoption is fostered by the "integration of the innovation" into adopters' daily or regular practices and lifestyles.[21] Their notion of integration is similar to the notion of satisfaction among consumers and others. The more a social product is able to deliver on its promises, the greater the satisfaction it gives target adopters; then, we can predict, the greater the chances a social marketing campaign will be free of dropouts.

CASE 6–1
Expanded Program on Immunization

Over the past 15 years, developed and developing countries of the world have experienced varied diffusion of immunization against the deadlier childhood diseases. Data on these experiences provide illustrations of the reality and usefulness of the social-diffusion prediction models that this chapter discussed. The World Health Organization's (WHOs) Expanded Program on Immunization (EPI) has gathered these data.

EPI

The WHO established the EPI in 1974. In 1977, EPI set the long-term objective of immunizing all the world's infants and pregnant women against six major diseases by 1990. These six diseases are

1. Measles, which affects practically all unimmunized children and kills over 2 million of them every year.
2. Pertussis, or whopping cough, which kills some 0.6 million children each year.
3. Neonatal tetanus, which is contracted at birth through contamination of the umbilical cord and kills about 0.8 million infants each year.
4. Polio, which is a principal cause of lameness in developing countries and kills about 30,000 children each year.
5. Tuberculosis, which attacks about 10 million children each year.

SOURCE: J. D. Sherris and R. Blackburn, "Immunizing the World's Children," *Population Reports,* Series L, No. 5, pp. 153–192. Baltimore: Johns Hopkins University Population Information Program, 1986.

6. Diphtheria, which although less common, still kills 10–15 percent of its victims each year.

In 1985, together with the United Nations Children's Fund (UNICEF), WHO took specific measures to speed up EPI. These included getting its member-countries' health ministries to see that their health care centers (1) provide information on immunizations at each health contact, (2) reduce the dropout rates, (3) raise the priority of controlling measles, polio, and neonatal tetanus, (4) bring the immunization services to more of the urban poor, and (5) use ''special events'' immunization campaigns like ''a national immunization week.''

An effective immunization diffusion program prevents dis-

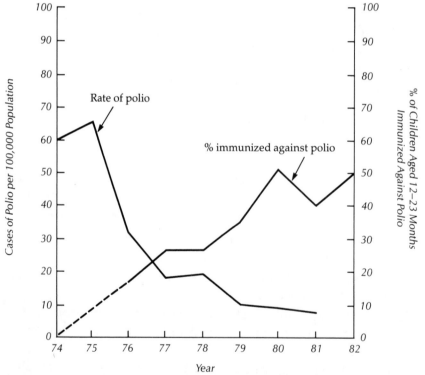

Note: No data on percentage of children immunized before 1976

FIGURE 6–A Percentage of Children, Aged 12–23 Months, Who Were Immunized Against Poliomyelitis and the Rate of Poliomyelitis, Yaounde, Cameroon, 1974–82

SOURCE: J. D. Sherris and R. Blackburn, ''Immunizing the World's Children,'' *Population Reports*, Series L, No. 5. Baltimore: Johns Hopkins University Population Information Program, 1986.

abling and disfiguring sicknesses and saves lives. A study of the West African immunization campaigns against measles estimated that they saved at least 170,000 lives each year. The Sri Lankan DPT (diphtheria, pertussis, and tetanus) immunization program was said to have reduced deaths from neonatal tetanus to a tenth of the previous level. Brazil's antipolio campaign, introduced as a "Twice-Yearly Vaccination Days" special event, is estimated to have cut polio cases to less than 0.06 per 100,000.

Diffusion of Immunization Adoptions

The data on immunization adoptions in Cameroon and in Sri Lanka are of particular interest. The gradual-penetration diffusion model fits the adoption-diffusion data of Yaounde, Cam-

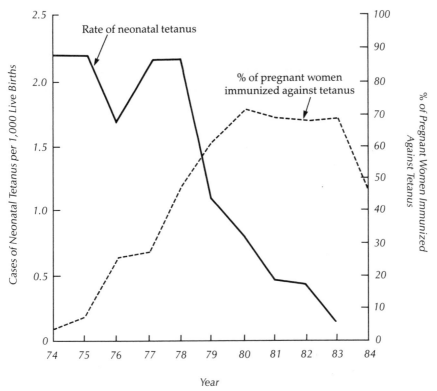

FIGURE 6–B Percentage of Pregnant Women Who Were Immunized Against Tetanus and the Rate of Neonatal Tetanus, Sri Lanka, 1974–84
SOURCE: J. D. Sherris and R. Blackburn, "Immunizing the World's Children," *Population Reports*, Series L, No. 5. Baltimore: Johns Hopkins University Population Information Program, 1986.

eroon, for oral polio vaccinations. Figure 6–A shows the data on the gradual increase in the adoption of the oral polio vaccine from 1974 to 1982. The benefit of this diffusion in terms of year to year polio rate reduction is also shown.

The data on the immunization of Sri Lankan pregnant women against tetanus from 1974 to 1984 are predictable under the contagionlike diffusion model. Figure 6–B presents these data, together with data on the incidence of neonatal tetanus over the same period. It is clear from these data that as the diffusion of neonatal tetanus immunization covered more and more pregnant women, the incidence of neonatal tetanus dropped.

If social marketers had planned the Cameroon oral polio vaccination campaign or the Sri Lankan immunization program, they would have asked how the campaign or program could have achieved the following:

1. A more rapid takeoff because the takeoff rate in both was gradual.
2. A more rapid or earlier acceleration, since acceleration took place after 1978 in the Cameroon program and after 1977 in the Sri Lanka campaign.
3. A higher penetration because the Cameroon program reached only 50 percent of the target children and the Sri Lanka campaign reached less than 50 percent of the target pregnant women.

These are answerable questions. As this chapter has illustrated, social marketers can exercise a measure of control over their determinant variables.

DEVELOPING SOCIAL MARKETING PROGRAMS

7

◆

Designing
the Social Product

Once social marketers have analyzed the social marketing environment, the behavior of target adopters, and the means by which adoptions of social products spread throughout a population, they are ready to define the product-market fit and design the social product and marketing campaign.

Designing the social product is the foundation on which all the elements of the marketing mix are built. Designing and developing a social product entails, primarily, identifying the needs of target adopters. Social marketers aim to develop new social products that satisfy the needs of the target adopters better than those that are available or to adapt social products so they fit the adopters' needs better than they did before. The tasks are twofold: to identify the distinctive needs of target adopters that a specific social product can satisfy and to determine how to present the defined product effectively to the target adopters. The second task involves positioning the product, dressing it up, and positioning effectively the social marketing campaign and program.

THE CONCEPT OF SOCIAL PRODUCT

Social change campaigns that seek to market human rights, literacy, the cessation of cigarette smoking, energy-conservation practices, and the rehabilitation of alcohol and drug abuse, among others, often find it difficult to explain their products. The tendency is to identify features of a product: what can be seen, felt, touched, sniffed, heard, or tasted. But these characteristics do not address what target adopters really seek. For example, family planning marketers who say their product is a condom misunderstand their market. Even those who say the product is family planning may be out of touch with what target adopters are really seeking in birth control and family planning. Case 7–1 shows that even the Peace Corps, which is considered a social product, had to undergo a changing definition of the product as the needs of the target adopters were better understood.

Types of Social Products

Social marketers typically find themselves in one of three situations. They may offer a social product that satisfies a need that no other product is satisfying (Type 1). Or they may offer a social product that satisfies a need that other social products are addressing but that satisfies it better (Type 2). Or they may offer a social product that cannot satisfy a need that target adopters currently perceive or have but that nevertheless addresses a real underlying need of people (Type 3).

In terms of the behavior of target adopters, the three types of social products represent increasing levels of difficulty in adoption and penetrating the market. Type 1 is the least difficult, while Type 3 is the hardest to market.

It is also useful to distinguish between a social product that has a tangible-product base (such as methadone treatment for heroin addicts or contraceptive devices for family planning) and a social product that is largely intangible (training in literacy, the cessation of cigarette smoking, and human rights, for example). In general, the former entails a more complex social marketing task than does the latter.

Another way to distinguish social products is according to the objective or end-result of adoption. There are three idea products—a belief, an attitude, and a value—as well as two practice products—one that calls for the performance of a single act (such as acceptance of a single smallpox immunization) and the other that requires the sustained performance of a behavior made up of repeated acts (for instance, acceptance of a continuous pattern of family planning behavior).

Demands of Target Adopters and Marketing Tasks

The types of social products are summarized in Table 7–1. Each type corresponds to a particular need or demand of target adopters, which in turn, corresponds to a particular social marketing task.

Latent demand. Uncovering a latent need or demand creates an opportunity to introduce a new social product. A demand is latent when a substantial number of people share a strong need for an effective social product or service that does not exist, as in the areas of the cessation of smoking, the control of pollution, the prevention of forest fires, the prevention of heart disease, and the like.

TABLE 7–1 Types of Products, Conditions of Demand, and Marketing Tasks

Type of Product	Condition of Demand	Marketing Task
By Difficulty of Market Penetration		
New social marketing product	Latent demand	Develop the demand
Superior social marketing product	Underfilled demand	Fill a subsatisfied demand
Substitute social marketing product	Unwholesome demand	Destroy the demand
By Complication of Marketing Task		
With a tangible-product base	Dual demand	Satisfy both demands
Without a tangible-product base	Single demand	Satisfy the single need
By the Object of Adoption		
Idea	Abstract demand	Evidence the demand; evidential marketing
Practice: single act	Irregular demand	Synchronize the demand
Practice: sustained act	Faltering demand	Revitalize the demand

The practical problem for social marketers is how to convert latent demand into actual demand by means of an effective product or service. A social marketing campaign first has to determine the specific unmet need and the product that can solve it. One useful technique is problem-detection analysis (PDA).[1] PDA assumes that people are often not able to define what they need but are able to talk about their problems and concerns.

An illustration of how the technique works is a campaign to have cigarette smokers give up smoking. In this PDA survey, the first question asked was

Think about how you would feel now if you have really given up smoking? Will you tell me all the personal concerns, worries, and fears that you would have about this condition? What else?

The respondent's answer may be short or long. When the respondent is finished, the interviewer proceeds to the second and third questions:

For each concern, please tell me how frequently you feel it? Would you say you feel or encounter [problem]:

4 = practically all the time you think of giving up smoking
3 = quite frequently
2 = only every now and then
1 = very infrequently

Let's go back to each concern. Please tell me how serious you regard each concern? Would you say [problem] is

4 = extremely serious
3 = quite serious
2 = somewhat serious
1 = not really serious

The two ratings, multiplied for each identified problem or concern, yield an importance index, which helps identify the respondent's major concerns.

The final question asked for each identifiable concern is this:

Can you think of something you know that can offer a satisfactory solution to each concern? Let's start with [problem]?

The answers to this last question underscore the usefulness of PDA. They help social marketers categorize identifiable problems and their product solutions into the following:

1. Problems for which a respondent is unable to identify any available solution. For example, in terms of giving up smoking, this may be the wish to have a cigarette made of a tobacco substitute that is as tasty as real tobacco but without the nicotine and tars that are damaging to health. This type of concern calls for product innovation.

2. Concerns that may be solvable by supplying more information: "What if I keep putting on weight once I quit?" or "What do I do to keep down my stress?"

3. Concerns that illustrate latent demand, such as a smoker who says, "I've tried to quit before but it doesn't work. Others may be able to quit but I just can't give up smoking." In this instance, the target adopter must be given confidence that he or she can succeed; in this way, latent demand is converted into effective, actual demand.

Underfilled demand. In an underfilled demand situation, products or services that are available to satisfy the target adopters' needs do not fully satisfy them or the demand. In other words, a gap in feeling or experiencing satisfaction has to be filled. Social marketers must develop a new product or improve an existing one to fill that gap. In seeking to meet an underfilled demand that comes from such a gap, social marketers have to distinguish between a gap in the level of satisfaction and a gap in kind.

A gap in the level of satisfaction refers to a situation in which the available products are unable to provide the desired level, or degree, of satisfaction. A case in point is the demand by rural mothers in Third World countries for access to more physicians. Because of the scarcity of physicians and their geographic maldistribution there, few physicians serve in rural areas. Campaigns to combat malnutrition in Asia and Latin America suffer from this typs of gap.

A gap-in-kind exists when target adopters can obtain satisfaction only through an improved product or a new product that corrects the deficiencies in existing ones. When the smokers of filter-tip cigarettes began to ask for even greater protection from tar, the answer was not found in cigarettes with more filters but cigarettes with another kind of filter, namely, charcoal filters.

Unwholesome demand. Unwholesome demand exists when target adopters advocate socially harmful ideas, such as racial superiority and violence, or adhere to socially alienating practices, such as excessive drinking, drug abuse, and reckless driving.

This condition calls for social campaigns that aim to destroy the unwholesome demand. To do so effectively, social marketers must be able to provide a satisfying substitute idea or practice. A common strategic mistake is always to try to market a diametrically opposite substitute to the undesirable idea or behavior. For example, in family planning campaigns, it is often assumed that to "unsell" or replace large family units requires marketing small family units. However, the concept of a small family may not be the effective substitute value that would motivate couples to commit themselves to family planning.

Dual versus single demand. A dual-demand situation exists when target adopters may have to be created for both a product concept, such as family planning, and a tool or means to realize the value of the social product (a tangible product), as in the marketing of condoms that accompanies a family planning campaign. There are four possible situations of dual demand:

Situation	Demand for the Product Concept	Demand for the Tangible Product	Social Marketing Task
1	low	low	creation of a dual demand
2	high	low	creation of a tangible product-led demand
3	low	high	creation of a product concept-led demand
4	high	high	maintenance of a dual demand

A dual demand has to be created when the demand for both the idea or practice and for the related tangible product is low. One example is the case of countries in which family planning campaigns face resistance to the concept of birth control as well as to contraceptive techniques and devices, such as intrauterine devices and condoms.

The creation of a tangible product-led demand is called for when the demand for the product concept or campaign objective is high while the demand for the related tangible product is low.

For example, because of a major government-supported campaign to ban smoking in Singapore, the demand for ways to quit smoking is high and people are seeking cigarette substitutes to achieve this goal. However, the demand for one type of cigarette substitute, sugar-free lozenges (the campaign's tangible product base) is low.

When the demand for the social campaign's objective or product concept is low but there is broad acceptance of a related tangible product, the social marketer's task is create a product concept-led demand. In Thailand, for example, the demand for family planning (the product concept) was relatively low before a major family planning program was launched in the 1970s. However, the demand for condoms (the tangible product) was high in Bangkok, where condoms were being heavily promoted as a protection against sexually transmitted diseases. In this situation, the social marketer would have to find a way to link the high acceptance of condoms to the idea of the value of their use for the desirable goal of family planning.

Finally, the task of maintaining the dual demand relates to those marketing situations in which the demand is high for both the product concept and for its tangible-product base. The case of the Low Cost/No Cost (LC/NC) Program for energy conservation, discussed in Chapter 5, is an example.

Abstract demand. When a social marketing campaign seeks to win only the adoption of an idea, the demand may be referred to as an abstract demand. Some may argue that all social marketing programs ultimately seek behavioral change, including those that only seek the adoption of an idea. What the aim should be is really an issue of timing. For some programs, it makes practical sense to limit the objective for a time just to diffusing public awareness of a social problem. Consider the following two cases.

An antigraft movement gained currency in the Philippines after President Corazon Aquino took office. An organization called "Operasyon Walang Lagay" (OWL) was launched to discourage the giving or taking of bribes. OWL's organizers defined the movement's mission as raising "the level of awareness among the different sectors of the Filipino society, both government and private-sector, of the value of honesty as a way of life." Later, OWL added an additional objective of "reducing if not eliminating, the practice of bribery, grease money, 'tong,' and ten percent."[2]

Philippine society has had a long history of campaigns to weed out graft and corruption, and many laws, governmental policies, and monitoring agencies were already in place. Nevertheless, corruption had become a way of life in the Philippine bureaucracy. According to OWL-sponsored studies, these efforts failed because of a combination of "problems of organizational instability, frequent changes in leadership, political pressures in employee recruitment, public apathy, strained relationships with other branches and agencies of government, and legal impediments."[3] Given the history of failures, OWL executives initially were satisfied to raise consciousness about the value of honesty and honest official behavior. Later, they decided that awareness of the problem was not enough; changing the behavior of bureaucrats and eliminating bribery and corruption were the necessary goals.

Another illustration of the fine line between changing ideas and behavior is the experience of the Hunger Project, a nonprofit organization established in 1977. The goal of the Hunger Project is to eliminate hunger throughout the world that, it claims, is taking the lives of 15 million people each year. The campaign leaders assert that humanity "now possesses the resources, technology and know-how to end hunger." Yet the Hunger Project lacks the wherewithal to get every nation to take actions to end hunger. Instead, this campaign has focused on what it regards as the missing ingredient to make things happen: "the will to act on the ability to actually bring hunger to an end."[4]

The mission of the antihunger campaign is "to generate that will, that global commitment to eliminate the persistence of hunger and starvation by the end of this century."[5] To this end, its programs consist of educational forums, printed and electronic materials, media events, and the like that are directed at opinion makers, policymakers, educators, and development experts. For the Hunger Project, the acceptance of a new idea (that humanity together now can eliminate hunger with existing resources) has to precede and trigger behavioral changes (the commitment and will of governments to make the necessary choices to end hunger).

Irregular demand. Marketing some social products involves meeting irregular demands. The marketing of blood donations, for example, calls for single acts by target adopters that are often irregularly performed. Since "professional" donors, who repeatedly donate blood, do not constitute a big-enough segment on which the Red Cross can depend, the Red Cross has to find ways to attract new blood donors during periods of irregular demand.

Faltering demand. Once a social product has been marketed successfully to the entire target-adopter population, the social marketer may then face a faltering demand. If the demand for a social product begins to weaken, thought may have to be given to "remarketing" the product—launching a new marketing program that will support the desired level of demand. For example, the fall in oil prices has led the public to buy larger cars and to lessen their previous concern with conserving oil. A new campaign is needed to remind people to husband resources even when they are plentiful.

POSITIONING THE SOCIAL PRODUCT

After social marketers have gauged the market need, or demand, and the marketing task, they are ready to define the product-market fit. This task is called "product positioning."

Segmenting the Target-Adopter Population

Positioning must start with dividing the diverse population of target adopters into homogeneous segments any of which may be selected as the one to be reached with a distinct social marketing mix. Segmentation has three benefits:

1. It enables social marketers to target their efforts to those groups of target adopters who need a product most or who can be served best by the product.
2. It enables social marketers to tailor a product to the target adopters' needs and hence to provide greater satisfaction to adopters and to make it likely to sustain adoptions.
3. It enables social marketers to tailor communications and distribution more effectively to meet the adopters' needs and to win adoptions.

A target-adopter population can be partitioned into many segments. Table 7–2 lists the most frequently used segmentation vari-

Table 7-2 Major Segmentation Variables for Consumer Markets

Variable	Typical Breakdowns
Geographic	
Region	Pacific, Mountain, West North Central, West South Central, Central, East South Central, South Atlantic, Middle Atlantic, New England
County size	A, B, C, D
City or SMSA size	Under 5,000; 5,000–20,000; 20,000–50,000; 50,000–100,000; 100,000–250,000; 250,000–500,000; 500,000–1,000,000; 1,000,000–4,000,000; 4,000,000 or over
Density	Urban, suburban, rural
Climate	Northern, southern
Demographic	
Age	Under 6, 6–11, 12–19, 20–34, 35–49, 50–64, 65+
Sex	Male, female
Family size	1–2, 3–4, 5+
Family life cycle	Young, single; young, married, no children; young, married, youngest child under 6; young, married, youngest child 6 or over; older, married, with children; older, married, no children under 18; older, single; other
Income	Under $5,000; $5,000–$10,000; $10,000–$15,000; $15,000–$20,000; $20,000–$25,000; $25,000–$30,000; $30,000–$50,000; $50,000 and over
Occupation	Professional and technical; managers, officials, and proprietors; clerical, sales; craftsmen, foremen; operatives; farmers; retired; students, housewives; unemployed
Education	Grade school or less; some high school; high school graduate; some college; college graduate
Religion	Catholic, Protestant, Jewish, other
Race	White, black, oriental
Nationality	American, British, French, German, Scandinavian, Italian, Latin American, Middle Eastern, Japanese
Psychographic	
Social class	Lower lowers, upper lowers, working class, middle class, upper middles, lower uppers, upper uppers
Lifestyle	Straights, swingers, longhairs
Personality	Compulsive, gregarious, authoritarian, ambitious

Variable	*Typical Breakdowns*
Behavioral	
Occasions	Regular occasion, special occasion
Benefits	Quality, service, economy
User status	Nonuser, ex-user, potential user, first-time user, regular user
Usage rate	Light user, medium user, heavy user
Loyalty status	None, medium, strong, absolute
Readiness stage	Unaware, aware, informed, interested, desirous, intending to buy
Attitude toward product	Enthusiastic, positive, indifferent, negative, hostile

SOURCE: Philip Kotler, *Marketing Management: Analysis, Planning, and Control*, 6th ed. © 1988, p. 287. Reprinted by permission of Prentice-Hall, Inc., Englewood Cliffs, NJ.

ables in U.S. social marketing. Segments can be formed by using single variables or several variables in combination. For example, Figure 7–1 shows a complex segmentation of the market of visually impaired persons. In this instance, a social agency can perform more effectively if it limits its service to one or a few segments of visually impaired people, instead of trying to serve all groups.

Choosing Segmentation Variables

Which variables should social marketers use in segmenting their market? The most appropriate segmentation variables are those that best capture differences in the behavior of target adopters. In certain cases, the differences in behavior are a function of demographics. For example, age is a factor in drug-addiction behavior, and this variable defines the segments of children, teenagers, young adults, older adults, and senior citizens. These age-defined segments differ in their propensities toward drug addiction and drug-use behaviors. Therefore, age may be the most useful segmentation variable for marketing therapy programs for drug addicts. In other cases, geographic or psychographic characteristics are the primary segmentation variables.

In cases when multiple segmentation variables apply, data analysis will help. The cross tabulation of adoption/nonadoption data

		Single Handicapped		Multiple Handicapped	
		Partially sighted	Totally blind	Partially sighted	Totally blind
Congenital	Elderly				
	Working-age adult				
	Child				
Adventitious	Elderly				
	Working-age adult				
	Child				

FIGURE 7–1 Segmentation of the Market of Visually Impaired Persons
SOURCE: Constructed from Roberta Clarke under the supervision of Benson P. Shapiro, "Teaching Note, The Richardson Center for the Blind," no date.

against the demographic, geographic, or psychographic variables will reveal which variables best differentiate the target adopters from the nonadopters.

A social marketer should not use too many segmentation variables. For example, if eight variables were used, each at two levels, this would yield 256 ($=2^8$) market segments. This is too great a number of segments to reach successfully, since it would require tailoring marketing programs to each of these segments—a task that is too complex for the objectives that are sought. However, suppose a voluntary sterilization agency's analysis of data on knowledge, attitudes, and practices found that only the three variables of age, number of children, and level of income were closely associated with the acceptance or nonacceptance of a vasectomy. Retaining two levels of each variable yields only 8 ($=3^2$) segments. Now the segmentation would be more manageable.

Market Targeting

The marketer's next step is to evaluate the different segments to decide how many and which ones to serve. This step is called market targeting.

Suppose the following four target-adopter segments for an oral rehydration program were identified by using the following geographic and income variables: (1) very poor rural households, (2) marginally poor rural households, (3) very poor urban households, and (4) marginally poor urban households. Because of limited funds, the marketing campaign might have to choose to target only the third and fourth segments, rather than scatter the resources over all four segments.

Product Positioning

Social marketers must next determine what product positioning is most suitable for each target-adopter segment. How is this positioning to be determined? Two tasks are involved: to identify the major needs of the target-adopter segment and to develop a product advantage to satisfy these needs. Both must be determined for the product to be distinctive and motivating. A product that meets a major need of a target segment but is unable to meet that need better than other products is not distinctive and will not motivate adoptions. A product that is superior in satisfying minor needs but that fails to satisfy a major need also will not be motivating.

The concept of a product's distinctiveness can be illustrated in the case of a new product, a superior product, and a substitute product. When the 1973 oil crisis hit the industrializing East Asian countries of Singapore, South Korea, and Taiwan, office workers in these countries felt the need for a cheaper means of transportation. They wanted something to take them from their home to their office and back without the burdensome cost of using their cars. Someone introduced car pooling as the answer to this need. As a social marketing product, car pooling was distinctive. It addressed a major need and served that need uniquely. It was far superior to public transportation or taxis in convenience and cost. Car pooling was the new product that served an untapped need of the target adopters.

The Low Cost/No Cost (LC/NC) energy-conservation project was a superior product to Project Payback. Although both projects satisfied a major need for doing something about energy conservation, LC/NC delivered the better solution. It called for a simple, concrete, and action-oriented energy-conservation practice that focused on "individual action to counteract feelings of helplessness in the face of an energy crisis and rising fuel costs."[6]

An example of a substitute product is a drug-addiction program that offers the youth segment the means to satisfy a major need while effectively challenging the need underlying the drug abuse. A noted social psychologist says that taking drugs is attractive to young people "not in spite of its dangerousness but rather because of its dangerousness."[7] If this is the case, then, according to the concept of a substitute product, the effective way to counter drug taking in this segment is to offer a substitute product that meets a higher need. For example, high school athletes, when told that any team member who uses drugs will be dropped from the team, may refrain from using drugs because being on the team meets a higher need.

This discussion leads to an important principle of product development in social marketing. The challenge is not so much to come out with superior products but to develop effective substitute products. Effective substitute products are the motivating base for asking people to give up their currently undesirable practices, such as in smoking, excessive drinking, drug abuse, and poor nutrition.

POSITIONING THE TANGIBLE-PRODUCT BASE

What about the social marketing product that has a tangible-product base? What is the social marketers' positioning problem for this class of products?

Product Concept Versus Tangible-Product Positioning

Let us tackle this problem by considering the case of a family planning program that targets newly married and one-child couples. For these target-adopter segments, family planning itself is the product concept. The need it will satisfy is "to express one's love to one's life partner." For the husband, this need includes "seeing that the wife is protected from the weakening effects of frequent pregnancies."

Having been "sold" on family planning, a couple must now choose a contraceptive technique or device—a tangible product—to achieve the objective of birth control. The product they chose will have to satisfy the couple's needs. Each alternative contraception product may suit a different need. For the pill, the need may be to maintain "spontaneity" in intercourse without risking pregnancy; for the diaphragm, it may be to avoid the side effects of the pill; and for the condom, it may be the husband's need to share the burden of preventing unwanted pregnancies.

Social marketers normally plan their product-diffusion campaign for tangible products by adoption of the product concept and then by adoption of the tangible product. Proceeding in this sequence can require a long time, similar to the pitfalls involved in efforts, discussed earlier, to change attitudes first before influencing behavior. Promoting both the social product concept and a related tangible product at the same time will bring about earlier trial adoption and possibly a change in attitude.

Branding and Packaging a Tangible Product

After having determined the product-market fit, social marketers have to present the fit to target adopters. This stage involves branding and packaging the tangible product.

Branding and packaging is an important stage. The first thing that potential adopters see is a name and the packaging of a product. Often, these are the earliest sensory stimuli to reach target adopters. The brand name should not be a casual afterthought but an integral reinforcer of the product concept. A brand name should have four qualities:

1. It should be easy to pronounce, recognize, and remember.
2. It should capture or define the product's benefits.
3. It should define a product's qualities or appeal.
4. It should be distinctive.

Marketing research firms have developed elaborate tests for researching the effectiveness of brand names: association tests, which tap the images evoked when the name is mentioned; memory tests, which measure how well a brand name is remembered; and preference tests, which probe consumers' preferences for brand names. Normally, marketers generate a number of brand names through brainstorming and later evaluate the choices made by consensus by applying these tests.

What about the packaging? Whereas a brand name is a singular thing, packaging consists of several elements or dimensions, including the material, shape, color, size, weight, symbols, label, and copy, which makes it harder to test.

The oral rehydration solution package, mentioned earlier, is worth examining in this regard. The product is a small bag. The bag is divided into two sections, one containing glucose, and the other, salt. The printed words, or copy, on the package instruct the mother to tear the top of both sides and then to pour the glucose and the salt powder into a liter of water. In the Honduran oral rehydration program, the package carried the name "Litrosol," reinforcing the idea of the solution's "liter" size when dissolved in water. In the Philippines, the brand name is "Oresol," which combines the first syllables of the product's generic name, "oral rehydration solution."

Tests are available to elicit target adopters' reactions to the packaging of a social product. Engineering tests are conducted to ensure that the package stands up under normal conditions; visual tests, to ensure that the printed copy on a package is readable and the package colors and design are pleasing; dealer tests, to ensure that dealers find the packages attractive and easy to handle; and consumer tests, to measure consumers' responses to particular types of packaging.

POSITIONING THE ORGANIZATION AND PROGRAM OF THE SOCIAL MARKETING CAMPAIGN

The final consideration in designing a social product involves conveying an acceptable image of the social campaign behind the product, its staff, mission, and competence and the value of its goals. When a product or a message communicating a product arises from a campaign or campaign staff that enjoys great credibility and respect, the likelihood that the product will be adopted is greatly increased.

For example, in 1978, to get customers to cut down on electricity consumption, one set of households received the campaign's message from Con Edison (a low credibility source); a second set, from the New York State Public Service Commission (a high credibility source); and a third set, the control group, received no communications.[8] The households received the marketing messages with their monthly electric bills.

In the month following receipt of the energy-conservation communications, the electric bills of the three groups were compared. The two groups that received the electricity-conservation messages used significantly less electricity than did the group that received no such communication, and the group that received the message from the Public Service Commission used substantially less electricity than did the group that received the message from Con Edison.

What can social marketers do to raise or improve the credibility of their campaigns and programs? Research indicates that credibility is a function of three things: expertise, trustworthiness, and likability.[9] Expertise is the specialized knowledge and skills a campaign appears to have, which reinforces the image of the objectives that are being marketed. Physicians, scientists, and professors rank high in terms of expertise and the authority of their communications. Trustworthiness is related to how objective and honest the source is perceived to be. Organizations with a record of good public service are considered trustworthy. Likability describes the source's attractiveness or appeal to a public or to a target-adopter group. Organizations and social marketing campaigns that have the highest credibility have achieved high scores on all three.

If a target adopter has a positive attitude toward a social marketing campaign and its communicated messages or has a negative attitude toward both, a state of congruity is said to exist. But what happens if a target adopter has a positive view of the one and a negative view of the other? Suppose an adopter regards a social marketing organization as highly credible, but finds it unappealing. Osgood and Tannenbaum posited that attitudes change in the direction of increasing the amount of congruity between the two evaluations.[10] The consumer may end up respecting the organization somewhat less and respecting the campaign or its objective somewhat more. The notion of congruity suggests that social marketing campaigns can utilize a positive, credible image to reduce negative perceptions toward other campaign aspects, such as its communications or even the brand name used for a product.

SOCIAL MARKETING OF SERVICES

Social services are an adjunct and instrument of social product marketing. The change agent must not only market an idea, such as quitting smoking, but provide clinics to serve prospective target adopters who want to quit smoking. Administering the clinics involves managing professionals and volunteers who interact with prospective target adopters, since their competence, attitude, and behavior will affect the target adopters' level of adoption and commitment. The clinic's convenience and ambiance will also influence the adoption decision. Consequently, social marketers must be skilled not only in marketing ideas and practices but in marketing services.

Providing services to a market has some special characteristics that are not normally found in providing goods. Here are four distinguishing characteristics of service-oriented social products:

Intangibility. Unlike goods, services cannot be seen, tasted, felt, heard, or smelled before they are adopted or purchased. For example, first-time blood donors cannot really sense what giving blood is like. To reduce uncertainty, they will look for signs or evidence of what the service will be like. Therefore, the social marketer's task is to "manage the evidence," to "tangibilize the intangible."[11]

Suppose that a clinic wants to convey the efficiency and safety of donating blood. Making such a claim would not be enough. To demonstrate efficiency, the clinic would answer telephone calls without delay, schedule appointments efficiently, admit donors with a minimum of waiting time, and so on. To demonstrate safety, the clinic would look clean and orderly, health questions would be answered promptly before blood is taken, and needles would be disposed of carefully. The key is to identify and demonstrate tangible qualities or characteristics that appeal to target adopters.

Inseparability. Practices, such as donating blood, typically are produced and consumed at the same time. This is not true of physical goods that are manufactured at one point, placed into inventory at another, later distributed through multiple outlets, and still later, consumed. Provider-client interaction is a special feature of service marketing. For example, if a nurse at a blood-donor clinic is unfriendly or clumsy, she can affect the client's perception of the quality of the entire social campaign or service.

Variability. Services are highly variable because they depend on who provides them and when and where they are provided. Thus, two nurses in the blood-donor clinic can create different impressions of the quality of a clinic. Tangible goods or products, on the other hand, are far more uniform.

Marketers of services can take two steps toward quality control. The first is to invest in high-quality personnel and their training. The second is to monitor the satisfaction of customers continuously, by means of suggestion and complaint systems, customer surveys, and comparison shopping to detect and correct faulty service.

Perishability. The perishability of services is not a problem when demand is steady because it is easy to staff the services in advance. When demand fluctuates, service organizations face difficult problems. If they staff for peak demand, their staff and resources will be idle when the demand is not high. If they staff for average demand, they may have long lines of waiting and irritated customers some of the time. Service marketers try to adjust their service capacity to the varying levels of demand by using reservation systems, part-time employees who are on call, differential pricing, and other devices.[12]

It should be clear that social marketing campaigns typically place greater emphasis on the staff who provide social products and on the interaction between the staff and the target adopters of a social product than often is the case in commercial, business marketing. To succeed in a competitive environment, social marketing campaigns, particularly those that market services, must create differentiated benefits and features, offer high-quality service, and find ways to increase the productivity of the staff who provide the social products and services.

CASE 7–1

The Peace Corps: A Product in Search of a Market

The Product Concept

In his first State of the Union address of January 30, 1961, President John F. Kennedy said the United States must help construct ''a sound and expanding economy for the entire non-communist

SOURCES: Robert L. Gaudine, *The Uncomfortable Learning: Some Americans in India* (Bombay: Popular Prakashan, 1974); and K. Lowther and C. P. Lucas, *Keeping Kennedy's Promise: The Peace Corps* (Boulder, Colo.: Westview Press, 1978). Quotations are drawn from these sources.

world. The problems in achieving this goal are towering and un-precedented. The response must be towering and unprecedented as well." Kennedy established the United States Peace Corps to help achieve the goal of improving the quality of life in Third-World countries. Kennedy's remarks were the mandate of the Peace Corps. Sargent Shriver, the first Peace Corps director, made two assumptions in organizing the Peace Corps.

1. Because Kennedy received more than 30,000 written pledges before and after his election from individuals who were will-ing to serve in an "International Youth Service Agency," Americans, therefore, were ready to serve in Third-World countries.
2. Third World countries needed and would welcome the skilled assistance of young Americans.

The Peace Corps staff conceived of the Peace Corps volunteer as "a legitimate instrument of human development, . . . and [an affirmation of] Americans' pride in themselves as a practical [and] peaceful people." Peace Corps volunteers were going to be Amer-icans who, in Kennedy's words, "are wanted by the host coun-try, who have a real job to do, and who are qualified to do that job."

Peace Corps as a Social Change Campaign

The campaign to create the Peace Corps sought to distinguish it from the foreign-aid bureaucracies and from federal foreign-aid specialists. The Peace Corps volunteer would have "the freedom to exercise initiative and respond to people's needs as he found them." This meant that the volunteer would work without a clear job description.

The first group of volunteers started with "little planning of jobs" but a lot of faith in their adaptability. Many volunteers dis-covered that "their jobs either did not exist, did not need doing, were beyond their ability and training, or were better left to local nationals." A volunteer working on an Applied Nutrition Pro-gram in India put it this way: "Nothing's definitely defined. I don't think we can really help in this program. We're not quali-fied." The first big and serious embarrassment occurred in the Philippines. Volunteers who were to serve as "teachers' aides" arrived only to find that the country had an oversupply of teachers.

Peace Corps Campaign and Product Modification

When volunteers could find no real place in teaching or public health, they were assigned to "community development." The assumed qualification for this type of work was the same as before: the volunteers' sincerity and conviction that they were uniquely qualified to assist people in developing countries to build a better way of life.

An Indian commented on what he observed in Peace Corps volunteers who performed community service: "The volunteer assumed he would be fairly treated, even appreciated. At least not thwarted. He was not made aware how deep the stress, discomfort, isolation of work in India goes. He was not told. There was no honest examination of what actually happens to Americans in [this] country. The recruit was never exposed to the full reality ahead." There were of course exceptions like the volunteer from Mississippi who was working in Brazil, of whom an evaluator wrote:

> He was spending his time surveying the community, getting to know the people, their interests and the structure of the town. His ultimate purpose was to help the local residents develop their own resources . . . and to show them that they could bring political leverage to bear in the capital. He was purposely holding back from participation. . . . His patient activism had the deceptive appearance of passivity; he had carefully established himself as someone who had come to share and not to impose. . . . And the people in the town were coming to him for ideas, which he skillfully transformed into their ideas.

Product Development in Retrospect

There is evidence that the Peace Corps was launched on too large a scale without sufficient definition and testing of the product. Before John F. Kennedy became president, he acknowledged, in a January 9, 1959 press release, the risk of building a big Peace Corps without adequate knowledge of the target adopters' needs and without product testing. "Because of the experimental nature of the program, and the limited information now available

about needs, it should certainly be started on a small scale. . . .
There should be no pressure to achieve greater volume until there
is sufficient experience and background study to give some confidence that expanded numbers can be wisely used." Yet contrary
to Kennedy's caution, Warren W. Wiggins, the first director of
program development and operations, believed that the Peace
Corps could have a significant impact only by delivering volunteers "in the largest measure possible."

Ten years later, the Peace Corps learned its lesson. It came to
view developing countries and the tasks of development more
realistically. Developing countries were trying to help themselves
but recognized the need for capital assistance and technical skills.
Peace Corps volunteers would have to learn to relate sensitively
and empathically with persons in other cultures before they could
perform useful work. The Peace Corps evolved in this period
from a provider of untrained "generalist" volunteers to a provider of trained, skilled volunteer specialists, positioning itself
more effectively to distribute technical resources that better fit the
development agendas of developing nations.

8

Making the Social Product Available: Distribution Channels

After planning a social product's positioning and presentation, marketers must turn their attention to making it available. If a social product is not available, target adopters will not be able to act on the information and persuasion presented through promotional activities. Nor will they be able to adopt it on a trial basis or have any direct experience of it. For these reasons, we deal with distribution channels before the rest of the social-marketing mix elements. Distribution channels (such as health clinics, governmental agencies, retail stores, and the media) are the outlets for making social products available. We will first consider planning for the distribution of social products with a tangible-product base and then intangible products.

DISTRIBUTING A TANGIBLE PRODUCT

A distribution channel is a network of "institutions and agencies involved in the task of moving products from points of production to points of consumption."[1] In social marketing, the point of production is the social change campaign and the points of consumption are the target adopters. Managing a distribution channel involves managing a network of intermediaries. Two issues have to be considered: how intermediaries are linked both to the marketing campaign and to the adopters and what the significant elements are in managing intermediary networks.

Channel Levels

Each type of intermediary in a network constitutes a channel level and defines the length of a channel. Figure 8–1 illustrates several distribution channels. A zero-level channel (direct distribution) consists of a change agent that directly makes its product available to target adopters—house to house, by mail, or through its own outlets. A one-level channel has one distribution intermediary, such as retail drugstores. A two-level channel contains two intermediaries, for example, wholesalers used to reach the retailers. A three-level channel has three intermediaries: distributors, wholesalers, and retailers.

Why would social marketers distribute their products through intermediaries rather than directly? The issue is this: Who can do the distribution job better? If a social campaign had many target adopters to distribute its tangible product to, it would require storage facilities, retailing facilities, and transportation costs. Intermediaries may be more efficient in making products widely available. "Through their contacts, experience, specialization, and scale of operation [they] offer the change agent more than it can usually achieve on its own."[2]

Social marketers face two decisions regarding distribution: the type of distribution outlets and the number of outlets and their locations. A family planning agency, for example, can deliver its social product through clinics, hospitals, and retail outlets. The choice of distribution outlet should take into account the preferences and behavior of the target adopters. As a case in point, Philippine people who adopt family planning prefer not to do so in a hospital. They dislike the connotation that they are "patients" and, therefore, that they are "sick."

The number of distribution outlets depends on the resources of the change agent and the number and location of potential target adopters. For example, since a small family planning agency may have resources for only a single outlet, its location should be convenient, minimizing the distances that target adopters have to travel.

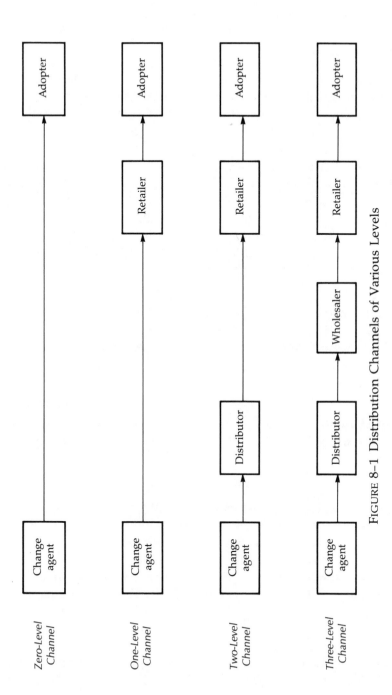

FIGURE 8-1 Distribution Channels of Various Levels

In their research on the optimal number of locations for distribution outlets, Ghosh and Craig identified the rule of weighing the costs of establishing and operating additional outlets against the expected gains in new and repeat adoptions that would accompany the increased coverage.[3] When the change agent already has several outlets, setting up additional outlets could undermine the distribution objectives of the existing outlets. The social marketer must analyze the impact of a new outlet on the entire distribution network, rather than treat each outlet discretely and independently of the rest. Social marketers may be called on to forecast gains in new and repeated adoptions that would result by adding other outlets. Studies of the behavior of consumers have uncovered several influences on the patronage of outlets that are particularly relevant to the delivery of social services.[4]

- An outlet's patronage by target adopters is an inverse function of the outlet's distance from where a target adopter is located; it is directly related to the distance of alternative outlets from both the target adopter and the primary outlet.
- Target adopters will travel only within a certain threshold distance or travel time.
- Adoptions also are dependent on transportation factors, including alternative transport modes and perceptions of comfort and reliability.

Channel Position, Role, and Conflict

Channel position refers to the location of a member of the channel in the distribution network. Channel role is the set of behaviors that are expected from a channel member who occupies a particular channel position. Social campaigns depend on the reliability and predictability of their channel members, just as much as do businesses. Retailers will know when wholesaler-salespersons will call and when shipments from wholesalers will arrive. Wholesalers, in turn, will know when manufacturers will send their merchandise, when bills will arrive, and when promotional plans will be executed. Intermediaries in a distribution network are highly dependent on one other. Yet their interests, goals, and resources may be divergent. Small retailers may think that they are exploited by large wholesalers, and wholesalers may believe that many retailers do not perform their jobs well.

When conflict arises among intermediaries in a distribution network, how can social marketers manage the situation? Four approaches to managing conflict in a distribution channel have been identified.[5]

1. When intermediaries try to resolve their conflict through negotiation, each must consider whether concession and compromise is necessary and how the other side can be induced to accept less than what it wants. Negotiation depends on making the right assessment of the conflict and the relative strength of each party.
2. Intermediaries seek to settle a conflict from the outside, utilizing respected leaders and mediators to help the parties resolve the conflict and, if necessary, sponsor or impose a solution.
3. Sometimes attempts are made to strengthen the mutual interests of the intermediaries. Increased interaction and cooperation, it is assumed, will lessen conflict among intermediaries. The formation of trade associations among intermediaries is one approach. This strategy may promote the formation of a coalition and co-optation.[6] A social marketer may seek allies to increase his or her bargaining power or bring rivals into his or her camp to win their trust and support.
4. Conflict may also be resolved through legal processes, such as conciliation, mediation, and arbitration. Arbitration, which is often used, can either be compulsory or voluntary. It requires conflicting parties to submit to final, binding decisions.

Channel Management: The Case of CSMP

A channel's problems in distributing a tangible product may be illustrated by the experiences of the Condom Social Marketing Project (CSMP) in the Philippines. The distribution objective of CSMP was to set up a two-level channel: wholesalers and retail outlets. This arrangement, it was assumed, would facilitate distribution to the most distant target adopters whose need for contraceptive devices often was the greatest.

Management issues arise at each level in the channel. In CSMP, for example, wholesalers perceived their role differently from what CSMP perceived it to be. CSMP expected a wholesaler to view the family planning campaign as potentially profitable over the long term and as a contribution to national development. A CSMP team described the project to wholesalers: "Where can you find an enterprise where you can make money and also do good for people? It's clean profit with a clear conscience." Unfortunately, the wholesalers did not see things the same way. They perceived CSMP as distributing a product (namely, condoms) in retail outlets (such as groceries and bazaars) that were not equipped to sell the product; therefore, they judged the project to be risky and for the added risk, they demanded higher-than-normal commissions. Although CSMP was willing to offer some concessions, it could not meet all the demands of the wholesalers. CSMP then decided to use a three-level channel, hiring a distributor to oversee the distribution of condoms to wholesalers who, in turn, would reach retailers.

Social marketers must determine the commitment that each distribution intermediary is willing to make in promoting the "sale" of their social products. They must check the retailers' attitude toward the product and the level of support they are willing to give it. Social marketers must take responsibility for the product's movement throughout the distribution channel. Figure 8–2 illustrates the movement of a product through intermediaries, or channel movement, and the movement of a product between an outlet and the target adopters, or the adoption movement.

Channel movement is the equivalent of product placement. When a tangible product "moves" from CSMP to the distributor, this means that the condoms are available at the distributor's warehouse. Similarly, with the "movement" from the distributor to its wholesalers and from the wholesalers to the retail outlets, condoms are being placed in a great number of outlets. Distribution management focuses on moving the product efficiently

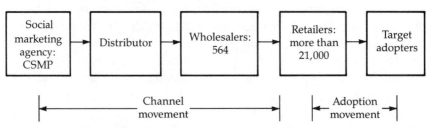

FIGURE 8–2 Channel Movement versus Adoption Movement: The CSMP Case

through the intermediaries. The movement of a product from retail outlets to target adopters is primarily an adoption-promotion issue, which will be discussed in later chapters.

DISTRIBUTING AN INTANGIBLE PRODUCT

The Media

Consider the distribution problem of the social marketer in charge of the Philippines antibribery program or the Swedish campaign to change driving habits. In the first case, the social product is first a "value," the value of honesty in government, and, second, a "practice," the practice of abstaining from giving and receiving bribes. In the second case, the social product is a new behavior or practice—driving on the right, rather than on the left. Ideas and practices are intangible products. How can social marketers make these intangible products available to individuals, groups, or entire populations of potential target adopters? What are the channels for distributing such products?

Advertising researchers refer to mass communication media as being engaged in "message distribution" or "message delivery." Therefore, the media are the prime channels for marketing and distributing intangible social products. Advertising media are available in many different forms. In the Philippines, for example, they include

Television	5 originating, 18 replay, and 49 relay stations; 2 cable television channels (1 in English and 1 in Chinese), operating in Metropolitan Manila
Radio	308 stations on the AM Band and 78 on the FM Band
Newspapers	19 national and 54 provincial
Magazines	31 local and national
Comic books	36
Trade journals	13
Foreign publications	53 newspapers, magazines, trade journals, yearbooks, and in-flight magazines

Outdoor advertising	billboards, illuminated posters, and overpass signs sold by 65 outdoor advertising companies
Cinema	over 1,000 movie houses in over 300 cities
Transit advertising	buses, jeepneys, commuter trains, and tricycles
Point-of-purchase shopping cart posters	in 12 supermarket chains in Metropolitan Manila alone

The estimated size of the audience in each outlet indicates its potential distribution capability. For example, social marketers can count on radio to reach 77 percent of all Philippine households; television, 37 percent; newspapers, 30 percent; and magazines, 19 percent. These are message-placement capabilities. Whether a placement will result in acceptance of an idea or a practice depends on how effectively the social product is promoted.

The question for social marketers is, How many channel levels are involved in the movement of messages from the source to the destination? Researchers of mass communication differentiate among three models of flow, as shown in Figure 8–3.

The one-step flow model consists of the social marketer arranging for media that carry messages directly to the target adopters. In the two-step flow model, the messages carried by the media reach initial target adopters who carry messages to later target adopters. In the multistep flow model, the messages move in a more complex way between and through advertising agencies and the media to initial target adopters and later target adopters.

The distributional effectiveness of the media varies, when measured against a number of characteristics. Table 8–1 compares television, radio, magazines, and newspapers along 35 characteristics. One media channel may rate high on one set of characteristics and low on another set. Social marketers have to determine the mix of media characteristics they need to attain the efficient distribution of their particular messages. For example, if a social marketer wants to place an ad quickly and convey detailed information, then he or she will strongly favor newspapers.

Some products involve the distribution and delivery of information and related services of a highly intensive personal and interpersonal nature. The social marketing of family planning and of literacy, for example, is accomplished through institutions,

1. The one-step flow model:

2. The two-step flow model:

3. The multi-step flow model:

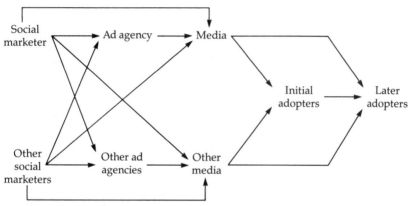

FIGURE 8–3 Flow of Distribution of a Nontangible Social Product: Three Alternative Models

such as health clinics and schools, that rely heavily on interpersonal communications between professionals and volunteers, on the one hand, and target adopters, on the other.

Still other social products are delivered best through specialized media, rather than mass media—channels of delivery that link specialists and professionals with particular segments of target adopters. Economic revitalization programs for cities that seek domestic and foreign investors for new industrial plants and expanded employment opportunities are an example. Some social change campaigns optimize distribution through a combination of mass and specialized media channels, as well as interpersonal channels. At times interpersonal channels are primary and supplemented by mass communications; at other times, mass advertising is the primary channel and is supplemented by interpersonal communications. Outlets are the delivery points of

TABLE 8–1 Gross Comparisons of Mass Communication Media

Comparison Items	Television	Radio	Magazines	Newspapers
Total population reach (adults and children)	Very strong	Good	Fair	Good
Selective upscale adult reach	Fair	Good	Very strong	Good
Upscale adult selectivity (per ad exposure)	Poor	Fair	Very strong	Good
Young adult selectivity (per ad exposure)	Fair	Very strong	Very strong	Fair
Cost per 1,000 ratios	Fair-Good	Very strong	Strong	Good
National media availabilities and uniform coverage	Very strong	Poor	Good	Poor
Local market selectivity	Good	Good	Poor	Very strong
Ability to control frequency	Fair	Good	Good	Very strong
Ability to pile frequency on reach base	Very strong	Very strong	Good	Fair
Ability to exploit time-of-day factors (in scheduling)	Fair	Very strong	Poor	Poor
Ability to exploit day-of-week factors (in scheduling)	Fair	Very strong	Poor	Very strong
Seasonal audience stability	Poor	Very strong	Good	Good
Predictability of audience levels	Fair-poor	Good	Good	Very good
Depth of demographics in audience surveys	Poor	Poor	Very strong	Fair-good
Reliability and consistency of audience surveys	Fair-good	Good	Fair-good	Good
Ability to monitor schedules	Good	Poor	Very strong	Very strong
Ability to negotiate rates	Good	Fair	Poor	Poor

Criterion				
Fast closing and air dates	Fair	Good	Poor	Very strong
Opportunity to exploit editorial "compatibility"	Poor	Fair	Very strong	Good
Selective ad positioning	Poor	Fair	Good	Very strong
Advertising exposure	Good	Good	Good	Good
Advertising intrusiveness	Very strong	Good	Fair	Poor
Audience concern over ad "clutter"	Very high	High	Almost none	Almost none
Emotional stimulation	Very strong	Fair	Fair	Poor
Sensory stimulation	Fair-good	Fair	Very strong	Fair
Registration of brand name	Very strong	Good	Fair	Fair
Product or efficacy demonstrations	Very strong	Poor	Fair	Fair
Ability to exploit attention getting devices	Very strong	Poor	Very strong	Good
Ability to use humor	Very strong	Good	Poor	Poor
Ability to use slice-of-life approach	Very strong	Good	Poor	Poor
Ability to convey detail and information	Fair	Fair	Very strong	Very strong
Ability to stimulate imagination	Fair-good	Very strong	Fair	Poor
Package identification	Good	Poor	Very strong	Good
Prestige and respectability of the medium	Fair	Fair	Very strong	Strong
Ability to talk person to person with audience	Fair-good	Very strong	Poor	Poor

SOURCE: Quoted in M. L. Ray, *Advertising and Communication Management* (Englewood Cliffs, N.J.: Prentice-Hall, 1982), Table 15–2, p. 384.

products, but in the case of social products, a premium is placed on the exchange and delivery of products by individuals. High-quality services that are performed by professionals and volunteers are likely to be an essential adjunct to the distribution of social products. Thus, two types of interpersonal distribution channels are professionals and volunteers.

Professionals. Social campaigns to persuade people to quit smoking use professionals as primary distribution channels. Physicians often are enlisted as the "retailers" of this type of product; they are given primary responsibility for changing smoking behavior.

Social marketers have to work hard to obtain the cooperation of professionals. They do so in two ways: by requiring cooperation through coercive or legal means and by encouraging cooperation through rewards, benefits, and professional appeals.

The first approach requires social marketers to assess if they have any coercive or legal power over professionals. Do professionals perceive that the social marketing program has the ability to withhold prized resources, add to their operating costs, or bring about unfavorable publicity if they fail to participate? Do professionals perceive that the social marketing program has the force of law behind it and thus requires their participation?

The second approach would secure cooperation through rewards and benefits. Marketers have to evaluate the direct rewards they can offer professionals. Do professionals think that favorable publicity or funding grants and other sought-after financial resources will incur from their participation? Do professionals believe that they will gain prestige? Social marketers also can appeal to professionals' pride in their expertise and competence. Can professionals augment their expertise and skills by being associated with the social campaign? Does the social marketer have information that professionals may need?

Each time a professional agrees to participate, the social marketer should also try to get him or her to recruit other professionals. Professionals are typically more effective in recruiting other professionals than is the social marketing agency.

Volunteers. If there were no volunteer workers, the great majority of social change campaigns would either terminate or have to reduce their activities significantly. Volunteers are the lifeblood of many campaigns and social product adoptions. Studies on volunteerism have identified three sources of motivation for volunteering: a personal interest and need that is satisfied by a social campaign, a belief that a social campaign will benefit society, and a desire to help other people.

Social marketers who depend on volunteers have to understand the ways to meet and satisfy volunteers' needs. The motivations that have been identified are merely a starting point. Marketers have to analyze specific situations and specific motivating factors. Volunteers often are the front line for influencing social change and distributing the products of a social change campaign. Their linkage to potential target adopters often determines the success or failure of the campaign.

Once a social product is planned and designed, the critical issue is how to distribute and deliver the product to target adopters. Social campaigns that involve a tangible-product base have to distribute directly or through a network of intermediary channels. Wholesalers and retailers may be involved in product placement. Advertisers and the mass media are also likely to be involved in distributing information that will influence social change.

The delivery of a social product usually depends heavily on interpersonal communications as the points of delivery. Social marketers have to deal closely with issues and conflicts that may arise in distribution channels to ensure that the flow of social products to target adopters is working at maximum efficiency. With an understanding of the role of distribution in social marketing campaigns, we now can turn to dealing with the costs of adopting a social product from the point of view of target adopters.

9

Managing the Costs of Adoption

After a social product is distributed, it must be accessible to target adopters. Making a social product easy to obtain and to use is the task of managing the costs of adopting the product. Adam Smith, the founder of modern economics, expressed this view more than two centuries ago when he said that "the real price of everything, what everything really costs to the man who wants to acquire it, is the toil and trouble of acquiring it."[1] Adoption costs are either of a monetary or a nonmonetary kind. Monetary costs to target adopters inevitably accompany social campaigns with a tangible-product base.

MANAGING THE MONETARY COSTS OF ADOPTION

Many social change campaigns, such as family planning programs, drug abuse rehabilitation centers, and antismoking clinics, charge a price or fee for products and services. The higher the price charged, the greater the target adopters' costs of adoption and the fewer the target adopters. Therefore, social change campaigns must carefully price their products.

The Marketing Functions of Pricing

In considering what price to charge for a specific social product, social marketers should be aware of the several functions that prices serve.

The accessibility function. Pricing affects the ability of the target adopters to acquire the social product. In general, the higher the price, the harder it is to acquire the social product, and the lower the price, the easier it is to acquire the social product.

The product-positioning function. The rule regarding price is subject to some qualifications, however. Price can serve as a symbol and a surrogate for a product's quality. When target adopters have difficulty judging the quality of a social product, they often use price as a standard. A high price may lead target adopters to view the product as having high quality or prestige. A low price may lead target adopters to view the product as being of poor quality. A free product may lead target adopters to be casual in their interest in the product. Many "free goods," such as public health services or legal assistance, do not produce maximum demand because they imply that the product is "downscale." Consider the following episode:

> A city in South America built a modern hospital that offered free clinic services to indigent citizens. When completed, the hospital staff expected to receive a flood of new patients. But most indigent people continued to patronize private physicians and street clinics to whom they paid a fee. These target adopters were not convinced of the quality and attention they would receive in the hospital. To win clients, the hospital decided to experiment by announcing that a fee would be charged. Suddenly, many patients began to come to the hospital.

The demarketing function. Another function served by price is to "demarket" the demand when it is excessive or undesirable.[2] Demarketing occurs when the demand exceeds the capacity of the social program or when the social marketer wants to discourage the use of a product by raising its price, such as cigarettes or alcohol in antismoking or antidrinking campaigns. Under these conditions, the social marketer seeks to discourage, temporarily or permanently, some behavior of target adopters by raising the price of that behavior.

Demarketing can be accomplished by using the four Ps of product, price, promotion, and place. Specifically, the product's quality can be reduced, the price can be raised, promotion can be reduced or eliminated, and the place of delivery can be made inaccessible. Raising the price is often the most potent means. Consider the following extreme example.

> Malaysian laws raised the "price" of taking or possessing drugs to that of paying with one's life, if caught. The government implemented a "price" of capital punishment that has shown no mercy to either citizens or foreigners. Since 1982, ten foreigners have "paid" by going to the gallows. The Malaysian deputy prime minister stated, "We do not apologize, we do not intend to apologize and we simply cannot apologize for the very tough laws here. Whether British or Australian, you are subject to the laws of Malaysia when you come here. Nobody can ever say, 'I'm sorry, I am not aware of it'."[3]

In some cases, demarketing may appear to be hard-hearted or even immoral. Suppose that an epidemic of infant diarrhea led to an overfull and possibly unfillable demand for the oral rehydration product. If a governmental agency raised its price for oral rehydration solution or limited the accessibility of the solution in other ways to allocate its supply, it would be attacked as immoral.

Setting the Objectives of Pricing

In developing a price policy, the first thing a social change campaign with a tangible-product base must decide is the objectives it seeks to achieve. We have seen how price can be used to ration demand and to serve as a product-positioning device. Here we are asking what the broadest alternative objectives might be in determining the pricing strategy. Suppose a drug-abuse rehabilitation center wanted to set a price on its service. It might have five pricing objectives.[4]

- *Maximizing Profits.* The center would examine the likely behavior of demand and costs at different possible price levels and settle on the price that would maximize the center's profit.

- *Recovering Costs.* The center would have to consider its ability to raise money from donors as a factor in setting the price of its services. It might seek a price that would recover a "reasonable" part of its costs. The aim might be to recover part of the costs and make up the difference by raising a subsidy or funds from public or private sources to recover the full costs because sufficient funds could not be raised from other sources.
- *Maximizing the Number of Target Adopters.* If the center wanted to attract the most target adopters it could, it would charge a low price or offer its services at no charge. However, as was mentioned earlier, potential target adopters might interpret the low prices to be a reflection of the quality of the services.
- *Social Equity.* Many social campaigns favor policies that increase social equity among citizens. Specifically, they would like poorer citizens to pay less and richer citizens to pay more. Thus, the center might decide to charge different prices according to the income of the target adopters.
- *Demarketing.* Pricing, as stated earlier, might be used to discourage as many people as possible from adopting a particular social product. Thus, governments establish a high tax on cigarettes and liquor to discourage their use. The only reason that the center might establish a "demarketing" price would be to handle an overdemand for its services.

Method of Price Setting

Once the pricing objective is clarified, a campaign can proceed to set a specific price or prices. The agency should take three things into consideration: costs, the prices of competitors, and target adopters' sensitivity to the price. Costs usually set a floor on the price, particularly if a social agency is interested in recovering the full costs. The prices of competitors often set a ceiling on the price, particularly if competitors offer a better product. Between this floor and ceiling, a campaign has to consider the target adopters' sensitivity to the price.

Cost-based pricing. The two most popular cost-based pricing methods are markup pricing and investment-return pricing. In markup pricing, the marketer seeks a given percentage return on sales. In investment-return pricing, the marketer figures a price that will yield a given rate of return on the program's invested capital. These two pricing methods are illustrated in Case 9–1.

Two major questions are raised by cost-based pricing methods: Is it safe to assume that the agency will achieve the specified level of sales? Is it right to set a price that produces a surplus over costs? The first issue can be readily answered. Adoptions of a social product, or its "sales," are not a "given." Adoptions are influenced by several factors, one of which is the price that cost-based methods establish. That is why marketers regard the cost-based price as providing only an initial benchmark, one that is to be modified by other considerations of competition and the target adopter's sensitivity to the price.

The second issue is more difficult. Crompton and Lamb suggested that prices, from a social point of view, should be based on how widely the benefits of a campaign or program are expected to be distributed.[5] The price should be lower when the benefits of the social product are widely distributed. If the benefits go primarily to a narrow group of target adopters, that group should bear the costs. This principle leads to distinguishing three types of social products from the perspective of pricing—public campaigns, public-private campaigns, and private campaigns.

Since everyone benefits from public campaigns, costs should be recovered mainly through the tax system, not through pricing. In public-private campaigns (private services that serve the public interest), the benefits accrue to discrete social segments and have spillover benefits to the rest; therefore, pricing should cover only part of the total costs. Because private campaigns benefit primarily particular target adopters, the benefits-received principle holds that the full costs of the services should be passed on to the target adopters.

The prices of competitors' products. Before setting the price, a social change campaign should survey the prices charged by others for the same or similar products. In the case of the Condom Social Marketing Project (CSMP) in the Philippines, this survey took the form of a "store check" and a "clinic check." The store check surveyed 84 randomly selected drugstores in the test area—

the only trade outlets carrying a significant volume of condoms. The clinic check surveyed 40 public health centers and family planning clinics.

The results of the store check are presented in Table 9–1. As can be seen, the retail prices of condoms were wide ranging. Brands of condoms sold for as low as 30 centavos a piece and as high as 2.50 pesos. Pricing was also undisciplined. The brand Sampoon sold in one drugstore for 35 centavos and in another, along the same street, for 2.50 pesos. CSMP concluded that it could price its condom anywhere from 30 centavos to 2.50 pesos.

In the clinic check, condoms were advertised in clinic posters and handouts as available at no charge. However, in practice, clinics asked for "donations" from clients. The average donation amounted to 50 centavos per condom. CSMP took this average as a sign that its target adopters were ready to pay 50 centavos for a condom.

Target adopters' sensitivity to prices. A second adjustment to the cost-based price requires attention to what the target adopters are willing to pay. Nagle identified nine ways to research target adopters' sensitivity to prices.[6] They are described in Case 9–2.

TABLE 9–1 Condom Pricing in Metro Manila, June 9, 1975 (Base = 84 Drugstores)

Price Per Piece (Pesos)	Percentage of Stores Charging Different Prices for the Same Brand			
	Gold Coin	Sampoon	Jellia	Sultan
0.30	8			
0.35	21	10	8	20
0.40	21	8	12	
0.50	50	36	40	30
0.75		21	20	14
0.80		7		11
0.85				8
1.00			9	17
1.50		7	11	
2.00		7		
2.50		4		

SOURCE: Population Center Foundation, CSMP, Metro Manila, Philippines, 1975.

The nine approaches vary in the cost and characteristics of the research. For example, aggregate sales data may be the least expensive if the data is derived from accounting, but they may be the least useful because the price variations that are disclosed are minimal. In-store purchase experiments, however, are probably the costliest approach because a large panel of stores have to be monitored over a fairly long period.

Factors Affecting Sensitivity to Prices

To be able to measure sensitivity to prices is one thing. To be able to explain why it occurs is another. Nagle[7] identified nine factors that influence sensitivity to prices:

- Unique-value effect: Buyers are less price sensitive when a social product is unique.
- Substitute-awareness effect: Buyers are less price sensitive when they are unaware of substitute products.
- Difficult-comparison effect: Buyers are less price sensitive when they cannot easily compare the quality of alternative products.
- Total-expenditure effect: Buyers are less price sensitive the lower the ratio of the cost of a product to their income.
- End-benefit effect: Buyers are less price sensitive the lower the cost of the product is in relation to the benefits of the product.
- Shared-cost effect: Buyers are less price sensitive when part of the cost is borne by another party.
- Sunk-investment effect: Buyers are less price sensitive when a product is used in conjunction with an asset they previously bought (such as film and a camera).
- Price-quality effect: Buyers are less price sensitive when they assume a product possesses quality, prestige, or exclusiveness.
- Inventory effect: Buyers are less price-sensitive when they cannot store the product.

How is this list of factors used? If a social change campaign must put a high price on its product, this list of factors will help it determine what steps could be taken to gain acceptance of that high price. For example, the first factor, unique value, suggests that a campaign can enhance its product's unique value and characteristics and communicate them effectively.

MANAGING THE NONMONETARY COSTS OF ADOPTION

For target adopters, price constitutes the monetary cost of adopting a social product with a tangible product base. The total costs of adopting, however, extend beyond the monetary cost. This is evident in the following example:

> Consider the case of a woman with a family history of breast cancer who is deciding whether to go to a doctor's office for a breast examination. The woman has been exposed to a social marketing campaign advising women to have regular examinations. The visit to the doctor will cost her money. If she is an hourly worker and has no automobile, she will have to pay for transportation and lose perhaps three hours of wages. If she is at home with a young child and drives, she may have to pay for a baby-sitter.
>
> Getting to and from the doctor involves nonmonetary costs in terms of physical energy, as well as the following psychic costs:
>
> - Awkwardness at having to ask for time off from work
> - Embarrassment at having to explain the situation to co-workers
> - Aggravation at having to find a taxi or a parking space
> - Embarrassment at having her breasts examined
> - Fear that the examination might hurt
> - Fear that a cancer will be found, and so on

Thus, it is not enough for a social marketer to promote breast examinations. The marketer must also help the adopter reduce the monetary and nonmonetary costs. Nonmonetary adoption costs fall into two categories: time costs (such as travel time and waiting time), and perceived risks (psychological risks, social risks and physical risks).

Time Costs

Social marketers normally will attempt to help target adopters reduce time costs. Reducing travel time is a matter of managing the distribution channel. The more outlets and the better their locations, the less the travel time. When the social product is an "idea" or "behavior," distribution also involves managing communication "messages" efficiently via the media or interpersonal contacts.

Social campaigns should minimize adopters' waiting time for the delivery of a social product. Usage time can be reduced, according to Fox with the strategy of "embedding." To embed a target behavior, Fox noted, means to find ways "in which the new behavior can be carried out simultaneously with present activities."[8] Consider a program to prevent gum disease, which attempts to get people to floss their teeth. The usage time of teeth flossing may be reduced by encouraging people to floss their teeth while they watch television. Embedding one behavior in the course of carrying out another comfortable behavior does not involve additional time. Habit-forming time can be reduced, according to Fox, with the concept of "anchoring." To get people into the habit of adopting a new behavior, such as flossing teeth, the social marketer can persuade them to link its performance to some already habitual behavior, such as brushing their teeth.

Perceived Risks

Another category of nonmonetary costs involves perceived risks. What can social marketers do to reduce perceived risks? Gemunden[9] proposed the following model:

1. Against a perceived psychological risk, provide social products in ways that deliver psychological rewards.
2. Against a perceived social risk, gather endorsements from credible sources that reduce the potential stigma or embarrassment of adopting a product.
3. Against a perceived usage risk, provide target adopters with reassuring information on the product or with a free trial of the product so they can experience how the product will do what it promises to do.
4. Against perceived physical risk, solicit seals of approval from authoritative institutions, such as the American Dental

Association, the American Medical Association, or other highly respected organizations.

In addition, target adopters can perform on their own preventive and corrective measures to manage products with highly perceived risks. Roselius identified several self-managed risk-reducing approaches: remaining loyal to a "proved" brand, buying only the major brand, choosing on the basis of an outlet's reliability, relying on the results of governmental testing, pretesting through trial adoption, paying attention to favorable word-of-mouth communication about the product, shopping around for alternative products, accepting credible endorsements, and privately testing a product.[10] Each of these risk-reduction strategies can be built into the marketing mix of a social product. For example, providing high-quality interpersonal transactions is part of delivery, while offering extensive, informative instructions on usage is part of the promotion and presentation of a product. The use of endorsements is handled by advertising. Giving target adopters the experience of a free trial of a product by means of small-sized packages is a form of promotion called product sampling. Social marketers can utilize all marketing instruments in reducing the product-adoption costs for target adopters.

Case 9-3 presents an example of consumers who are disappointed with a product. It vividly highlights all the specific adoption costs that consumers bear who chose to complain. A consumer protection agency would need to understand and reduce these costs if it really wanted to facilitate more consumer complaining behavior.

Social marketers need to pay close attention to the consumer's costs—monetary and nonmonetary—of adopting a social product. Social marketers may place a price on the social product to affect its accessibility and positioning, as well as to return some funds to cover the costs of marketing it. Price setting should take into account the change agent's costs, the prices of competitive products, and target adopters' sensitivity to prices. Social marketers should also seek to reduce the prospect's time, energy, and psychic costs. Once the costs and prices are established, the social marketer can start arranging effective communication/promotion programs for the social product, a task to which we now turn.

CASE 9–1
Setting the Price for Oral Rehydration Packs

Assume that an oral rehydration campaign in Honduras incurs the following costs (the L is the Honduras currency called a lempira):

Variable cost per pack	L 0.30
Annual fixed overhead	L 120,000
Annual fixed depreciation and maintenance expense	L 80,000
Total invested capital	L 800,000

Assume further that the project expects to distribute and sell 400,000 packs its first year and regards a 20 percent return on its total sales and on its total invested capital to be satisfactory.

To determine its markup price, the project's social marketer must first estimate the product's average cost per packet:

Average cost = average variable cost + (fixed costs ÷ total quantity sales)

In the present example, this would be

Average cost = L 0.30 + [(L 120,000 + L 80,000) ÷ 400,000]
= L 0.80

The markup price that will yield the target return on sales is obtained from the formula:

Markup price = Average cost ÷ (1 − target return on sales)

For our current example, the markup price would be

Markup price = L 0.80 ÷ (1 − .20) = L 1.00

Then the markup is 20 percent of the sales revenue. To determine its investment-return price, the project first estimates the average cost as in the previous markup and then uses the following expression:

Investment return price = Average cost + [(target rate of return × total invested capital) ÷ total quantity sales].

For our example, this price would be

Investment-return price $= L\,0.80 + [(.20 \times L\,800{,}000) \div 400{,}000]$
$$= L\,1.20.$$

Note that the markup price would be L 1.00, but the investment-return price would be L 1.20.

CASE 9–2
Nine Ways to Research
Target Adopters' Sensitivity to Price

Approaches using actual purchases measured under uncontrolled conditions:

1. The aggregate sales approach, in which data on the marketer's adoptions or "sales" are collected.
2. The store-audit approach, in which data on outlets' "sales" are gathered by an independent retail-audit firm.
3. The consumer-panel approach, in which data on "sales" are gathered from a panel of households by an independent market-research organization.

Approaches using actual purchases measured under experimentally controlled conditions:

4. The in-store purchase experiment, in which the basis for estimating price sensitivity comes from monitoring sales at the conventional price and then changing the price from the base level.
5. The laboratory-purchase experiment, which gathers data in a controlled environment, such as intercepting target adopters in the experiment as they walk into a retail outlet.

Approaches using preferences/intentions data measured under uncontrolled conditions:

6. The direct survey, in which respondents are asked what they are willing to pay for the product and at what price they expect it to sell.

SOURCE: Thomas T. Nagle, *The Strategy Process and Tactics of Pricing: A Guide to Profitable Decision Making,* © 1987, p. 2. Reprinted by permission of Prentice-Hall, Inc., Englewood Cliffs, NJ.

7. The buy-response survey, in which respondents are shown the product at different preselected prices and then asked if they would purchase it at a given price.

Approaches using preferences/intentions data measured under experimentally controlled conditions:

8. The simulated purchase survey, in which price sensitivity is estimated from responses of respondents who are asked to imagine that they are "shopping," then shown pictures or samples of different brands of the same product along with their prices, and then asked to choose among the brands at various prices.
9. Conjoint analysis, in which data on respondents' choices between paired products are subjected to the conjoint-analysis technique, which predicts at what prices target adopters will purchase products that contain combinations of product attributes.[11]

Case 9–3
Assisting Target Adopters with Complaints

Many target adopters and consumers are disappointed with a product, but relatively few complain. After buying a poorly made appliance or being overcharged by an auto repair shop, they might sulk, swear they will be more careful next time, and possibly complain to a few friends. They may complain to a retailer but are largely at its mercy. They rarely take their complaints to consumer protection agencies.

Consumer-rights advocates seek to encourage people to be more aggressive in seeking redress for their complaints. The question is this: Why do so few people complain even if they feel victimized by an adoption or an adopted product? The answer is that the costs of complaining often exceed the perceived gains. From 1974 to 1976, the Consumer Complaint Project of the Center for Study of Responsive Law (CSRL) in the United States studied 132 cases and surveyed 2,419 consumers in 34 American cities to determine the factors that inhibited complaining behavior. This project identified process that was marked at each step by numerous and diverse costs to the complaining consumer. The process consisted of the five steps shown in Figure 9–A. Steps 3, 4, and 5 are the major steps. The step of perceiving a purchase-failure problem (Step 3) is necessary if the consumer is to complain. Each difficulty provides a lead for a consumer-motivation campaign. The difficulty of voicing the complaint (Step 4) provides another set of useful leads. The list of rejection techniques shown, in Steps 5.1 and 5.2 show what consumers might confront from sellers or third parties if they seek redress. Figure 9–A can alert consumer advocacy groups to the potential services they can offer complaining or dissatisfied target adopters of social products.

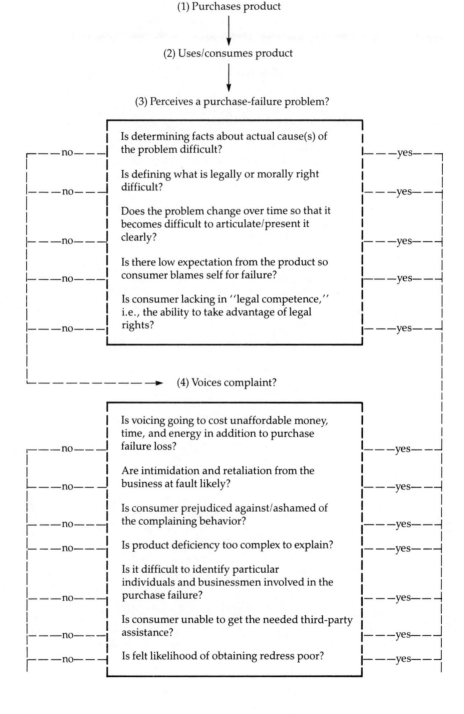

(1) Purchases product

(2) Uses/consumes product

(3) Perceives a purchase-failure problem?

—no— Is determining facts about actual cause(s) of the problem difficult? —yes—

—no— Is defining what is legally or morally right difficult? —yes—

—no— Does the problem change over time so that it becomes difficult to articulate/present it clearly? —yes—

—no— Is there low expectation from the product so consumer blames self for failure? —yes—

—no— Is consumer lacking in "legal competence," i.e., the ability to take advantage of legal rights? —yes—

(4) Voices complaint?

—no— Is voicing going to cost unaffordable money, time, and energy in addition to purchase failure loss? —yes—

—no— Are intimidation and retaliation from the business at fault likely? —yes—

—no— Is consumer prejudiced against/ashamed of the complaining behavior? —yes—

—no— Is product deficiency too complex to explain? —yes—

—no— Is it difficult to identify particular individuals and businessmen involved in the purchase failure? —yes—

—no— Is consumer unable to get the needed third-party assistance? —yes—

—no— Is felt likelihood of obtaining redress poor? —yes—

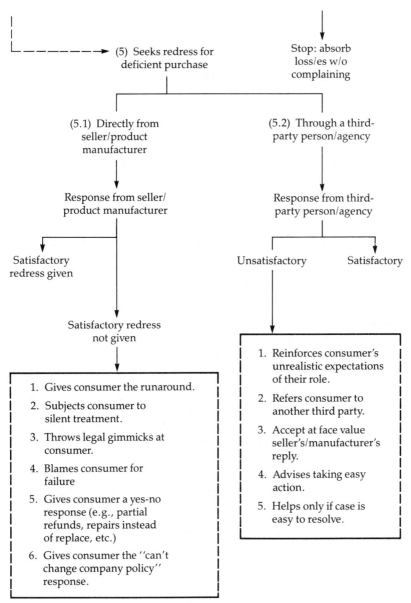

FIGURE 9–A The Complaining-Behavior Process

SOURCE: Constructed from Arthur Best, *When Consumers Complain* (New York: Columbia University Press, 1981).

10

◆

Promoting Through Mass Communication

After planning a social product's availability and accessibility through distribution and pricing, the social marketer will promote the product and its adoption through a communication program. The first step is to differentiate target adopters as a mass and as individuals. For target adopters as a mass, the most effective technique is the use of mass communications. For target-adopters as individuals, a direct approach is more appropriate, which includes both selective communications (direct mail and telemarketing) and personal communications (word-of-mouth and one-to-one communications). These three channels of communication are mutually reinforcing; they can and should be used together.

This chapter is concerned with the first of these means, mass communication. It examines the mass-communication process, mass-communication decisions to move target adopters closer to adoption, and the evaluation of the effectiveness of mass communication.

THE MASS-COMMUNICATION PROCESS

What is the distinctive function of mass communication? It is to inform and persuade, within a given period, the largest possible number of target adopters about how the social product fits into their needs and how it fits better than alternative products.

Hierarchy-of-Effects Model

How does mass communication inform and persuade? One school of thought argues that informing and persuading takes place in a "hierarchy-of-effects" process that starts with the learning effect. Figure 10–1 illustrates the relevant steps in this process. The left-hand column specifies the mass-communication tasks of informing and persuading. Informing encompasses the task of making target adopters aware of the communication and getting them to remember its content. Persuading consists of getting adopters to form a favorable attitude toward the social product, along with an intention to try it.

According to the model, after a mass communication campaign is launched, a certain portion of target adopters will become aware of the communication. This is specified by $p(A)$ in Figure 10–1, which is known as the probability of awareness of the communication. The likelihood of nonawareness is designated as $p(-A)$; if this happens, potential adopters are closed off from the other effects of the communication process and, thus, exit the process. Those who become aware of a communication message will include those with a likelihood of remembering the message, $p(R)$, as well as those who fail to recall the message $p(-R)$. Farther down the chain, only a portion of target adopters with recall will form a favorable attitude toward the communicated social product, the $p(I)$ likelihood. Some of this group of favorably predisposed target adopters may intend to adopt the product, as expressed by $p(AI)$. However, only a portion of this group will implement their intention through trial adoption, defined by the $p(TA)$ probability. Finally, out of those who tried a product, some portion will repeat the adoption, as designated by the $p(RA)$ probability.

Figure 10–1 also indicates that the transition from one communication effect to the next depends on the level and quality of the factor that is responsible for that transition, as shown in the right-hand column. For example, the transition from exposure to a communication to awareness of a communication is a function of a communication's reach and frequency. (Multiplying these two characteristics yields the "media weight," according to the lan-

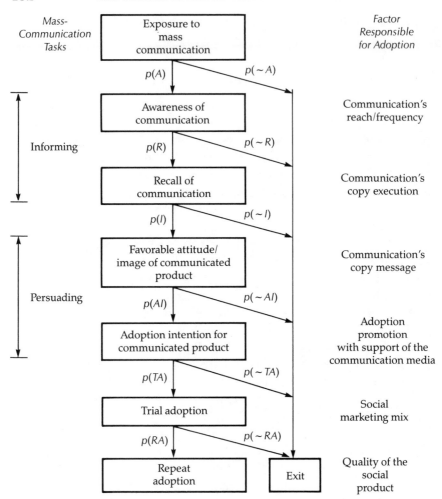

FIGURE 10–1 Hierarchy-of-Effects Model of the Mass-Communication Process

guage of mass communication. The extent to which awareness is converted into recall will depend on the effectiveness of the communication's copy execution—how successfully the communication framed its message. The rest of the process and its corresponding "causes" are read in a similar fashion.

Alternative Hierarchy-of-Effects Models

Do target adopters respond to mass communication only according to the one-directional sequence of responses shown in Figure

10–1? Today's communication researchers recognize that adoptions result from several possible sequences of learning behavior by target adopters, such as the do-feel-learn or learn-do-feel sequence outlined in Chapter 5. Therefore, the informing and persuading function of mass communication must be adapted to what is known about the variations in this behavior. In other words, choices about communication should be tailored to the behavior of target adopters. Specifically, the learn-feel-do model suggests that informing and persuading have to be logical and clear cut in the presentation of arguments. Similarly, the do-feel-learn trial-adoption model suggests that informing and persuading reassure target adopters that they have made the right choice in trying the product. The learn-do-feel model suggests that mass communication informational and persuasion messages should be attention getting, when target adopters have little involvement with a product.

MASS-COMMUNICATION DECISIONS

In using mass communications, the social marketer has five decisions to make: (1) what communication objectives should be set, (2) what to say in the communication, (3) how to say it, (4) where to place the communication, and (5) how to time the communications. Each decision is examined in sequence.

Communication Objectives

The social marketer draws the communication objectives from the objectives of the social change campaign. The campaign objective is to encourage adoption of an idea, a practice, or both, and adoption may include a tangible-product base or an intangible product. The key question is, What behavioral process of target adopters is likely to be involved? If the behavioral process is one of learning, then the objective of the communication is to promote awareness, recall, and a favorable image of the product. If the target adopters' behavioral process starts with low involvement, then the objective of the communication is to create awareness through attention-getting devices so that a trial adoption of the product can be triggered.

The Communication Message

The purpose of a communication message is to convey the superiority of the social product in satisfying the target adopter's need. This purpose is illustrated in regard to adopting a new social product, a superior product, and a substitute social product.

A new social product. In 1975, the British government launched a "Save It" energy-conservation program to inform and advise consumers how to use household energy more efficiently.[1] A survey of British households revealed that although most people believed that energy saving was important, they felt no apparent sense of crisis, since petrol and coal were available and no major power outages or reductions had occurred. Furthermore, despite their readiness to suggest ways in which energy could be saved, people did not believe that their energy-saving behavior could make a difference to the country or that it was their responsibility to save energy. In general, the public was ignorant about how to save energy. People tended to think exclusively in terms of switching off lights and appliances, but they were often not aware of the need for insulation in homes. The few who knew about the benefits of insulation had mistaken ideas of how it fit into an energy-conservation effort.

The survey of attitudes established the target adopters' latent need. The social product involved in the campaign was new because no other solutions for conservation existed. The advertising agency that was hired to develop the information campaign decided that three messages had to be communicated: the energy crisis was serious, small energy savings by each household would help solve the crisis, and there were affordable and relatively easy ways for a household to save energy.

A superior social product. The social marketing campaign by the Swedish Government to change driving habits by moving to a right-hand rule of the road reflected the growing rate of accidents by Swedes who increasingly were driving in other European countries with a right-hand rule, as well as the rate of accidents by foreigners who were driving in Sweden in increasing number.[2] For example, motor vehicle accidents had increased from 1,850 in 1957 to 7,788 in 1966. A communication campaign had to be designed that would emphasize the superiority of driving on the right over driving on the left. The communication program's messages emphasized safety—that driving on the left is far more dangerous than driving on the right. The entire population was told that safety considerations were more important than the convenience of habitual driving practices. The communication message, therefore, conveyed the long-term safety advantage to the Swedish people in switching to another practice.

A substitute social product. The target adopters in the anti-cigarette-smoking campaign initiated by Ejnar og Meta Thorsens Fond, a Danish Foundation, in 1974 were "children below the typical habituation age" of 13–14 years.[3] The communication objective was "to build up a firm motivation against smoking, . . . an anti-smoking attitude before the powerful, social pro-smoking forces set in."

Research indicated that children develop the desire to smoke from what they see around them: the "normal" nature of smoking among adults; the many proofs that most people at home, on television and movies, and in tobacco advertisements seem to be unconcerned about smoking; and the fact that smoking is a social symbol of group identification and hospitality. Data also showed that children knew early that smoking is harmful. Specifically, children were most concerned about tobacco's "steady, cumulative" harm on the body rather than that smoking involves the risk of cancer at some remote, unreal future. So for children, nonsmoking involves the need to maintain health.

The decision on the communication message was reduced to the question, Is the need to maintain health greater than the need to have something with which to relax and to be accepted by others? The idea of smoking's cumulative harm to health was judged to be the more potent message to direct to children. Nonsmoking was presented as a desirable substitute behavior for children to adopt.

Execution of the Communication: How to Inform and Persuade

After deciding what the communication should say, the social marketer must then frame the message so it is attention getting and persuasive. Three types of execution are available: (1) rational execution, (2) emotional execution, and (3) nonverbal elements execution.

Rational Execution

In choosing rational execution, an initial question is, Should the message state the desired behavior or allow target adopters to complete the message and draw their own conclusions? Consider, for example, the *Reader's Digest* campaign against drunken driving featuring the blind musician Stevie Wonder in a poster whose headline was "Before I'll Ride with a Drunk, I'll Drive Myself." Suppose that this headline read instead: "Before I'll Ride with a Drunk, I'll Drive. . . " or "Before I'll Ride with a Drink, I'll Dri. . . My. . . . " Which headline would be more easily recalled?

To answer the question, Zeigarnik conducted experiments in which every seventh letter of printed advertising slogans was removed; Zeigarnik found that the subjects remembered the incomplete slogans more than they did the complete ones.[4] Subsequent experiments by others indicated that the Zeigarnik effect holds largely for people who have a need to complete messages. Therefore, it is risky to assume that target adopters, left on their own, will complete the message and draw the right conclusion. It may be more effective to present a complete message.

Another question is whether a communication should take the form of rational argument and whether an argument is more effective if it presents one or both sides of an issue. For example, the message in a wear-your-seat-belt campaign can either be, "Seat Belts Will Save You from Disfigurement in a Car Accident," or "Seat Belts Are Inconvenient but They Will Save You from Disfigurement in a Car Accident." Studies have identified that one-sided messages appear to work best with people who are already favorably predisposed to an idea or practice and who have a low level of education but that two-sided messages work best when people are not predisposed to the product and have a higher level of education.

To what extent does a message have to be believable to be effective? Consider the campaign to introduce a cholesterol-free egg substitute called "Second Nature." Here are three alternative messages:

Second Nature	The Nutritious Safe Egg Substitute (believable)
Second Nature	The Egg Substitute with All the Flavor and Quality of Eggs but Without the Cholesterol (relatively unbelievable)

Second Nature   The Harmless Egg Substitute that Is a Real
                 Egg in Every Detail (unbelievable)

According to Maloney, people have a "latitude of acceptance" and a "latitude of rejection" for messages on the basis of their believability.[5] A believable message falls within a person's latitude of acceptance. The same message, executed in a nonbelievable way, will fall within the audience's latitude of rejection. Yet another type of message execution will land in a person's "zone of noncommitment," lying between acceptance and rejection. This type of message execution, according to Ray, moves the message "from dull believable advertising to a strength of message that creates curiosity and eventual action."[6] It accomplishes this because it generates responses such as, "It can't be true, but is it?" or "I'll have to try it and find out for myself."

Emotional Execution

Are messages more effective when they appeal to emotion rather than to rational argument? Should an emotional appeal be negative or positive? In the case of an antismoking project, for example, is it better to describe the harmful effects of smoking or the healthy feeling that comes with giving up the smoking habit?

Research has shown that negative messages work better when a social product presents a real solution to a problem, while positive messages are appropriate to social products that offer a means of satisfying a personal goal or objective. The most often used negative appeal is "fear," and the many positive appeals feature people in normal life situations. Furthermore, fear messages work best with segments of target adopters who have not thought of themselves as a market for a social product. For example, Ray stated that "strong [fear-oriented] Cancer Society appeals might be more effective for younger than older smokers, since younger smokers are less likely to see themselves vulnerable to the cancer threat."[7] Similarly, appeals to adopt the use of safety belts would incorporate fear messages for certain segments: "Infrequent drivers who have not considered the dangers of short trips in the city." A social marketing campaign has to evaluate each situation to determine whether a particular segment is more responsive to appeals to fear or to positive messages.

Suppose a social marketer chooses a fear-based appeal. Should it be moderate or strong? In an anti-drunk-driving campaign, should the gory details of a drunk-driver's accident be shown? Or should the appeal be moderately executed by showing a grieving family at the funeral services of the father who died in the accident?

Research suggests that decisions to execute fear-based messages should take several factors into account.[8]

1. A strong fear-based appeal works best when it is accompanied by forcefully stated solutions to a perceived fear that can be easily implemented. Otherwise, a social marketer may be better off with a moderate appeal to fear.

2. Specifically, a strong fear-based appeal is persuasive to those who have previously been unconcerned about a particular problem. Those who already have some concern may perceive a message of fear as going too far, which will inhibit their change of attitudes or behaviors.

3. An appeal to fear may work better when it is directed toward someone who is close to a potential target adopter rather than to the target adopter. For example, in a television commercial against teenage drinking,[9] announcer David Janssen said:
   Does your child . . . have a drinking problem?''
   [accompanying the visual of a boy going down the stairs]
   If . . . you do. . .
   [with shift of visuals to parents holding drinking glasses]
   . . . he does.
   [visual goes back to the boy and closeup on his face looking at parents).
   The persuasive power of this execution is traceable to its correct choice of the target adopter.

4. The more credible the source, the more persuasive the fear-based appeal. A credible source stops people from discounting or underestimating a fear-based appeal.

Messages may be more effective in raising the visibility or salience of an idea or issue when they are surrounded by and project a mood or atmosphere, such as humor or background music, that reinforces them. However, several factors have to be taken into account in using humor.

First, humorous messages are more effective when the prevailing communications in the field are not humorous. Second, humor becomes stale if it is repeated too frequently, so it needs to be varied if it is not to become irritating. Third, humor works well as long as the basic message is simple; it is inappropriate for complex messages. Fourth, the amount of humor in a message should not be too little, in which case it is hardly noticed, or too much, in which case it is either irritating or distracting.

Some communication specialists believe, however, that irritants can be attention getters. Consider the following two anti-drug-abuse television (TV) commercials. The first is an execution that the viewers liked, while the second is an execution that the viewers found irritating.[9a] In the "liked" execution, the audio stated:

> You're 17—old enough to know about things like speed, grass, acid, and smack. We don't intend to give you any advice. You wouldn't listen. But the trouble is neither will your kid brother. He doesn't know one-half of the things you know about drugs, like how they affect your body.
>
> He's really a set up for the guy selling the stuff. We can't warn your kid brother but maybe you can.

The visual was a rear shot of a blond teenage boy, dressed neatly in jeans, walking under trees in a suburban area in the spring. The camera pointed to his younger brother, who was dressed like him and was walking beside him. Then it shows a closeup of their faces. The commercial ends with the boys walking across the street, away from the camera.

In the irritating execution, the audio said:

SON Hey Dad, what's happening?

DAD I'll show you what's happening, get in that room. Now your mother found that in your room, would you please explain it?

SON It's nothing.

DAD What's it called, Johnny?

SON Dope, grass, whatever you want to call it.

DAD Then you must be known as Junkie?

SON No Dad, I'm sorry but it's just what I like to do. Look, you drink. I see you stumbling from the kitchen.

DAD My son, my marvelous son is a junkie. We're just looking for respect in this town. Why are you tearing us down?

SON I'm not tearing you down. I'm the only one that I'll hurt.

DAD What's the next step?

SON You people are fools; you don't know what you're talking about.

ANNOUNCER Before you talk with your child, you ought to read this free booklet about drug abuse. It's written by people who know what they're talking about. Write Drug Abuse Information, Box 1080, Washington, D.C. Do it before it's too late.

The visual showed a closeup of a disturbed mother and the enraged father who is talking with their son in the living room. There are three different still shots of three disturbed faces. The commercial ended with the boy slamming the door as he walked out of the room.

The target audience for these two antidrug abuse messages were parents. The test of these two executions showed that the irritating message made a stronger impression on the parents and, therefore, was more persuasive.

Nonverbal Elements

Some messages rely heavily on nonverbal elements. Nonverbal cues or images are often more influential than are verbal ones in getting the message across. Mehrabian found that media viewers regard the nonverbal elements of a message (such as voices, facial expressions, and body movements) as important indicators of what the message is actually saying.[10] DeLozier suggested that nonverbal communication can be more important in communicating an idea than the verbal expression of an idea and that nonverbal cues or images are often a potent elicitor of feelings and emotions.[11]

Six nonverbal elements influence the effectiveness of a communication:

- *Vocal Expression.* Mass-communication audiences are often heavily influenced by vocal characteristics: messages articulated with a consistent and forceful volume and by spoken voices that are neither "throaty" nor "breathy." Vocal characteristics are particularly critical in radio messages. Thus, social marketers in the Third World who depend heavily on radio media should carefully choose speakers with desirable language and vocal characteristics.

- *Facial Expressions.* Researchers have concluded that facial expressions are an extremely important communicator of information and emotion. Facial cues can convey any of the seven primary emotions: happiness, surprise, fear, sadness, anger, disgust/contempt, and interest.[12]
- *Body Movement.* Research has shown that media viewers pay attention to body movements and gestures as cues to character and intention. Media figures who are given to more gestures and facial activity and who display a body-open position are more likeable and persuasive. Those who use more hand shrugging and more facial control are more suspect.[13]
- *Eye Contact.* Media figures who sustain eye contact with their audience have a persuasive effect. However, sustained eye contact in the context of an aggressive message can have a negative effect.
- *Spatial Distance.* The execution of a message can be affected by the spatial distance between senders and receivers. Appropriate spatial distance varies with the social situation. The projection of intimate space is suited to intimate situations and nonintimate space is suited to nonintimate situations. The violation of the norms of personal space may render a message ineffective.
- *Physical Appearance.* A physically attractive media figure is more persuasive than is an unattractive one. However, under some circumstances, physical attractiveness can overwhelm a message so the viewer will recall an attractive communicator rather than the message that was conveyed.

Communication Media: Where to Inform and Persuade

The next decision in planning mass communication is to select the media through which to channel the message. Our concern here is to investigate the informational and persuasive characteristics of the media.

The first task is to find media that match the communication program's requirements. Suppose an oral rehydration therapy campaign determined that a dramatically emotional execution of the program's message was called for. Then, newspapers and magazines would be inferior to radio, television, and films, given the objective of an emotional appeal and the need to include nonverbal cues to elicit emotions. Visual and audio media, therefore, are the more effective for this objective.

The second task is to find media that match a social product's "personality." The media conduct surveys to gauge the images that audiences have of them, since it would not make much sense, for example, to utilize the magazine *Christian Century* to communicate pro-abortion messages. Media have the potential to reinforce or weaken a communication message. To look only at their reach and frequency is to view media as simply a distribution vehicle. The social marketer must also evaluate media for their informational and persuasive appeal and impact.

Timing of the Communication:
When to Inform and Persuade

The timing and phasing of a communication is a scheduling decision. The aim is to synchronize the timing of a media message with the hierarchy-of-effects stage of the target adopters. For example, the first family planning campaign in India sought to create awareness of the idea of family planning. After a few years, when a large part of the target population was familiar with family planning, the campaign proceeded to communicate the benefits of family planning. Still later, the campaign sought to explain how families could undertake family planning. Thus, the messages were changed over time as the target audience moved to higher stages of awareness, knowledge, and motivation.

Social marketers must make specific decisions about the timing of communications, involving the best months, weeks, days, and hours when the target-adopter audience will be the greatest. If young Indian families, for example, listen to the radio primarily between 8 PM and 9 PM and most heavily in the winter, this would be the best time to broadcast family planning messages.

EVALUATING THE EFFECTIVENESS
OF MASS COMMUNICATION

Once the social marketer has put together a mass-communication program, the program should be pretested. After the program is launched, it should be posttested. Here we examine techniques for pretesting and posttesting.[14]

Pretesting

Several pretesting techniques are available to evaluate each type of media. Here we describe one such technique for evaluating TV commercials.

The technique involves bringing a sample of potential target adopters to a central location where they are asked to view a 10-minute pilot television program, along with several interspersed commercials. The respondents are told that their reactions and opinions will be collected about the pilot. Respondents are seated together in a viewing room to watch the pilot program, which contains four or five test commercials. One of the commercials is the social marketer's test communication, and the rest are nonrelated commercials. After the viewing, the respondents' reactions are gathered according to a test design, as outlined in Case 10-1.

The responses obtained from the pretesting procedure are processed to yield alternative effectiveness measures of the social marketer's test TV commercial. The measures are shown in Case 10-2.

Social marketers have to review each indicator of effectiveness. They should be primarily concerned about "low-scoring" measures of effectiveness that relate most closely to what their communication was specifically designed to do.

Posttesting

To obtain feedback about the campaign's effectiveness during or after a campaign, social marketers posttest data. Suppose a pretested TV commercial carried messages of the "Save It" energy-conservation campaign, and social marketers wanted to evaluate its effectiveness three months after the launch. The task calls for selecting a sample of respondents and asking them approximately the same questions and a few additional ones that were asked in the pretest. From the answers to these questions, social marketers could derive the following information on the communication's effectiveness.[15]

1. Recall of energy-saving messages.
2. Source of energy-saving messages.
3. Expected sources of advice on saving energy.
4. Claimed behavior with regard to saving energy.

5. Perceived relative cost of different uses of energy within the household.
6. Reasons for starting to save energy.
7. Perceived price increases in energy, compared with other goods and services.
8. How people will cope with price increases.
9. Ownership of energy-saving installations.
10. Planning of energy-saving installations.
11. Attitudes toward energy-saving installations.
12. Consumers' perception of the importance of saving energy.
13. Reasons why saving energy is important.
14. Detailed recall of advertising and claimed action following it.
15. Deterrents to the installation of energy-saving devices.
16. Thickness of owned and planned insulation.

As in pretesting, social marketers will be most concerned about the measures of the effectiveness of communication that reflect the objectives of the communication that the campaign seeks to achieve. Case 10–3 brings many of the topics discussed in this chapter to bear on the challenge of developing effective mass communications for the AIDS problem on a global scale.

Case 10–1
Pretesting Procedure for Pilot TV Commercials

Following the viewing of a pilot TV commercial, several questions are asked of respondents. The reactions are rated on a 5-point scale of

    5 = one of the best TV programs I've seen
    4 = better than most TV programs
    3 = about average as a TV program
    2 = not as good as most TV programs
    1 = one of the worst TV programs I've ever seen

A second question asks the respondent if he or she would recommend the program to friends.

Then comes a series of open-ended questions that measure the relative impact of the TV commercials in the aggregate. First, the respondents are asked an "unaided" recall question of what products were advertised in the TV program. Then, for those products not mentioned, an "aided" recall question is asked. This question is followed by "postcommunication questions" about the social marketer's test TV commercial: (1) everything that the respondents remember about, (2) what else was shown in, and (3) what else was said in the test commercial.

The respondents then are reexposed just to the social marketer's test TV commercial. Right afterward, they are asked seven "diagnostic" questions:

1. What message the test commercial was trying to get across
2. An overall rating of the test commercial along the 5-point scale of

   5 = one of the best TV commercials I've ever seen
   4 = better than most TV commercials
   3 = about average as a TV commercial
   2 = not as good as most TV commercials
   1 = one of the worst TV commercials I've ever seen

3. Interest in trying or adopting the advertised product, expressed along a 5-point scale of

   5 = definitely will try/adopt this
   4 = probably will try/adopt this
   3 = might or might not try/adopt this
   2 = probably will not try/adopt this
   1 = definitely will not try/adopt this

4. An open-ended opinion question on what the respondents liked and did not like about the test commercial
5. A rating of the test TV commercial along a 5-point scale of the extent to which it is appealing, believable, and understandable
6. An open-ended opinion question on what the respondent regards as the social product's advantages and disadvantages versus the advantages and disadvantages of alternative products

7. An image rating along a 5-point scale of the advertised social product attributes

Case 10–2
Measures of the Effectiveness
of Communication in Pilot TV Commercials

- Awareness of the effectiveness of the communication: the percentage of the respondents who are aware of the test TV commercial, as shown in the TV pilot.
- Effectiveness of the recall of the communication: the percentage of the respondents who are able to recall the social product that was advertised. The target audience may be aware of the communication but fail to recall it spontaneously. When this happens, the test TV commercial is said to have awareness effectiveness, but poor recall effectiveness.
- Comprehension of the effectiveness of the communication's copy: inferred from the percentage who were able to articulate correctly what the test commercial sought to communicate.
- Comparative overall effectiveness of the communication's image: the percentage of respondents who positively rated the test TV commercial.
- Effectiveness of the communication in motivating respondents to try or adopt the social product: the combined percentage of respondents who "definitely" and "probably" are interested in trying/adopting the social product.
- Attitude toward the effectiveness of the communication: the percentage of respondents who expressed favorable attitudes toward the social product.
- Effectiveness of the communication in conveying a specific image: the percentage of favorable ratings of the test commercial on each of three attributes in the pretest.
- Effectiveness of the image of the social product: the percentage of favorable ratings of each attribute of the social product.

CASE 10–3
Mass Communication for a Global Problem: AIDS

When a social change issue is of global proportions, social marketers are likely to emphasize global mass communications as a dominant element of the marketing mix. The urgency of communicating information worldwide on the detection and prevention of AIDS is a case in point.

Special Program on AIDS

The United Nations World Health Organization (WHO) developed the Special Program on AIDS (SPA) in 1986. SPA's three basic objectives were as follows:

1. To help governments create national strategies to control AIDS and develop, implement, and monitor activities to teach people how to prevent the further spread of HIV infection.

2. To support, promote, and coordinate research on AIDS in medical, social, behavioral, and other fields.

3. To gather data on AIDS epidemics and predict future trends.[15]

To achieve these objectives, SPA pursued a three-tier strategy of immediate, intermediate, and long-term interventions. In the immediate "emergency" phase, a government enlists SPA's assistance to (1) assess the extent of HIV infection in that country and the resources available to combat it, (2) conduct specific

SOURCES: Greg Harris, "The Globalization of Advertising," *International Journal of Advertising*, 3 (1984), pp. 223–234; Warren J. Keegan, *Global Marketing Management*, 4th ed. (Englewood Cliffs, N.J.: Prentice-Hall, 1988); Charles Krauthammer, "AIDS Hysteria," *The New Republic*, 197 (October 5, 1987), pp. 18, 20; L. Liskin and R. Blackburn, "AIDS: A Public Health Crisis," *Population Reports*, 14 (July–August 1986), pp. 193–228; William McGuire, "Theoretical Foundations of Campaigns," in R. E. Rice and W. J. Paisley, eds., *Public Communication Campaigns* (Beverly Hills, Calif.: Sage Publications, 1981), pp. 41–70; Renée Sabatier, "AIDS in the Developing World," *International Family Planning Perspectives*, 13 (September 1987), pp. 96–103; and Yoram Wind, "The Myth of Globalization," *Journal of Consumer Marketing*, 2 (Spring 1986), pp. 23–26.

AIDS-education programs for health workers, and (3) start new or strengthen existing public health education programs.

The intermediate phase consists of working with health authorities to develop or strengthen an AIDS-control plan and offering assistance of one to three years' duration to monitor the spread of AIDS; assembling laboratory, hospital, and other resources for AIDS screening; and educating the public, specific high-risk groups, and medical workers. The long-term aspects of the program seek to provide long-term support for monitoring AIDS and assessing its social and economic impact. The assisted countries participate in a global AIDS prevention and control network on a continuing basis.

Mass Communication Component

SPA's mass-communication program is targeted to two overlapping audiences: the general public and specific high-risk groups. The public education program aims to inform people on the prevention of AIDS and to assuage unfounded fears and prejudices. Liskin and Blackburn[16] listed seven AIDS-information elements that a mass communication-oriented public education program should include (as the basis for designing messages):

1. AIDS is fatal for which there is no known cure.
2. Nonsexual casual contact and blood donation do not spread AIDS.
3. AIDS infection comes from sexual intercourse, from contaminated blood, and from contaminated hypodermic needles.
4. An infected woman can transmit AIDS to her child in pregnancy.
5. Reducing the number of sexual partners lowers the chances of AIDS infection; a stable relationship with a single uninfected partner is safest.
6. For the sexually active, the use of condoms offers protection against AIDS.
7. An AIDS-infected person can appear and feel healthy yet still spread the infection to others.

For reaching high-risk groups, the communication task consisted of providing information to lessen the likelihood of contracting and transmitting the AIDS virus. This information included the following messages:

1. Limiting the number of sexual partners lowers the chances of contracting AIDS; and avoiding intercourse with someone who has many sexual partners.
2. Both vaginal and anal intercourse can spread the virus.
3. The use of condoms provides protection against the risk of infection.
4. If the AIDS virus is detected, avoid getting pregnant or getting your partner pregnant, since an infected pregnant woman can transmit AIDS to her baby; do not donate blood, semen, or body organs.
5. Avoid sharing needles and use of someone else's needles; and sterilize needles and syringes before use.
6. As extra precautions, avoid sharing razors, toothbrushes, or other intimate items that could get contaminated with blood.[17]

SPA reached agreement on the types of communication messages but encountered sharp differences on the manner of executing the messages. Social change campaigns in some countries, including Australia, used fear-inspiring images, such as a bowling ball that topples ordinary men, women, and children in its path. This message created a misleading and panic-arousing impression that AIDS can randomly strike all segments of society. The British campaign, the first nationwide AIDS campaign in the world, also was based on fear, carrying the thematic slogan, "AIDS. Don't die of ignorance." Critics of this message argued that it "ended up spreading more fear than enlightenment."[18] The extreme case of a fear-oriented campaign was South Korea's. South Korea enacted laws mandating health ministers, provincial governors, and mayors to isolate AIDS carriers from the general public, with the eventual imprisonment for up to seven years of "those who knowingly transmit the AIDS virus."[19]

Other countries, such as the United States, pursued mass-communication programs that focused on factual presentations with a minimum of fear-inducing elements. The Surgeon General's Office of the U.S. Department of Health and Human Services distributed a report on the prevention and control of AIDS to every American household and established more specialized communications that were targeted to schoolchildren in the belief that the best prevention consists of teaching about AIDS in the primary and elementary schools.

SPA's Global Communication Challenge

In managing a global mass-communication program, SPA faced a particular global-communication issue: Should the AIDS messages be standardized or differentiated to reflect particular cultural patterns?[20] Ultimately, nations have employed culturally specific communications programs. Some communications analysts believe that the execution of uniform messages throughout the world is not feasible.[21] Their analyses of so-called global brands suggests that standardization is feasible and beneficial for "product and market planning" but not for mass communications. Other analysts have a different viewpoint. Drawing on survey data of the experiences of multinational advertising agencies, Keegan stated that standardization of messages is practical and desirable, but message execution has to take account of natural cultural differences.[22]

Regional and national differences can determine how effective a particular AIDS communication is. In the United States, for example, graphic and explicit advertising is a popular mass-communication style. The 1987 AIDS advertising campaign in New York City reflected this style. One newspaper ad depicted the spilled contents of a woman's purse, including a comb, lipstick, and condoms, and offered the bold warning: "Don't go out without your rubbers." Another ad showed a picture of three unpackaged condoms and the headline "Smart sportswear for the active man." On the other hand, a poster in Trinidad sought to sell the idea of monogamy rather than active but safe sex. The poster showed a man and his girlfriend sitting on a park bench and looking happy, with the headline: "You're safer with one partner. Avoid AIDS." In northern European countries, mass communications generally adopt a calm, frank, and factual stance; therefore, communications on AIDS are typically low key. The leader of Sweden's AIDS task force observed: "We decided early that we didn't want a message of catastrophe. We wanted a consistent responsible line in our information over time. Otherwise, people won't listen."[23] The French approach also is low key

FIGURE 10–A Market Segmentation: Different Strokes for Different Folks

SOURCE: Petra Rohr Rouendal/IPPF. Taken from *Preventing a Crisis*, International Planned Parenthood Federation, PO Box 759, Inner Circle, Regent's Park, London NW1 4LQ.

and factual and counteracts appeals based on fear and panic. The Japanese, reflecting the puritan and modest characteristics of their culture, have utilized discreet and euphemistic messages with low-key execution styles.

Although each country may set a certain tone for its general AIDS message, its social marketers must develop specific messages for the different target-adopter groups in the country, as is dramatically conveyed in Figure 10–A. This figure shows six target groups and the message that each needs or wants to take from an AIDS campaign. Even here, debates rage about the specific message for each group. For young single women, should the message be no sex (chastity), less sex (monogamous relations), or safe sex (condoms—safer sex practices)? For drug users, should the message be no drugs (drug rehabilitation), less drugs, safer drugs, or clean needles? One can expect that all the many pressure groups in a country will take different stands on what they consider to be effective and appropriate messages to send to each target group.

11

Promoting Through
Selective Communication

Mass communications can inform and persuade a large group of people in a brief time. For example, because of mass communication-oriented campaigns to alert people to the danger of AIDS, the disease now is familiar to 90 percent of Americans. But although most people are aware of the disease, they do not know the precise nature of the HIV (human immunodeficiency virus) infection or of AIDS and how to take the necessary protective measures. This knowledge, which depends on intensive, detailed communications, may be beyond the ability of the mass media to communicate.

Some target-adopter segments, such as high-risk people, however, need even more information than do others. This information is likely to come from selective types of media, rather than from the mass media. Selective communication can do what mass communication cannot, namely, it can inform and persuade a predetermined set of target adopters in an interactive and flexible way. Selective communication, it should be noted, may be used to supplement mass communication, both as a follow-up technique that offers more intensive information and as a market-segmenting technique, which more precisely targets segments of a mass audience that a social marketer is seeking to reach. The two principal techniques of selective communication are direct mail and telemarketing.

DIRECT MAIL

Direct mail has at least four advantages in the promotion of a social product:

1. It can segment the target-adopter population into more uniform and definable clusters than can the mass media and thus cuts down on wasted media reach. Advertising space in a magazine or newspaper or advertising time on radio or television locks social marketers into a fixed reach that includes people that they do not need to reach. With direct mail, social marketers can use mailing lists of people who are the most likely prospects in the target-adopter market.
2. Communications can be personalized. Each target adopter can receive a letter with specific messages that are tailored to his or her attitudes and needs.
3. Direct mail is more flexible than is mass communication. Unlike a magazine or newspaper, the volume of direct mail can be calibrated to reach a specific audience that is as small or large as a social marketer requires. It can assume a format of any size or shape and present its message in a complex or simple way.
4. Direct mail can present an opportunity for adoption. It can provide directions on how to adopt a product, unlike most mass media ads, which seek primarily to generate awareness or interest.

The Audience

Direct mailers have to make a series of decisions in launching direct-mail promotions. The audience for selective communication—the potential target adopters of a social product—is reachable through mailing lists. These lists differentiate potential target adopters by numerous characteristics, the basis for segmenting the adopter market. For the U.S. market, Standard Rate and Data Service (SRDS) provides a directory of *Direct Mail Lists Rates and Data* that identifies 28,000 mailing lists that may be rented. Mailing lists are available for rental or purchase from business firms known as "list brokers." Since lists and list brokers are usually not found in developing countries, social marketing organizations in these countries may have to create their own lists.

Direct mailers distinguish between house lists, responder lists, and compiled lists. A house list contains the names of a given organization's clients or members, usually separated into active and inactive groups. A marketer may first aim to promote a social product to persons on the active list to see if there is sufficient response; if the response is weak, the marketer will not have wasted money promoting to the whole list. Many organizations and campaigns will not rent out their house lists to others because they want to avoid competition or protect confidentiality. For example, organizations with names of AIDS patients are mandated by law not to reveal their names.

A responder list contains the names of individuals who have responded earlier to direct-mail promotions by other organizations; therefore, it is equivalent to the active segment of a house list. Although a responder list has been used successfully by another organization, a social marketer has to determine whether the list's high response rate will be applicable in promoting his or her specific social product.

A compiled list contains names of potential target adopters or consumers that have been gathered from several different sources, such as motor vehicle registrations, telephone books, voter registration lists, hospitals, schools, churches, professional directories, and social and civic associations. These large lists are generally more useful for large-scale or mass mailings.

Whichever mailing list is used, a social marketer should look for indicators of the most likely target adopters on the lists. Addresses may indicate the likelihood of adoption insofar as they reflect socioeconomic status or educational level. Recently listed names are better than are older ones because people change their addresses frequently. Sometimes the ethnic or religious characteristics of a person's name may indicate the probability of adoption, as in the December 1988 campaign to gather financial aid for the victims of the Armenian earthquake. In organizing a direct-mail effort, social marketers should use only a small percentage of names in the first mailing to evaluate whether the response rate is high enough to justify the further use of the mailing list.

Communication Message

Direct-mail literature refers to the communication message as "the offer." This is an appropriate term because the promotion objective is not only to inform and to persuade but to induce adopters to take action to adopt a product. The offer may or may not involve a tangible-product base. It includes a social product and a set of incentives to push target adopters to take action, that is, to make a phone call, fill out and return a coupon, sign a petition, and the like. The more attractive the incentives, the more probable the action. Therefore, choosing the right set of incentives is critical. The major categories of incentives are risk-reducing incentives, free items, and economy incentives.

The two most popular forms of risk-reducing incentives are the free trial offer and the money-back guarantee. In the free trial offer, the prospective adopter's fear that a social product may be disappointing is mitigated or removed. The length of the trial period, according to experts, varies with the nature of the product; 10 days are more than enough for target adopters to evaluate such products as books and other merchandise, 15 days are more appropriate for products requiring habituation, and 30 days may be needed for more complex social products that require some effort by target adopters. The money-back guarantee is a way to raise the incentives of a trial offer when the product is a single whole product or indivisible. For example, a person cannot get one-third vaccinated for trial purposes. In a money-back guarantee, the reduction of the risk is largely psychological. Target adopters can count on receiving their money back if they are not satisfied.

Direct mailers can offer target adopters a free product, such as a booklet, to induce them to take a specific action. Sometimes they can indicate that the target adopters can keep the free item whether or not they adopt the social product.

Economy incentives come in at least three forms. A discount offer appeals to the target adopter's sense of a bargain. An example is the American Heart Association's short-term introductory offer of a $1 EKG test for hypertension. This special price can break down the target adopter's normal inertia. The real test is whether a high percentage of trial adopters are converted into committed adopters. A second form is the sale offer, or, in effect, a limited-time discount. Because people are generally suspicious about sales, it is useful to give a reason why the sale is being held. One way to do so is to call it an ''Anniversary'' or ''Summer'' sale. A third form is the sample offer, which may carry a nominal charge. This charge removes suspicion about the value of the social product if it were merely a free sample and can screen out the merely curious target adopters from the truly concerned ones.

Execution of the Communication

In preparing a direct-mail communication, one must prepare a direct-mail package that includes four items: the mail envelope, the letter, the brochure, and the response form. If an analogy were drawn between direct-mail communication and selling, the mail envelope is equivalent to the physical appearance of the sales representative; the letter, to the sales presentation; the brochure, to the sales pitch; and the response form, to the closing documentation of a sale.

The mail envelope's function is to attract the target adopter's attention, hold it, and then induce the adopter to open the mail. If the adopter is not moved to open the mail, the process is aborted. The adopter's attention can be captured by the envelope in a number of ways. A headline can be placed on the envelope carrying the basic message about the product, such as "Save a Life." This technique is particularly effective with target adopters who already are predisposed to the product. Or the envelope may carry a teaser headline, such as "Earn Money by Doing Good." The size, shape, and color of the envelope also must be carefully designed to draw attention to it.

The direct-mail letter carries the sales presentation. It has several dimensions: tone, salutation, length, opening and closing paragraphs, and postscripts and headings. The letter's tone is often conveyed through the salutation. A "Dear Friend" salutation versus a "Dear Mr. Jones" salutation immediately sets a contrasting tone: the former, a familiar tone; the latter, formal and businesslike. The letter's length should be long enough to convey the message, yet short enough to hold interest. There are no clear rules; consequently, the right length is best determined by pretesting.

Depending on the reading style of a target adopter, either the letter's opening paragraph or its closing paragraph will get the most attention.[1] Both portions of the letter must be carefully crafted. The opening paragraph must create an immediately favorable impression and should introduce the main message. The closing paragraph is typically the postscript. Most people will read the P.S. at the end of a letter. Headings within a direct-mail letter can be used to attract the reader's attention to different parts of the message and providing breaks to what otherwise would be boring-looking copy.

The brochure is a reinforcing device: it illustrates, dramatizes, exemplifies, and demonstrates what the letter says in words. It does so through appropriately chosen pictures, colors, drawings, and artwork. The net effect should be to reinforce the message with a degree of realism and concreteness. The response form is the channel through which readers are able to indicate the type of response they wish to make. The mailing usually includes a postage-free envelope in which the reader can mail back the response card.

Distribution of the Communication

The distribution system for direct mail is the postal system. In industrialized countries, almost all direct mail is reliably delivered. In developing countries, the postal service is not as efficient or reliable. Social marketers in developing countries might consider hand delivery as an alternative to postal delivery.

TELEMARKETING

The other major selective marketing tool for communications is telemarketing, namely, the use of a telephone to perform the needed communication and promotional tasks. The telephone can be used in two ways: "inbound telemarketing" and "outbound telemarketing." Inbound telemarketing occurs when a social marketer makes use of a toll-free number that persons can call when they need information. Thus, a health agency that deals with the AIDS problem can put an ad in a newspaper suggesting that people who are concerned about AIDS can call its toll-free number. The advantage of inbound telemarketing over the mails is that it permits two-way interaction as well as anonymity for the caller. Outbound telemarketing occurs when the social marketer actively phones target adopters to inform or persuade them about some idea or practice. For example, a health agency can obtain a list of subscribers to a gay or homosexual magazine and then telephone readers with offers of information and assistance regarding the AIDS problem.

When to Use Telemarketing

The most basic requirement of telemarketing is widespread telephone ownership among target adopters. Telemarketing is useful primarily in industrial countries with high rates of telephone ownership. It is less appropriate in countries like the Philippines and Indonesia, where telephone ownership is limited to only a small percentage of the population.

Research has shown that telemarketing is most suitable for carrying out the following communication functions:

1. *To Follow Up Mass Communication and Direct Mail.* Roman cited a U.S. survey of women shoppers in which the vast majority said that they acted on telephone calls from retailers about advertised sales and specials.[2] Political organizations also find telemarketing to be effective in reaching voters who are otherwise unreachable.

2. *To Encourage and Reinforce Adopter Loyalty.* Abrams reported that telemarketing that was designed to resolve complaints raised repeat patronage or adoptions from the persons called in 95 percent of the cases.[3] Katzenstein and Sachs called this function the telephone's "servicing function."[4]

3. *To Obtain Names of Target Adopters Who May Be More Effectively Persuaded by Personal Communications.* Telemarketing may not complete the persuasion process, but it can serve as a ground breaker to arrange for a follow-up personal visit by the social marketer. The AIDS information hot line in the U.S. was set up by American Red Cross with this specific purpose in mind.

Telemarketing can be used to reach new adopters and to serve current ones. New prospects are reached by acquiring call lists containing the names of people who are good prospects for adoption. The quality of any call list can be evaluated quickly by telephoning a small sample of names on the list and noting the percentage who are qualified. The social marketer may then use the lists that show a high percentage of qualified prospects. Telemarketing can also serve target adopters in active or passive ways. Social marketers can initiate calls to target adopters to audit their satisfaction and to uncover potential problems, or they can simply make their telephone number available to target adopters as a hot line.

The Message and Its Execution

A telemarketing message is designed to support the informing, persuading, and promotional objectives of a social change campaign. However, the execution of the message on the telephone requires fine tuning.

The first challenge is to get the target adopter on the receiving end to listen to the caller. Telemarketing representatives should have a pleasant voice and a good opening, such as, "Mr. Smith, I know that you may be busy. I just want a minute of your time. My name is John Jones, and I'm a volunteer worker for the American Heart Association. Do you have a minute?" The second challenge is to hold the target adopter's interest while presenting the message. The message will normally take the form of a scripted presentation that all telemarketing representatives will utilize. However, the representatives should be trained and rehearsed so they do not sound like they are reading from a script. Scripted or canned presentation can be enhanced by asking the caller to listen to a recorded message from a celebrity or well-known public figure. Thus, the voice of John Denver, an American singer, might urge a listener to consider sending money to aid the fight against world hunger. When the recorded message is completed, the telemarketing representative concludes the message.

The most canned form of telephone message delivery is the prerecorded message—a completely automated communication system, known as Automatic Dialing and Recorded Message Player. The system dials programmed telephone numbers and automatically plays the prerecorded message when a target adopter picks up the phone. Listeners are told that they may respond in either of two ways: by calling an answering telephone machine where they can leave their names, addresses, or telephone numbers for a follow-up call or by staying on the phone until the message is over and a telemarketer continues the call.

Whatever telemarketing technology is used, research has shown that the voice that is heard is as important a factor of persuasion as the message itself. The use of language and the sound of a voice are particularly critical when communication is heard but not seen. Mehrabian and Williams showed that high volume, vocal inflection, and vocal speech are associated with persuasiveness and credibility.[5] Packwood concluded that the louder the statements, the more persuasive they are, up to a point.[6] Addington found that the least credible vocal attributes are "throaty, tense, nasal, monotone, and breathy" characteristics.[7] All these findings emphasize the importance of carefully selecting and training telemarketers.

Timing of the Communication

The Direct Marketing Association in the United States recommended that telemarketing calls be made "during reasonable hours," which it defines as the period from 9:00 AM to 9:00 PM weekdays.[8] This time period is appropriate in the United States, but the situation may be different in other countries. In Latin American countries, for example, the hours of 1:00 to 3:00 PM are unreasonable because of the traditional siesta break. In the Philippines, Chinese traders do not like to receive sales calls during office hours. Even in the United States, some people are uncomfortable with receiving phone calls at dinner time or during the evening hours when they are watching a favorite television show. For this reason, telemarketing depends on research to determine the optimal times to reach target adopters.

12

Promoting Through Personal Communication

Social marketing can be viewed as both labor intensive and service intensive. The promotion and delivery of social products, with or without a tangible-product base, are heavily dependent on the quality of interpersonal communication, interaction, and service provided by all those who are working in a campaign. Personal communication is embedded in virtually every facet of the promotion and adoption of social products.

WHAT IS PERSONAL COMMUNICATION?

Social change campaigns typically involve a flow of intensive interactions and communications between change agents and target adopters. This flow of messages includes information and instruction, persuasion, advice and motivation, and the provision of assistance and services to target adopters. The personal communicators of a social change campaign assume a variety of roles, including motivators, outreach workers, facilitators, field workers, volunteers, professionals, recruiters, educators, counselors, missionaries, community organizers, extension workers, social workers, service providers, and service deliverers. These roles suggest the variety of the tasks that are performed in campaigns.

Of the three main promotional communication tools, personal

communication exercises the most powerful influence, particularly at certain stages of the adoption process. It is highly influential because of its three distinctive characteristics:

1. Personal communication entails numerous, diverse, and continuous interactions between the communicator and the recipient, or the target adopter. Thus, two participants in the communication process give and receive immediate and continuing feedback about each other's needs and reactions.

2. Because of the interactive nature of personal communication, the personal communicator has the opportunity to initiate, build, and maintain a full range of relationships with the target adopter. The deeper the relationship, the better the chance that the communicator can achieve the objective of the campaign.

3. As interactions increase and intensify, the target adopter's sense of obligation ''to return the favor'' grows and brings him or her closer to adopting the social product.

Social marketers can take advantage of these attributes but at a price: it is the costliest of the three promotional communication tools. On the basis of target adopters who were contacted, estimated costs for 1984, by type of media, were as follows:

Communication Media	Cost Per Contact
Mass communication (such as magazines)	$ 0.03
Selective communication (for example, direct mail)	$ 0.25
Personal communication	$102.00

Thus, direct mail costs about 10 times as much as mass communication, but personal communication is 4,000 times more expensive. Even when personal communicators are volunteers, the costs of personal communication are not eliminated, since a campaign still must recruit, train, and motivate volunteers. Ironically, volunteerism is likely to be more expensive than is mass communication or selective communication, when viewed from a communication campaign perspective. Is the greater impact of personal communication worth the extra costs? Under what circumstances?

THE AUDIENCE

According to Roberto, the selection of a personal-communication strategy will depend on two factors: whether the communicator is addressing one, several, or many target adopters, and whether the links are mediated and indirect or through word of mouth.[1] Accordingly, three strategies can be distinguished, as shown in Table 12-1.

Outreach Strategy

An outreach strategy occurs when the communicator is dealing directly with one person at a time, as when a social worker explains nutrition to the mother of a family. In this case, the communication can have a strong impact on the target adopter because of its one-on-one characteristic. However, the drawback of this strategy is that it reaches a limited number of people. Therefore, outreach is used sparingly. When it is used, the problem is how to distribute, in a given period, a communicator's time between new and continuing adopters to yield the best overall results. Much depends on how rapidly a target adopter can be converted into a trial adopter and then a committed adopter. If it can be done rapidly, then personal communicators should spend most of their time focusing on new adopters. If most trial adopters do not become committed adopters without intensive support

TABLE 12-1 Types of Personal Communication Strategies

Number of Linkages	Number of Recipients	
	One	Some
One	Outreach Strategies	Education Strategies
Two or More	Word-of-Mouth Strategies	

SOURCE: Eduardo L. Roberto, *Strategic Decision Making in a Social Program* (Lexington, Mass.: Lexington Books, 1975), p. 88.

from the communicator, then more time should be spent in sustaining the commitment of those who have already adopted.

Education Strategy

An education strategy is called for when the communicator deals directly with a group of people, such as in Alcoholics Anonymous sessions, drug-rehabilitation counseling, and "teach-ins." The choice of the educational forum is based on what social marketers are capable of organizing and what the budget will allow. The nature of the campaign agenda and the needs of the target adopters also are major factors. For example, it is feasible for AIDS-prevention counselors to exchange views in an open workshop, but it may be less feasible for victims of AIDS to do so.

Word-of-Mouth Strategy

A word-of-mouth strategy is called for when the communicator arranges for members of a target-adopter population to function as secondary communicators, who pass on the messages to their acquaintances, who, in turn, will pass on the messages to their acquaintances, and so on. The success of this type of communication will determine the adoption-diffusion rate. The major risk in word-of-mouth communication is the likelihood that a message will be distorted, especially when a social product is complex or controversial. In such an event, the social marketer must take steps to simplify the message and, if possible, the way it is transmitted.

THE MESSAGE

Social marketers must answer three questions before deciding what to say in a personal communication program: (1) Should the message be universal or varied? (2) How should the message be selected? and (3) How should the message be presented?

Universal or Varied Messages

When the positioning of a social product indicates that a large proportion of the target.adopters are highly motivated to try the product, the use of a single universal message is sound. However, when the target-adopter audience consists of many segments with different needs and levels of motivation, a universal message may be too rigid or limiting. In this case, several types of messages will be generated. Personal communicators often are in the best position to recognize the appropriateness of a message for individuals and for groups. They may have to draw on a "bank" of messages.

Social marketers normally will first develop a universal message for their social product. In an antidrug campaign directed at teenagers, for example, the message may be, "Say No to Drugs." This universal message anchors the campaign and gives it a consistent identity.

Which Message to Use

Because target-adopter audiences vary in their needs and motivations, it has become standard practice for social marketers to develop multiple messages about a social product for use in personal communications. The development of multiple messages can be guided by the elements shown in Figure 12–1.

Two features of a social product can be distinguished in designing messages. Physical/technical features, such as size, weight, temperature, shape, materials, consistency, ingredients, and other observable qualities, are of concern to research and development specialists. Sensory features are those that prospective target adopters can feel, see, sniff, hear, or taste.

Two types of benefits can also be differentiated in designing messages. Functional benefits relate to what the social product does or is intended to do for target adopters. Emotional/psychological benefits are those that prospective target adopters believe they are getting from using the social product. They are described as emotional and psychological because their reality lies inside the target adopter's mind.

These characteristics help the personal communicator choose a message that is most salient to the prospective target adopter. Consider, for example, an anti-AIDS educational campaign addressed to high-risk groups, whose aim is to persuade target adopters to take an AIDS screening test. The most widely used screening test, known as ELISA, has the following features and benefits:

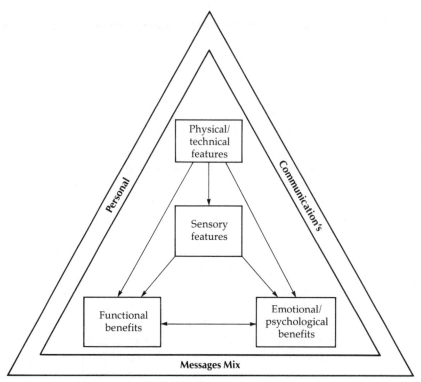

FIGURE 12-1 Presentation of Personal Communication Messages

Technical Features

1. The acronym ELISA is derived from "enzyme-lined immunosorbent assay," the technical description of the test.
2. The test uses a special electronic instrument that measures changes in the color of serum when antibodies are exposed to the human immunodeficiency virus (HIV), which causes AIDS.
3. As a screening test, ELISA sometimes produces a false positive, that is, a positive indication of the AIDS virus that turns out to be false.

Sensory Features

1. It is the cheapest test, costing $1 to $3, depending on the number of tests performed. In contrast, the Western blot, or immonoblot test, costs $90.

2. It is easy to administer. In contrast, the Western blot HIV test requires trained laboratory workers to interpret the results.
3. It is a quick test. It takes 2 to 5 hours to perform, compared to the Western blot, which takes as much as 2 days.
4. It is a very sensitive test. It identifies almost all blood containing antibodies to HIV.

Functional Benefits

1. Positive test results indicate infection.
2. It detects antibodies to HIV in the blood but does not diagnose AIDS.
3. It is a valuable test for screening blood and blood products.
4. It is an efficient test for large-scale screening.

Emotional/Psychological Benefits

1. The test enables AIDS-infected persons to know their status so they can take appropriate steps to obtain medical help and to prevent the further transmission of the virus.
2. The test motivates infected persons to seek appropriate counseling.

This framework helps the social marketer develop a checklist of the product's features and benefits that can be turned into messages.

How to Present Messages

Personal communicators can choose from a variety of messages. It would be inappropriate, however, to use too many types of messages, since doing so would produce information overload and fatigue. A smaller set of feature- and benefit-messages should be chosen. Then the question arises, How should the various features and benefits be related and sequenced in messages? One well-known rule of salesmanship says: ''Don't sell what you want, sell what they want.'' Personal communicators must start with who the prospective target adopters are and what they believe they will get out of a social product. Therefore, they should start their presentation with the benefits of the product to target adopters, not with the features of the product.

Personal communicators should start with those benefits that

are most credible and that can be accompanied by sensory reinforcement because such benefits are less subject to doubt, misunderstanding, or objections. Sales people put it this way: The sale
depends on emotion backed by logic. Benefits are the "emotion";
the physical/technical and sensory features are the "logic." Personal communicators should bring up only the features that are
of direct benefit to target adopters. Although they may be
tempted to mention a feature that is interesting, impressive, or
unique, they should not use it if it is not benefit related.

By following these rules, one can construct an effective presentation to promote the adoption of the AIDS screening test. The
benefits will be presented in the following sequence, with technical and sensory support whenever appropriate:

- Benefit 1: This is an efficient test.
- Benefit 2: It meets the need for safer sexual behavior.
- Benefit 3: If the test is positive, it indicates infection, which
  is the basis for seeking medical help and counseling.
- Benefit 4: The test can also detect the presence in the blood
  of antibodies to HIV.

EXECUTION OF THE COMMUNICATION

Mass communication has to prepare only for a single execution
because there are no direct interactions with a communication audience. Personal communication, however, must prepare for as
many executions as there are repeated and varying interactions.

Type of Interactions

Blake and Mouton distinguished several personal communication
orientations toward sales prospects or target adopters, as shown
in Figure 12-2.[2] This Grid® says that the personal communicator's
orientation is determined by the mix of concern for the customer
and for the sale. These two concerns are measured along a nine-
point scale, with one representing the lowest point and nine, the
highest. These two concerns give rise to the five styles of interaction shown in Figure 12-2.

A personal communication program is further complicated by
the fact that customers have their own interaction styles that are

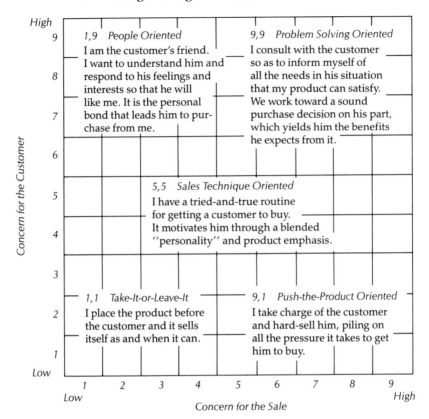

The Sales Grid

High
9 | 1,9 People Oriented
I am the customer's friend.
I want to understand him and
respond to his feelings and
interests so that he will
like me. It is the personal
bond that leads him to purchase from me.

9,9 Problem Solving Oriented
I consult with the customer
so as to inform myself of
all the needs in his situation
that my product can satisfy.
We work toward a sound
purchase decision on his part,
which yields him the benefits
he expects from it.

5,5 Sales Technique Oriented
I have a tried-and-true routine
for getting a customer to buy.
It motivates him through a blended
"personality" and product emphasis.

1,1 Take-It-or-Leave-It
I place the product before
the customer and it sells
itself as and when it can.

9,1 Push-the-Product Oriented
I take charge of the customer
and hard-sell him, piling on
all the pressure it takes to get
him to buy.

Concern for the Customer

Low
Concern for the Sale

FIGURE 12–2 The Sales Grid

SOURCE: *The Grid for Sales Excellence: New Insights into a Proven System of Effective Sales* (Second Edition), by Robert R. Blake and Jane Srygley Mouton. New York: McGraw-Hill Book Company, Copyright© 1980, 1970, page 6. Reproduced by permission.

based on their mix of concern for the salesperson and for the purchase. Figure 12–3 presents five customer interaction styles. By interfacing Figure 12–2 and Figure 12–3, one can begin to appreciate the many different outcomes that can take place when personal communicators interact with customers. For example, a specific interaction style of a personal communicator may work effectively, adversely, or indeterminately when matched with a particular interaction style of a customer. Blake and Mouton studied cases representing the possible pairings, as summarized in Table 12–2. Their findings indicate that the best match of styles are the problem-solving/solution-seeking interaction styles (see Figures 12–2 and 12–3).

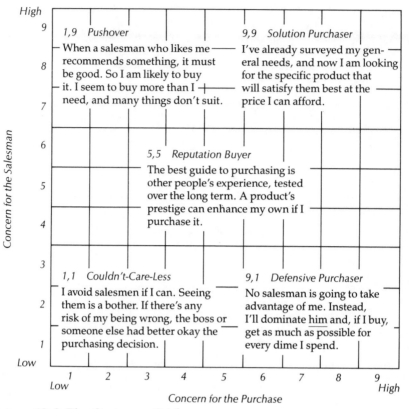

FIGURE 12–3 The Customer Grid

SOURCE: *The Grid for Sales Excellence: New Insights into a Proven System of Effective Sales* (Second Edition), by Robert R. Blake and Jane Srygley Mouton. New York: McGraw-Hill Book Company, Copyright© 1980, 1970, page 10. Reproduced by permission.

Relationship Marketing

Personal communicators may seek to frame their messages on the basis of their relationship to a target adopter, rather than on the interaction alone. Since they view their challenge as helping prospective target adopters solve their problems, they must spend more time with target adopters to learn about these problems. They must move from "transaction marketing," with its focus on making the initial sale, to that of "relationship marketing," with its focus on building a supportive relationship with target adopters over time.

Relationship marketing must start from a conceptualization of how target adopters solve problems. The process through which

TABLE 12-2 Probable Effectiveness of the Five Interaction Styles of the Personal Communicator[a]

Salesman Grid Style	Customer Grid Style				
	1, 1	1, 9	5, 5	9, 1	9, 9
9, 9	+	+	+	+	+
9, 1	?	+	+	?	?
5, 5	?	+	+	−	?
1, 9	−	+	?	−	?
1, 1	−	−	−	−	−

[a]The pairs of numbers refer to the styles noted in Figure 12–2 and 12–3.

+ = likely to be effective, − = likely to be ineffective, and ? = effectiveness cannot be determined.

SOURCE: *The Grid for Sales Excellence: New Insights into a Proven System of Effective Sales* (Second Edition), by Robert R. Blake and Jane Srygley Mouton. New York: McGraw-Hill Book Company, Copyright© 1980, 1970, page 16. Reproduced by permission.

target adopters go starts with uncertainty. Thus, the objective is to eliminate or reduce the uncertainty by trying to formulate the problem, finding alternative solutions and then the optimal one, and finally inducing the target adopter to implement the optimal solution. Only then does the target adopter's uncertainty diminish. The process can go wrong at several points. Target adopters may erroneously formulate a problem, they may not recognize optimal solutions, they may not evaluate alternative solutions correctly, or their implementation of a chosen solution may be faulty.

These errors point to the key stages in which a personal communicator may intervene effectively in a target adopter's problem-solving process. If the communicator arrives on the scene when the target adopter is trying to implement a solution, then the task of communication is to help the target adopter implement the solution. If the communicator arrives on the scene when a target adopter is first facing a problem, then the task is to spend much more time helping the target adopter to define the problem, generate alternative solutions, choose the best one, and implement it. When personal communicators succeed in getting involved in the early phases of the process, their value to the target adopters is greater and deepens.

Execution of the Communication

How should the personal communicator sequence the various steps involved in dealing with prospective target adopters? Two alternative approaches developed in commercial product marketing are applicable to social marketing. These are the classic model and the nonlinear model.

Classic Model

The classic model sees the communicator moving through seven steps: (1) prospecting and qualifying, (2) preapproach, (3) approach, (4) presentation and demonstration, (5) handling objections, (6) closing, and (7) followup (see Figure 12–4). The first step, prospecting and qualifying, consists of generating leads of potential target adopters, sorting these leads into poor versus promising ones, and then qualifying or evaluating the promising leads either through referrals, telemarketing or direct mail. The preapproach step involves the personal communicator in learning as much as possible about each potential target adopter before making an approach. On the basis of this information, the communicator can determine the optimal message and its optimal timing.

In the third step, approach, the personal communicator presents himself or herself with a certain look, opening lines, and follow-up remarks. The aim is to obtain and hold the target adopter's attention and interest. If this step fails, the personal communication process is aborted. The goal of the next step, presentation and demonstration, is to inform and persuade a target adopter to adopt a social product. There are three alternative approaches, according to Cash and Crissy:[3]

- The canned approach, in which the personal communicator conveys the social product's benefits and features through a standardized communication script.
- The formulated approach, in which the personal communicator conveys the product's benefits and features using a "selling formula" that is neither memorized nor rigidly followed.
- The need-satisfaction approach, in which the personal communicator chooses specific benefits and features to communicate only after determining a target adopter's needs.

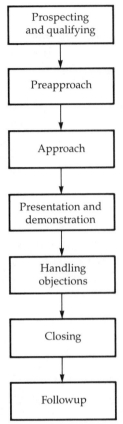

FIGURE 12-4 The Classic Model of Executing a Communication

The fifth step, handling objections, takes place during the pre-sentation and when the potential target adopter is asked to sign up or agree to another presentation. The important point is to anticipate the target adopter's objections and to know how to meet them. The sixth step, closing, involves gaining a prospective target adopter's commitment to become a continuing adopter. In the business world, effective closing is the most critical selling skill; it is equally important in social marketing. Those who are unable to close an adoption are conversationalists, not salespersons. The last step, followup, calls on the personal communicator to check up on the target adopter's satisfaction and continued adoption. At this time, the target adopter is fairly receptive to proposals to increase his or her commitment.

Nonlinear Model

When the actual communication between a communicator and a target adopter does not follow the classic model, the personal communicator must be prepared for contingencies. Figure 12–5 presents an example.

The sequence starts with an exploratory probe by the personal communicator to identify a prospect's problem or problems. The question may be broad, as in "Are you satisfied with your food habits?" or narrow, as in "How do you resist eating fatty foods? To this question, potential target adopters may (1) state a problem they are experiencing, (2) give a negative response, such as "That's none of your business," or (3) respond with indifference. To each response, the personal communicator can choose to confirm the response, explore it further, or try to identify the likely problem. If the personal communicator succeeds in identifying the target adopter's problem, then he or she can proceed with an appropriate presentation. There are at least six tasks to be performed during this stage:

1. Clearly restating the prospect's goal.
2. Referring to the social product.
3. Describing the social product's pertinent features.
4. Showing how the benefits are supported by pertinent features.
5. Relating the benefits to the target adopter's goal.
6. Exploring additional goals of the target adopter.

Prospective target adopters may respond to a presentation in any of three ways. If they want to discuss a specific benefit of the social product, the personal communicator should emphasize how the social product will deliver this benefit. If they indicate that the social product meets all their goals, the personal communicator should then move toward a closing. If they resist the presentation or conclusion, the personal communicator should search for the source of their resistance, which may be conflicting goals, doubts about the claimed benefits, or misunderstanding. Depending on the source of resistance, the personal communicator can attempt to refocus, prove, or explain. The nonlinear model shown in Figure 12–5 depicts the distinctiveness of personal communication, namely, its continuous and repeated interactive process.

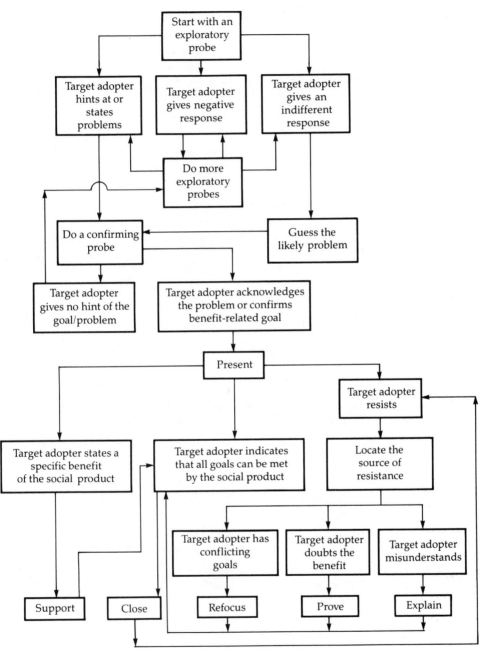

FIGURE 12-5 A Nonlinear Model of Executing a Communication

TIMING OF THE COMMUNICATION

The question is often raised, Is personal communication more effective when it comes after mass or selective communication or when it comes before? The normal answer is "after." This answer is based on the notion that mass communication is more cost effective in identifying target adopters and in presenting them with persuasive information. When the personal communicator arrives on the scene, the target adopter is half-sold.

Yet, there are exceptions to this practice, Swinyard and Ray's study provides an example.[4] Female residents in Palo Alto, California, were subjected to two message-timing executions. Six Red Cross volunteer workers first called on a random sample of respondents and delivered the following message:

> Hello, I'm a volunteer for the Red Cross Blood Center here in Palo Alto. I'm not here to ask for money; just for a minute of your time. March is Red Cross Month, and I am part of a program to help increase the neighbors' awareness of the Red Cross.
>
> The Red Cross is very short on blood of all types, and on blood donors despite the fact that it is so easy and convenient to give. You know, the Blood Center is less than a mile from here. We want to increase awareness of the importance of donating blood to the Red Cross, and we've found that every little reminder helps.[5]

Afterwards, respondents received direct-mail messages that appealed for blood donors and Red Cross volunteers. And at a later point, Red Cross volunteers called on the respondents again and presented the same message.

The results indicated that the personal/selective sequence of communications had a more substantial impact on the respondents' intention to donate blood than did the mass or selective communications alone. The direct-mail materials had a minimal effect on sensitizing respondents to the subsequent personal communication presentations. Swinyard and Ray concluded that the adverising-first-is-best rule did not work in this case. They explained the surprising results as probably being due to the target adopters' familiarity with both the social product (blood donation) and the marketing organization (Red Cross). They speculated that had the social campaign been less well known, nonpersonal/personal communication would have been the stronger strategy.

Social change campaigns usually depend heavily on personal communication between campaign staff and workers and target adopters. Winning adoptions of social products involve informing, persuading, motivating, educating, providing social services, and professional counseling, as well as advertising. Conventional marketing interactions between "sellers" and "buyers" in the social marketing context are supplemented by the building of personal relationships and reciprocity exchanges. In marketing social products, the flow of personal communications is heavy and intense. After determining the mix of communications in promoting social products, social marketers will need to focus on one additional and significant element in promotion, namely, triggering favorable responses from and adoptions by target adopters.

13

Triggering Target Adopters' Actions

When effectively implemented, mass communication, selective communication, and personal communication move potential target adopters to a state of positive motivation. The social marketing task at this point is to get target adopters to act on their intention, which we refer to as triggering the action.

There are two basic ways to obtain this result. One is to exert pressure on target adopters to act now, not later. This triggering strategy employs well-known consumer-promotion incentives, such as free samples, giveaway premiums, contests, and special sales. The other strategy solicits the involvement and participation of target adopters, which leads to trial adoption, which, in turn, can lead to committed adoption.

PRESSURE FOR IMMEDIATE ACTION

What factors keep motivated prospective target adopters from immediately carrying out their intention? Research on consumers' attitudes and behaviors has identified the following: (1) the lack of opportunity to carry out the intention, (2) the limited capacity to implement the intention, and (3) time constraints.

Opportunity to Act on the Intention

To carry out an intention, one must have an opportunity to do so. Such an opportunity may not be available when a prospective target adopter wants to adopt a social product. There may be no distribution outlet or the pressure of time or monetary costs may prevent action.

One technique for overcoming obstacles is product sampling. If the social product has a tangible-product base, it can be distributed to motivated target adopters in ways that minimize cost and inconvenience. If the social product is an idea, the sampling technique is more challenging but not impossible. Consider, for example, Canada's National Program to Reduce Tobacco Use among Teenagers.[1] In its mass communication phase, this program positioned nonsmoking to a target audience of 12–17 year olds as "the cool thing to do." To get the teenagers to "sample" this advertised experience, the Health Promotion Directorate of Canada provided them with the means to experience vicariously the cool-thing nonsmoking experience—a ten-minute video documentary entitled "The Making of Break Free." Both the English and French versions of the video were widely circulated in junior and senior high schools across Canada.

Capacity to Implement the Intention

The prospective target adopter's intention may be hampered by financial or emotional constraints. For example, although a person may be convinced to give up drinking, the cost of getting "dried out" in a hospital is beyond his or her means or the person is afraid to enter a group session, such as Alcoholics Anonymous.

Financial barriers can be lessened somewhat by providing substantial allowances or discounts to prospective target adopters. To overcome emotional constraints, personal promoters and role models may be effective. Personal promoters were used in Canada's program to reduce teenagers' use of tobacco. Student volunteers were recruited and trained to assist children, aged 11–17, to identify and overcome the social influences that reinforce smoking.[2]

Time Constraints

People have many things to do in a given day and thus may have little time to be induced to change a behavior or adopt a new behavior. In a study of primary health care programs in African and South Asian countries, Overholt et al. found that the average day of women is filled with activities whereas their husbands usually have a lot of idle time. What can social marketers do about time constraints? They can time their promotions of a social product to take place on or near special social and cultural occasions, such as holidays, days off from work, anniversaries, and religious celebrations. On these occasions, people may have more time to carry out their intentions.

Some business firms have responded to the AIDS epidemic, for example, by incorporating employee AIDS education into existing employee wellness programs.[3] By dispensing information on the prevention of AIDS during routine employees' health check-ups, they save their employees considerable time and, therefore, are more successful in triggering adoption than they have been with separate AIDS education programs.

Major Techniques

Marketers use several techniques to trigger the adoption of social products and services.[4]

- *Product Sampling.* A free sample of a product, such as new diet-control pills for weight reduction, could be distributed through the mail; door-to-door delivery; in outlets in the form of a help-yourself displays; or in packages for other uses, which are known as "carriers." A sample of a service, such as a weight-reducing exercise program, could be offered to prospective target adopters in the form of a free class before they sign up.

- *Couponing.* Coupons can be given to potential target adopters that entitle them to savings on the purchase of a specific product or service. They can be distributed by mail, through printed publications, or in other packages.

- *Premium Offering.* An item, called a "premium," can be offered free or at a nominal charge as a bonus to induce the purchase of a product or service. The free premium can be presented before or at the time the prospect adopts the product or service.

- *Contests and Sweepstakes.* Contests involve a display of skill or dexterity; sweepstakes do not. The skill may involve naming, guessing, estimating, or completing a jingle, the successful performance of which earns prospective target adopters prizes, such as money, merchandise, overseas trips, or free service.
- *Continuity Programs.* In this technique, the prospective target adopter collects coupons, proof-of purchase seals or labels each time he or she uses the specific product or service. The coupons can be accumulated to pay for a desired premium.
- *Special Events.* The social marketer can sponsor a public activity, such as an annual health fair or a "cleanup day," which motivates prospective target adopters to undertake a desired action.

PARTICIPATORY ADOPTION

Many social services are delivered on a nonparticipatory basis. Korten criticized nonparticipatory services because they have a limited reach, do not sustain beneficial action, fail to adapt to local circumstances, and create dependence.[5] He favored participatory, or "people-centered," development. Paul defined community participation as "an active process by which beneficiary or client groups influence the direction and execution of a development project with a view to enhancing their well being in terms of income, personal growth, self reliance or other values they cherish." The objectives are (1) to empower people "so that they are able to initiate actions on their own and thus influence the processes and outcomes of development" and (2) to forge an individual's initiative and capacity to sustain an adoption even after a social marketing campaign is completed.[6]

How are these objectives attained? Kelman (1958) identified three processes.[7]

In a compliance adoption process, prospective target adopters act on their intention not because they believe in the social product but because they expect to gain specific rewards or avoid specific penalties from its adoption.

In the identification adoption process, prospective target adopters are triggered to act by something other than the functional performance of a social product or an expected reward or gain. In this case, adoption occurs because of a target adopter's perception of a relationship with a social change campaign. Adoption yields satisfaction by virtue of the act of relating to a change agent; the motivation to act comes from a sense of "identification."

The internalization adoption process moves prospective target adopters to act because of the intrinsic meaning or value of adoption. Because the social product is congruent with the target adopter's value system, adoption is an expression of that value system, which, itself, is the source of satisfaction.

How does the social marketer implement these triggering concepts? Paul noted four ways to promote a prospective target adopter's participation in the adoption of a social product.

- *Information Sharing.* This is the lowest level of participation. The social marketer shares information with prospective target adopters to facilitate their taking action on their intention to adopt. The target adopter's need to understand, if adequately satisfied by relevant information, moves him or her to take action. In social programs that are burdened by misperceptions and controversy, such as AIDS-prevention campaigns, information sharing is critical.

- *Consultation.* At this level of participation, prospective target adopters are given the opportunity to share their questions, concerns, and reactions with social marketers and the campaign staff.

- *Decision Making.* At the next level, prospective target adopters are given an opportunity to play a role in determining the design and implementation of a social product or social change campaign. The sharing of planning and of control of the program becomes co-equal between prospective target adopters and the marketing campaign (see Figure 13–1).

- *Initiating Action.* When control of a social product or an entire social change campaign is passed on to prospective target

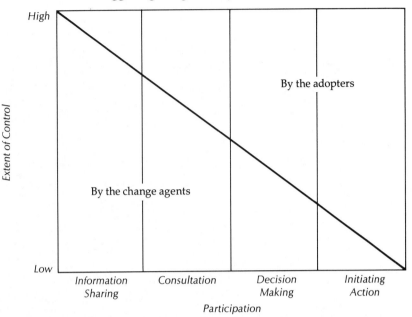

FIGURE 13-1 Sharing Control of the Program under the Four Levels of Participation

adopters and they take initiative and make decisions, then they have reached the highest level of participation.

What is a participation-driven social marketing program like? The program to control guinea-worm disease in Idere, Nigeria, is an illustration.[8] Guinea worm had plagued the 10,000 residents of Idere and the surrounding farm hamlets for many years. The disease reached epidemic proportions when the town's water system collapsed. The lasting solution was to build an adequate water supply, but that required time. Meanwhile, an interim control measure was needed. It was not economically feasible for the rural residents to protect themselves by boiling their water, since they could not afford to use fuel for this purpose. However, persuading residents to use filters when gathering their water proved to be the most practical interim control measure.

The campaign led to the development and distribution of a proper water filter, consisting of a cloth made of monofilament nylon gauze. It would be fine enough to block organisms that may have digested a guinea-worm larva, but would still allow water to flow through smoothly. Thirty volunteer health workers (VHWs), who were drawn from all areas of the town and surrounding countryside, participated in all phases of the campaign's design and implementation. Their participation in the marketing-mix activities, as outlined next, proved to be decisive in the campaign's success.

Design of the Social Product

1. VHWs discussed and determined the design of the filter.
2. VHWs identified and recruited local resources for producing the filter, including local tailors who were allowed to use their discretion in modifying and producing it.
3. VHWs monitored the quality of the production.

Decision on Pricing

1. The United Nations Development Programme, World Bank, and the World Health Organization funded a VHW-led community survey to determine the range of acceptable prices that would induce people to adopt the filter.
2. The VHW group discussed a fair price for the filter and decided to price the filter low enough so as not to sabotage the program.

Decision on Distribution

1. The VHWs organized themselves to market the guinea-worm-prevention filter, recruiting others to help them sell it. Of 35 members of the sales force, 27 were VHWs and the rest were townspeople.
2. The sales personnel received training from the African Regional Health Education Centre. They learned how to instruct consumers in the proper use of the filter.

Decision on Promoting Sales

1. The VHWs held demonstrations in the village and visited homes to explain the value and use of the filter.
2. The filter was the subject of announcements in churches and mosques.
3. The VHW group visited the leader of Idere to explain the

project and to urge him to endorse and promote the use of the filters.

Over a six-month period, evaluators of the filter campaign compared the results "favorably" with professionally run family-planning social marketing campaigns in the region.

Another example of participation by target adopters was a government-sponsored system of cooperatives in the Santa Valley of the northern coast of Peru.[9] In 1970, a devastating earthquake destroyed much of the countryside. This tragedy provided the impetus, aided by foreign loans and donor grants, for radical experiments in building a network of cooperative farms. Young agronomists who advocated the participation of farmers and peasants in the rebuilding of the valley became involved in the social change campaign.

The technical adviser to the Santa Valley campaign had been an administrator of a sheep-farming firm, and his outlook had been that of the landlords. However, after land reform, the adviser began working for a farming cooperative, and he became converted to the cooperative point of view. As he stated, "my point of view changed 180 degree to seeing everything from the point of view of the peasant. We live in peasant communities and spend each day working with peasants. Through this work we obtain the information needed to understand what commands interest among the people, and what they most need."[10]

The technical adviser provided the following assessment of the obstacles that the cooperative-farming campaign encountered in gaining the peasants' participation:

> There are practical problems in mobilizing the participation of peasants. These problems tend to be taken for granted or given only passing attention.
>
> The first problem is that the peasants' participation in a cooperative does not really change their daily work life. "He who previously was a manual laborer continues as such and those whose jobs were to irrigate or to cut crops keep doing the same. They feel [like] members of the cooperative only after 5 p.m., when they . . . have their meetings and assemblies."[11] This routine makes it difficult to demonstrate a better life and higher productivity.
>
> The second problem is that the participating peasants do not feel they own their land in a cooperative arrangement, thus,

they lack the motivation that can come from land ownership. Furthermore, the cooperative is always in debt to the government's Agricultural and Livestock Bank. Consequently, the peasants believe the land belongs to the government, not to them. It is hard to explain that the land is theirs when they know they are burdened with debt for 20 years.

It takes a long time to develop effective participation by peasants. Just in training alone, it was necessary to start with a preset agenda; otherwise there would be no participation. It was only after two years of daily nonstop work that the peasants began to choose plans of action on their own.

A massive study of cooperative programs whose aim was to gain the participation of peasants and farmers highlighted the barriers to organizing farming cooperatives. Sponsored by the United Nations Research Institute for Social Development, the study covered 37 rural cooperatives in 12 developing countries. Its major conclusions were as follows:

1. The participation of peasants cannot be imposed from above. For example, government-sponsored cooperatives in Latin America attempted to coerce peasants to participate. This coercion was both direct and indirect, depriving peasants of economic benefits if they refused to participate. Even church-sponsored programs obtained participation by coercing and stigmatizing nonparticipators as people who are heretics or subversives.

2. Governments that resorted to coercion acknowledged it. They justified coercion as the use of the power of the state to organize new groups that would be capable of transforming the traditional order.

3. Because peasants rarely participate, leaders of local cooperatives who are recruited become the instruments of coercion. For example, cooperatives in Latin America and Africa typically started out with independent local leaders. Later, these leaders allowed themselves to be co-opted by the government and ceased to be representatives of, or spokespersons for, the cooperative members. As a result, the power to make decisions was grabbed by governmental officials, rather than retained by the cooperatives' leaders.

4. The participation of peasants in the cooperative movement

contributed little to building the peasants' self-reliance. Local initiatives and peasant organizations were stifled. Dependence is not replaced by initiative, since the government replaces landowners as the new patrons.

5. Most cooperatives failed to advance economic and social equality. When they failed to meet the peasants' aspirations, they raised the levels of frustration and sowed discontent.

6. When peasants participated effectively, the cooperative organizations were small and pragmatic, rather than militant or ideological. Cooperatives with only an economic-development focus had the greatest impact.

Implications for the Participation of Target Adopters

There are limitations to inducing prospective target adopters to participate in social change campaigns, particularly those whose goals are massive personal and social changes. Many of these limitations stem from shortcomings in implementing the campaigns. The practical problem for change agents is to identify the conditions under which participation will work. One such condition may be strong grievances and discontent by a target-adopter population, which considers the status quo to be unacceptable. Tough, diligent work by change agents is another. As the example of peasant cooperatives in Peru demonstrated, social marketing campaigns often find it necessary to induce a shift from an "immediate-gratification" perspective to one that countenances "deferred gratification" and the expectation that the desired goals will require a great deal of time to implement. The success of getting prospective target adopters to participate in a campaign also depends on their motivation to band together around mutual interests and to organize themselves effectively.

The participation of target adopters is particularly appropriate when active dialogue and negotiation between target adopters and social change agents is required to move the campaign forward. The very nature of target adopters' participation in social marketing calls for the exchange of information, sharing control, and mutual trust. Where this condition exists, social marketers can effectively use participation-driven promotion programs.

14

◆

Managing Service Delivery and Target Adopters' Satisfaction

When triggering mechanisms work, they move potential target adopters into trial adoption. The result is that a Canadian teenager vicariously samples a nonsmoking day with the help of rock star Luba, a corporate employee joins an aerobics exercise group sponsored by the company's "wellness program," and a Peruvian peasant joins a farmers' cooperative. If the trial adopter's expectations are met, he or she is satisfied. Thus, social marketing campaigns can fulfill target adopters' expectations by providing a range of activities and services that effectuate and sustain the adoption of a social product. Service delivery is an important adjunct of the adoption of a social product; in fact, it supports the adoption process from start to finish.

SATISFYING TARGET ADOPTERS

The satisfaction of target adopters is the outcome of two forces: the target adopters' needs and expectations and a social change campaign's performance. A campaign's performance, in turn, depends on the quality of the social campaign's personnel, the place where the performance occurs, and the process—the sequence and flow of activities involved in transacting the adoption of a social product.

Prospective target adopters have expectations about each component. According to Parasuraman, Zeithaml, and Berry, there are ten sets of expectations for social marketers to consider: five related to personnel, three related to the place, and two related to process.[1]

The five types of expectations that prospective target adopters have of personnel are as follows:

1. Responsiveness

- "Personnel should be willing and ready to serve us."
- "They should arrange my appointment quickly."
- "They should be prompt in offering the service."
- "When personnel say they'll do something, it should be done quickly."

2. Competence

- "Personnel should know their job and how to do it."
- "All staff should be knowledgeable and skillful."
- "The behavior of personnel should reflect lots of experience in what they are doing."

3. Courtesy

- "Personnel should be polite, respectful, flexible, friendly, and accommodating."

4. Credibility

- "Personnel should be trustworthy, believable, honest, and have my best interests at heart."

5. Sensitivity

- "I want them to make some effort to understand my needs."
- "Instead of treating me like everyone else, personnel should find out about my specific needs and preferences."
- "I like getting individualized attention."

- "I'm a regular client and I want to be recognized and treated as one."

The three sets of expectations about place are these:

1. Access

- "A campaign and its offices should have convenient hours of operation."
- "Offices should be conveniently located."
- "When I call them, staff shouldn't be too busy."
- "I shouldn't have to wait too long in a line to get help."

2. Security

- "I want a place that's safe."
- "I want my dealings there kept private."

3. Appearance

- "Physical facilities should be attractive."

Finally, the two sets of *process* expectations are as follows:

1. Reliability

- "This is a vasectomy service. They must perform it right the first time."
- "Service should have consistent quality."

2. Communication

- "I like it when personnel explain to me what they are doing."
- "If there are risks and side-effects, they should tell me."

Social marketers need to know how prospective target adopters evaluate the quality of a service so they can influence these evaluations in a desired direction. Zeithaml suggested that target adopters evaluate their expectations along three lines.[2] First, target adopters can evaluate and confirm their sensory expectations even before they experience the service; for example, when they enter a hospital for a vaccination. Second, target adopters have expectations of the experience that relate to aspects of the product or service that they evaluate through trial adoption. Thus, target adopters can evaluate the promptness of the service of receiving a vaccination. Third, they have credence expectations, which refer to the qualities of a social product that they are unable to verify through their senses or experience but that they accept on faith, such as the effectiveness of the vaccination.

Which type of evaluation exerts the strongest influence on the satisfaction of target adopters? Parasuraman, Zeithaml, and Berry maintain that because sensory expectations are few and credence expectations are too difficult to evaluate, target adopters probably depend on experience in evaluating the quality of a service and, therefore, in expressing satisfaction or dissatisfaction.[3]

MANAGING SERVICE PERSONNEL

Service personnel play an important role in the satisfaction of target adopters. If personnel are aloof or rude, they can undermine all the marketing work done to attract target adopters. If they are friendly and warm, they can increase the target adopters' satisfaction and loyalty.

The social marketers' task is to ensure that personnel are friendly and warm, responsive, and sensitive to the needs of prospective and current adopters. They need a strong recruitment program and high-quality training, supervision, and evaluation.

Recruitment of Personnel

Four types of personnel can be identified, according to their visibility and the degree of contact they have with target adopters.[4]

1. Those who have high contact and high visibility, such as nurses who do blood tests in an AIDS screening facility.
2. Those who have high contact with target adopters but low or no visibility, including telephone counselors in a crisis-intervention center.
3. Those who have little or no contact with target adopters but are highly visible, for example, support personnel in an AIDS screening facility.
4. Those who have little or no contact and low visibility in relation to target adopters, such as, laboratory technicians who test blood samples for AIDS.

The first group is the one for whom interpersonal skills are most important. Employees in this group must be carefully selected for their personal qualities, such as warmth and responsiveness. However, other personnel who are visible to target adopters will also need some training in how to serve them. What kind of training should these personnel receive?

Training of Personnel

Several training methods are available.[5] One set of training techniques is on-the-job training, in which the trainee learns skills without sacrificing productivity. The most popular on-the-job training technique is job instruction. This technique introduces the trainee to the job through a step-by-step review and demonstration of the job functions. Then the trainee shares what he or she has learned by demonstrating the ability to carry out a specific task. This demonstration continues until the trainee performs at a satisfactory level.

Another technique is to place the trainee on a junior supervisory board that oversees service-delivery activities. By participating, the trainee acquires a sense of and appreciation for decisions that are being made. Presumably, this type of training engenders a positive attitude toward service delivery and permits others to assess the trainee's potential and problem-solving ability. In the third on-the-job training technique, job rotation, the trainee rotates through different service units in an organization. Rotation enables the trainee to view the sevice from different viewpoints and to assess better his or her aptitude for different roles in an organization.

A second set of training techniques consists of off-the-job training. These techniques include lectures, group discussions, the case method, and role playing. Organization research has contrasted the effectiveness of these techniques in forming and improving the skills of personnel, as shown in Table 14–1. The case method ranks as the most effective skill builder, except for building interpersonal skills, for which role playing is preferred.

Social marketers can optimize the performance of personnel by combining on-the-job and off-the-job training techniques. The particular technique they use depends on the type of personnel being trained and the training objectives that are to be accomplished.

TABLE 14-1 Comparison of Effectiveness of Off-the-job Training Techniques[a]

Techniques	Inter-personal Skills	Self-expression Skills	Practical Analytical Skills	Problem-solving Skills	Decision-making Skills
Lecture	2	1	3	1	1
Group dis-cussion	5	7	5	3	4
Case method	7	8	8	9	9
Role play-ing	9	8	6	6	7

[a]The rating of each technique is on an 11-point scale of 0 to 10 where 0 = extremely weak in forming/improving the skills concerned and 10 = extremely strong in forming/improving the skills concerned.

Supervision of Personnel

The supervision of personnel involves ensuring that their performance meets standards and, if necessary, helping them improve their performance. To ensure high-quality work, social marketers must supervise the performance of personnel in its earliest stages, identify problems quickly, and then make the necessary changes before a campaign is fully launched.

Evaluation of Personnel

What evaluation methods can a social marketer use to monitor and measure the staff's adherence to standards? There are several: (1) an operations-based method, (2) the solicitation of complaints, (3) the use of a suggestion box, and (4) surveys of target adopters.

An operations-based method makes use of techniques, such as the process chart, work-flow diagram, activity charts, man-machine charts, and operations charts, to generate the needed evaluation data.[6] The complaint-solicitation method calls on target adopters to provide feedback about the weaknesses of the service and needed improvements. In many instances, target adopters will not provide feedback; their dissatisfaction may lead them to withdraw from a campaign and tell friends about their unhappy experience. Surveys are devices for gathering a more representative sample of satisfied and dissatisfied target adopters, who are either given a structured questionnaire for expression their concerns or are interviewed after an adoption experience. For survey results to be useful, however, social marketers have to be quite specific in the questionnaire items they use and evaluate.

MANAGING THE PLACE OF SERVICE

The "where and what" of a social change campaign is also critical. The place where its services are provided, including the physical space, creates an atmosphere that either supports or undermines the task of meeting target adopters' expectations. The location of a social marketing program, both the headquarters and the field offices, can be either accessible or unaccessible, and the appearance of the facility can either be appealing or unappealing.

Physical Exteriors and Interiors

It is useful to think of the location of a campaign's services as a "store." The exterior consists of the frontage, architecture, size, entrances, signage, and other exterior spatial characteristics. The interior consists of decor, lighting, furnishings, layout, acoustical and ventilation conditions, cleanliness, and other spatial attributes.

The "store" becomes a facilitator of satisfaction when its attributes fall within a target adopter's latitude of acceptance, which has two threshold points: a lower threshold below which the target adopter finds too little physical quality and an upper threshold beyond which an adopter finds too much quality.

Atmosphere

A social program's field offices typically contain many target adopters or clients who are waiting for an activity or service to begin. During the process, they may interact with one another. The character of this waiting crowd can exert a subtle influence on their satisfaction. Certain social programs have no direct control over the people they draw; for example, an AIDS testing center is open to everyone. However, social marketers can employ demarketing measures to control the types of people they attract. According to Kotler, demarketing deals with

> efforts to discourage clients or customers in general (general demarketing) or a certain class in particular (selective demarketing) on either a temporary or permanent basis. . . . [It is] marketing in reverse. Instead of encouraging clients, it discourages the undesirable ones. Prices may be raised, and product quality, service, promotion, and convenience reduced.[7]

The physical atmosphere should be designed to satisfy the needs and expectations of the target adopters.[8] The physical appearance and layout must be attractive and comfortable to the target adopters, as well as to the service personnel. Good planning of the atmosphere does not necessarily involve extra cost. It requires being sensitive to what target adopters expect to experience in trying or adopting the specific social product.

MANAGING THE SERVICE PROCESS

Let us now move to the "how" of service delivery, the provision of activities and services that a social change campaign undertakes in its pursuit of its objectives.

Managing Technology

Social change campaigns can function as mom-and-pop operations or as modern enterprises with efficient technologies that facilitate their activities. In the business world, one can compare an old-fashioned restaurant with a single cook preparing one hamburger at a time with the modern hamburger-making technology of McDonald's, which produces thousands of hamburgers an hour. Likewise, one can imagine a blood-donation center that operates on a low-tech basis with one donor at a time versus a high-tech center in which several donors give blood at the same time and the blood is analyzed by a blood-analyzer machine. The high-tech approach promises more accurate and efficient service; it also runs the risk of being depersonalized. The trade-off between technological efficiency and personalized service has to be weighed in designing technologies that support social marketing campaigns.

Shostack suggested that a campaign's delivery of services should be designed using a three-step planning approach.[9] The first step maps all the processes that constitute a particular service. Figure 14–1 presents an example of the mapping of a family planning service process.[10] In this example, a social marketer would find it useful to disaggregate each component of the process, such as the "received individual family planning (FP) education" process, or the "choose sterilization" process, and so on. Disaggregating the processes of a campaign—the specific inputs and activities—can reveal the inputs that are needed and the steps that have to be covered in carrying out a campaign's objectives.

The second step calls for analyzing the "fail points" in the process. A social marketer can utilize a technique developed by Kepner and Tregoe, known as potential problem analysis (PPA).[11] PPA utilizes the following analytical questions and operations:

1. *What could go wrong?* Here social marketers will scrutinize their service processes and identify those elements where troubles can arise.

2. *What, specifically, is each problem?* An accurate answer helps the social marketer understand what each problem is, where it will crop up, when, and to what extent.

3. *How risky is each problem?* This question involves pinpointing the seriousness of a problem if it takes place and the likelihood that it will happen.

4. *What causes each problem?* Identifying the causes of each problem and the probability that each is responsible for a problem. This allows the social marketer to set priorities among the causes and to scrutinize them more closely.

5. *How can a problem's cause be controlled?* Identifying solutions to priority problems and, if they cannot be prevented, minimizing the effects.

In the third step, a social marketer incorporates a blueprint for implementing the service. Shostack regards this step as scheduling, since implementation of the service is time dependent, and time is a major determinant of the costs of a social service.[12] The blueprint provides an estimation of the time needed to execute each subprocess, both the standard time and the acceptable amount of deviation from the standard. The latter provides a social marketer with an important mechanism of control.

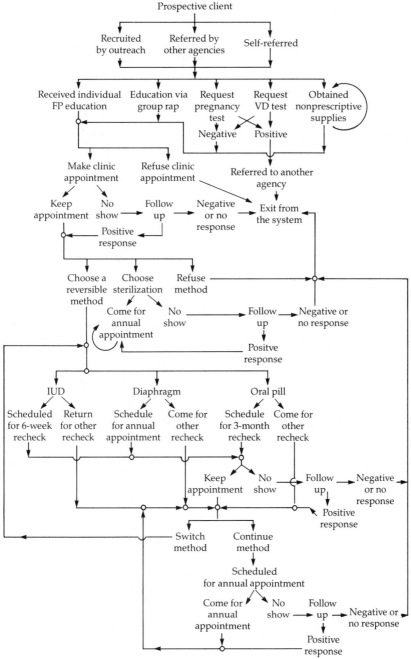

FIGURE 14–1 Clients' Use of Services at the Albany County Family Planning Service, Laramie, Wyoming

SOURCE: Eduardo L. Roberto, *Strategic Decision Making in a Social Program* (Lexington, Mass.: Lexington Books, 1975).

Managing the Performance of Activities

Every activity of a social change campaign can be viewed as a drama, or staged performance.[13] All the actors must behave in strict compliance with their individual, as well as their interactive, performance roles. If they do not and a campaign is staged badly, the result will be a countless number of dissatisfied target adopters. When campaign personnel and target adopters succeed in "reading from a common script," both are satisfied, and satisfaction is the ultimate aim in designing the delivery of a service.

15

Mobilizing
Influence Groups

Many social causes, including the peace movement, environmental protection, and the women's movement, take on the character of a public issue. Typically, these social change campaigns require the assistance of mediating institutions, such as governmental agencies, churches, consumer organizations, trade associations, and educational institutions, to reach their goals. These mediating institutions are variously called "gatekeepers," "opinion molders," "pressure groups," and "influence centers."

Three types of influence groups have to be identified in implementing a social change campaign: allies, opponents, and neutrals. Allies are groups that are supportive of a particular campaign. The peace movement, for example, counts among its allies peace activists, churches, political figures, and human rights organizations. The environmental protection movement has allies in conservation groups, ecologists, naturalists, and concerned legislators.

Opponents are groups whose interests would be hurt by a particular social change campaign. Among opponents of environmental protection are manufacturing and mining companies whose operations often result in pollution and the destruction of land. The women's movement is opposed by men's social clubs, some church groups, and so on.

Neutral groups are groups whose interests are not directly affected by a particular campaign. This does not mean that these groups will necessarily stay on the sidelines. Social marketers can solicit their social support using rational, emotional, or moral appeals and by showing indirect benefits that would accrue to a neutral group or to the larger society. Thus, an environmental group might solicit the support of the American Medical Association in funding an antipollution campaign even though physicians will not directly benefit.

Social marketers must identify and manage the groups and institutions that wield influence in their particular issue-area, raising support among allies and neutral groups and disarming the opponents. What can happen when they do not is illustrated in Case 15-1. Two useful approaches are the market-motivation approach and the power-politics approach.

MARKET-MOTIVATION APPROACH

In the market-motivation approach, a social marketer will mobilize an influence group by viewing it as an intermediate group of clients or target adopters that has needs it wishes to satisfy.

Analyzing the Motivation of Influence Groups

Planning must begin with an analysis of the specific motivations of allies and opponents. Neutrals can be turned into either allies or opponents.

Allies. Potential and current allies may be favorably predisposed to a social change campaign for a variety of reasons. Consider specifically the motivations of givers to fund-raising campaigns. Kotler and Andreasen categorized these motivations of allies in three broad categories:[1]

Responsibility (''we support without being asked'')

1. *The Need for Self-Esteem.* Giving may be motivated by the need to feel good and leads to an enhanced self-image.
2. *The Need for Recognition.* The motivation is increased social status or prestige that accrues from the act of giving.
3. *Concern for Humanity.* The motivation stems from concern for others for religious reasons or a sense of moral obligation.

4. *The Need to Empathize.* The motivation is an orientation to others and a wish to help less fortunate people.

Responsiveness ("we give when asked to")

6. *The Habit of Giving.* The motivation is a desire not to be embarrassed for the failure to give or the habit of giving.
7. *Nuisance Giving.* The motivation is to stop being annoyed by a requesting party.

Practicality ("we give because of pressure")

8. *The Fear of a Threat.* The motivation is protection from a threat or perceived problem.
9. *Succumbing to Pressure.* The motivation is a sense of being required to or being pressured to do so.

To the extent that each of these motivations is independent of one another, the social marketer theoretically can target nine potential segments of allies. In reality, however, these nine motivations usually combine to produce giving behavior, and hence the segments tend to be fewer in number. Influence groups tend to act out of mixed motives.

Opponents. Opponents can arise for at least two reasons: self-interest and a fear of what the change will bring.

Self-interest. Opponents can arise because they perceive a potential loss if the campaign succeeds. Consider the following example.

> In 1979, the U.S. assistant secretary of agriculture for food and consumer services favored a proposal to restrict the sale in schools of "junk" foods, such as soda pop, chewing gum, candies, and flavored ices. This effort, he believed, would boost children's health. The president of the National Confectioners Association—the trade association of candy manufacturers—countered with the following objections:
>
> Everything we eat need not have a scientific, medical, nutritional reason. . . . We sell our products for enjoyment, but many of them possess very substantial nutritional value. They contain milk, nuts, fruits, eggs and chocolate.

> The federal government in Washington [has no right] telling parents and school authorities what foods may or may not be sold in their own schools. . . . We think it's an insult to parents and local school authorities to assume they're incompetent to make their own decisions.[2]

The proposal to restrict school sales of junk food, therefore, had threatened specific groups with a loss of income.

As another example, consider the proposal to extend insurance coverage to home care of AIDS patients. For AIDS patients, the proposal is more beneficial than costly. Home care is much cheaper than hospital care. A San Francisco health commissioner estimated that the 1987 average daily cost of caring for an AIDS patient in a municipal hospital is about $800. The commissioner revealed that a visiting nurse program in New York City offered home care service for AIDS patients at a cost of $81.40 a day. Moreover, there are not enough hospital beds to accommodate AIDS patients. In Maryland, for instance, only one chronic care facility will take AIDS patients; it has only five beds for AIDS patients and, therefore, there always is a waiting list. It is not surprising that health insurance companies opposed the proposal. Hospital coverage would cost insurance companies less because few AIDS patients can be treated in hospitals, whereas home care would result in a far greater number of patients and a greater cost.

The Fear of Change. When a social change campaign entails new skills, new behaviors, or new ways of viewing and doing things, some opponents naturally will arise. The very changes that a social campaign promotes can be perceived as threatening the old ways of doing things. For example, U.S. government policymakers have rejected the proposal to subsidize day care centers for preschool age children that are operated by private for-profit enterprises. This proposal triggered a bureaucratic fear of loss of control. Some of the grounds for rejection were these:

> Unregulated private enterprise . . . does not take into account the public interest in quality child care. Children of disadvantaged families ought to have better care than that which their parents can afford to purchase. . . . Private enterprise is not to be trusted. Control exercised by consumer choice is not likely to be well informed about what is best for the children. The social responsibility in this matter requires better control.[3]

Strategies for Mobilizing Influence Groups

The motivation of an influence group provides the basis for formulating the social marketing strategy to gain its support. Consider the AIDS problem. A major issue that an AIDS program faces is the right to privacy versus the right to life. The former consists of the right of patients who test positive for AIDS antibodies to determine who should know about the test results. Protection of this right to privacy shields AIDS patients from public humiliation and discrimination that would arise if the results are not strictly protected. However, citizens have the right to protect themselves from a potentially lethal virus. One group of citizens, in particular, who have a real concern about AIDS patients are the surgeons who operate on AIDS patients. Physicians have a right to know about a potentially life-threatening risk to them.

Another influence group involved in this privacy issue are legislators who enact laws to protect human rights. On the one hand, an AIDS campaign to protect the privacy of AIDS patients will appeal to legislators to empathize with the plight of AIDS victims. On the other hand, an AIDS campaign that seeks to protect right to life over the right to privacy will appeal to legislators to consider the protection of those who are at risk of being exposed to the virus. Social marketers will frame appeals to influence groups that are most likely to raise support for their objectives in ways that meet the needs of these influential groups.[4]

Another key influence group in AIDS campaigns are entertainers. The actress Elizabeth Taylor, for example, has participated actively in fund-raising campaigns for AIDS research as a result of the death of an AIDS victim/friend and fellow actor, Rock Hudson. Famous soccer players, including retired soccer great Pele, have held exhibition soccer games, billed as "Kick AIDS '88," to raise funds to fight AIDS. Appeals to civic responsibility and to humanity have been used to mobilize support from these celebrities.

What about mobilization strategies that are based on an influence group's need to be responsive? Consider the task of an AIDS campaign in mobilizing support from employers. The campaign can approach employers with an appeal to provide their employees with AIDS-prevention information:

AIDS is the type of issue which can disrupt the conduct of business, interfere with employee and customer relations, and result in legal actions and extensive medical care expenditures.

With intelligent planning, a company has the ability to make an important contribution to alleviating and overcoming a public health calamity for their employees and the public as a whole.[5]

What about mobilization strategies that are based on an influence group's sense of practicality and sense of responsibility? In campaigns to educate young people about AIDS, school authorities are key. A school board, for example, was a target influence group in Fairfax County, Virginia, in a campaign to extend AIDS education to seventh and eighth graders. The Fairfax school board was urged to drop its policy prohibiting teaching about homosexuality and contraception. Supporters of the education campaign argued that students need to learn as early as possible how AIDS is transmitted so they can adopt protective measures later in their sexually active years.[6]

Tactics for Mobilizing Influence Groups

Tactics, or techniques for putting a strategy into action, will require social marketers to answer the following questions:

1. How should an influence group be informed and persuaded about a campaign?
2. How should the support of an influence group be gained?
3. How can costs incurred by the influence group's support be minimized?
4. How can an influence group's support be facilitated so the group acts without delay?

Answers to these questions must take account of an influence group's decision-making process.[7] For example, the rational decision-making style of one group will call for a particular set of campaign tactics, and the bureaucratic or political decision-making style of another group will dictate a different set of tactics. A rational style means that an influence group is oriented to gathering extensive information before making a decision. The group is likely to define its needs, scrutinize the campaign's objectives, identify alternatives, and finally make a choice of strong, weak, or no support.

The decision-making style of a bureaucratic organization will involve consistency with past decisions and respect for precedents and rules. A bureaucratically oriented influence group is likely to make decisions on the basis of routines spelled out in organizational manuals. Knowledge of these routines and rules will help social marketers win the support of such groups. Politically oriented groups, such as interest groups, must be handled differently. For them decision making usually follows negotiation and bargaining. Such groups typically use and withhold information selectively to gain a strategic advantage.

POWER-POLITICS APPROACH

Winning support of influence groups for a social marketing campaign often is a matter not of market motivation but of power. The art of politics, rather than the art of applied social psychology, determines whether a campaign will earn an influence group's support.

Sources of Power

Managing political power for the purpose of winning support for a campaign is the ability to get another person or group to do what that person or group would not otherwise do. Social marketers may exercise power over influence groups through any one or any combination of five bases of power.[8]

- *Rewards.* A social marketer may exert power over an influence group by being in a position to furnish rewards to it. Such rewards may take the form of a payment or gift or the extension of recognition and visibility.

- *Coercion.* A social marketer's power may derive from an influence group's perception that a campaign possesses the leverage to punish (inflict social or financial harm) the group if it fails to be responsive. For example, a social change campaign may be in a position to expose information about an influence group that would undermine its operation and its base of support.

- *Expertise or Information.* A social marketer's power may be based on an influence group's perception that a campaign can offer needed technical assistance or special information and expertise that the group or a governmental agency sorely needs.

- *Legitimacy.* An influence group may give its support because it perceives a campaign has a moral legitimacy that is widely recognized or has goals that are strongly favored by the public.
- *Prestige.* An influence group's support may arise from its desire to be identified with a social marketer's organization and objectives and a campaign's successes.

Strategies of Power

Power strategies refer to the "how" of effectively influencing an influence group through the use of rewards, coercion, expertise, information, legitimacy, or prestige. Two types of strategies are the facilitation strategy and the identification strategy.

The facilitation strategy seeks to minimize the costs or discomfort of change that an influence group may experience. A social change campaign may gain the support and acceptance of an influence group by conducting itself with a minimum of public visibility, obtrusiveness, and fanfare. Or it may provide a solid public rationale for an influence group's support that the group will feel comfortable in having for its supportive actions.

The theory behind the identification strategy is that when an influence group perceives its interests to be aligned with the objectives of a social change campaign, it will be receptive to a social marketer's efforts. To achieve identification, a social marketer has to understand how power is distributed in the networks and institutions of which a targeted influence group is part, sometimes referred to as the "power structure."

Three types of power structures may exist: pyramidal, factional, and coalitional.[9] In a pyramidal power structure, an "elite" influence group wields decisive power and promotes its agenda through a layer of "deputy" groups that, in turn, wield influence over lower-level groups. When faced with this power structure, a social marketer must focus on winning the support of the elite group, for without its approval or tolerance, the other influence groups will not act.

In a factional power structure, two or more influential factions are competing for dominant power in the community. In these circumstances, social marketers must determine to which faction the targeted influence group belongs and then ally itself with that faction. Such an alliance, however, is likely to result in the loss of goodwill of the other factions.

In a coalitional power structure, influence groups typically form temporary coalitions. Thus, social marketers are challenged to determine the changing characteristics of coalitions and the vagaries of power shifts and to identify from which influence groups it is most critical to win support at a given time.

Power Tactics

How can the strategies of facilitation and identification be implemented? Social marketing campaigns have employed a variety of power tactics to win the support of influence groups.

Influencing the evaluation process. When an influence group has to determine whether to lend support to a social change campaign, it will decide after evaluating its alternatives. Social marketers can try to influence this decision. One is to persuade a target influence group that the social marketer's organization represents a better opportunity to extend its power base. Another way is for the social marketer to solicit support by influencing the criteria that a target influence group uses to make its decisions about support. This approach is less obtrusive and makes it easier for an influence group to rationalize its decision to its members and the larger public.

Influencing the agenda. Pfeffer stated that ''the nice thing about agendas is that few people regard them as elements of political strategy.''[10] For this reason, the determination of an agenda is an unobtrusive tactic for effecting responses from influence groups. Setting an agenda in a way that wins favor from an influence group can be productive. The literature on agenda setting presents considerable evidence that agendas can be manipulated effectively. A campaign might first focus attention on noncontroversial items on the agenda and then build up to more controversial ones. Or a campaign can start out by seeking support for a weak item. When a weak item is presented first, an influence group may be predisposed to present a tough front to this easy prey. Having demonstrated that it is no pushover, an influence group can then be more flexible on subsequent items. Thus a social marketer can present a dummy agenda item first before trying to win support of an entire campaign.

Coalition and alliance building. Coalition and alliance building is a consensus-building approach. It operates on the basis of offering rewards. In using this approach, social marketers can begin with the premise that the interests of their campaign can be made to converge in significant respects with those of an influence group. Building consensus and coalition can take several forms. One is to organize numerous constituency groups who can be mobilized to pressure a target influence group to offer its support. This tactic was applied in connection with President Lyndon Johnson's War on Poverty. The War on Poverty was organized with support from community-based manpower planning, housing and development, and community groups. Later, when the program sought support for its budget in the U.S. Congress, it utilized these local-level groups to rally support for the necessary funding level.

Another tactic is to organize a same-level coalition of constituency groups. The school system in Fairfax County, Virginia, for example, promoted its AIDS education campaign by organizing support from groups, such as the student advisory councils, Parent-Teachers Association (PTA), and the American Association of University Women. In seeking support from the U.S. Department of Education for an AIDS-education program, the school system applied pressure through these constituency groups. Pressure tactics were needed because of the department's reluctance to act favorably on the proposed AIDS education program.

The co-optation tactic. The co-optation tactic involves trying to convert an opposition individual or group into a supporter of a social change campaign. One tactic is to place a supporter in a key position within the opposition group. Another tactic is to invite a member of the opposition group to participate in the social marketing campaign. These tactics are designed to win the support of an influence group by generating identification and ultimately commitment from its co-opted representatives. A third tactic involves knowing when committees are formed and then recommending key individuals to membership in them. Committees are often formed to build a consensus. They do so by providing a place for the resolution of multiple and conflicting interests through representation, negotiation, and resolution.

The success of a social change campaign often depends on the support it receives from influential public figures and institutions, both private and public. This support is particularly necessary when a campaign involves social objectives that are controversial and do not have a solid base of public support. In such cases, an effectively run campaign will seek to generate support among favorably disposed groups, convert indifferent groups to a supportive role, and defuse the opposition of hostile groups. Mobilizing support involves identifying the needs of influence groups and offering them benefits in exchange for their support. Once they have gained the support of influence groups, social marketers then face the critical task of developing a social marketing plan that systematically and comprehensively integrates all the elements and phases of the social change campaign.

CASE 15–1

The Teacher Corps: Changing the Unchangeable

An example of a social change campaign that failed to build support among influence groups is the U.S. Teacher Corps, established in the early 1970s. The concept behind the Teacher Corps came from John Kenneth Galbraith's recognition of a social need in American education. The social need was how to educate the poor effectively and how to prepare the teachers for this role. Galbraith reasoned that it takes a different set of skills to teach in low-income schools than the skills that are taught in conventional teacher training programs. The Teacher Corps was designed to transmit those skills. The legislation creating the corps set these objectives: (1) ''to strengthen educational opportunities for children in areas with concentrations of low-income families, (2) to attract and prepare persons to become teachers in such areas

SOURCE: Summarized and adapted from Ronald G. Corwin, *Reform and Organizational Survival: The Teacher Corps as an Instrument of Educational Change* (New York: John Wiley & Sons, 1973). Quotations are drawn from this source.

through coordinated work-study experiences, and (3) to encourage colleges and universities, schools, and state departments of education to work together to broaden and improve teacher education programs.''

Target Adopters and the Social Product

The target adopters of the Teacher Corps were liberal arts graduates. The corps offered a teacher education program built around teams of 30 to 40 teaching interns. Five professional teachers were selected to be team leaders for each of the five teams. In launching the Teacher Corps, President Lyndon B. Johnson spoke of its concept with pride and hope: ''Our country is blessed with young men and women who desire to serve those less fortunate than themselves. The Teacher Corps offers a practical means of uniting the idealism and wisdom of each, young graduates and accomplished teachers, and thus enriching the lives of coming generations.''

The teacher education program of the Teacher Corps involved an eight-week special preservice training course at a college or university. At another stage, interns were divided into teams of at least six interns each under a team leader. Each team then was sent to an elementary school in a poor area. A team worked with small groups of children on specific lesson plans. Later, it went into more complex tasks. A team spent about 20 percent of its time in academic work at the university, 60 percent of its time working in the schools, and 20 percent of its time working on community activities that affected the social and home environment of the students. Some of this work could lead to teacher certification and a master's degree within two years.

Target Influence Groups and the Social Product

For a number of influential educational groups, such as the more than 100 participating universities and 250 participating school systems, the Teacher Corps represented a new social product—''a federal intervention in local educational institutions . . . an attempt by the federal government to establish and to guide a network of educational organizations within its jurisdiction.'' Other influence groups in the educational system included school accreditation agencies, professional educational associations, textbook publishers, local school boards, and PTAs.

When the Teacher Corps proceeded to carry out its mandate, it had the potential of either changing the system or having the system change it. The latter happened. Congress delegated the program's management to local universities, which shared authority with local school districts. The Teacher Corps office in Washington, D.C., exercised little real control over the subcontracted universities and schools.

The universities that applied for the Teacher Corps were interested primarily in federal money and only secondarily in the teacher training program. They resisted the changes that the program required by branding the participants of the Teacher Corps as trouble makers and outsiders, conspiring to break up the team structure mandated by the program, appointing team leaders who could coercively control the interns, and replacing dissident interns and faculty members with those who were loyal.

In the end, the Teacher Corps program enjoyed little support from local educational institutions and had difficulty competing for congressional appropriations alongside more established programs. An evaluation study concluded that "whereas the program was intended to effect change, it became modified by the same principles and processes that had shaped the organizations it was trying to alter."

MANAGING
SOCIAL MARKETING

16

Developing the Social Marketing Plan

Social marketers will develop an integrated social marketing plan whose mix of elements is coherent and appealing to the target adopters. It is not sufficient to develop each element of the marketing mix separately. Putting together disparate elements will not necessarily result in an optimal plan for a social change campaign. One marketing element or phase may be incompatible with others when combined in a mix. For example, low pricing may be incompatible with high-quality positioning, meager advertising expenditures may be incompatible with high-quality positioning, and intensive sales-promotion efforts may be incompatible with social-product positioning. Ultimately, adoptions of a social product will depend on an optimal mix of elements, rather than on the discrete separate elements themselves.

CHARACTERISTICS OF A SOCIAL MARKETING PLAN

Social marketers will plan a campaign and establish its objectives systematically, comprehensively, and deliberately, in writing and with a purpose. A marketing plan establishes standards for implementing a campaign and evaluating its outcomes. What does a social marketing plan look like? Case 16–1 presents a detailed example of a social marketing plan; it should be examined first.

Parts of the Plan

A marketing plan has several parts: an executive summary, assessment of the current social marketing situation, identification of opportunities and threats, objectives for the social product, proposed social marketing strategies, action programs, budgets and controls.

A social marketing plan begins with a brief summary of the principal goals and recommendations in the plan (the executive summary). A table of contents is included to identify the plan's major elements. The executive summary is useful to the staff of the social marketing campaign, as well as to influence groups and benefactors, because it allows them to grasp its main thrust quickly.

The plan's first section describes the target-adopter population and its segments and the social product's position in those segments. This information includes (1) the profile of the target adopters, (2) a review of the social product (3) an assessment of alternative sources that could satisfy the target adopters' needs, and (4) a scan of the environment.

The profile of the target adopters characterizes the target-adopter population and its segments, measuring their sizes with available social-demographic data. Use is made of an up-to-date awareness, knowledge, attitude, and practice survey, which indicates the status of the target-adopter population in relation to desired responses from the segmented target-adopter group.

The review of the social product is an inventory of the social product's past performance and its impact on target-adopter markets. This section analyzes the needs of each segment of the target-adopter population that the social product aims to satisfy.

The assessment of alternative sources of satisfaction for the target-adopters' needs, is a marketing plan that not only identifies these principal alternative sources but examines the appeal of substitute products to the target-adopter segments.

In the scan of the environment, the key demographic, economic, physical, technological, political/legal, and sociocultural environmental forces that affect the social product are assessed. The scan's function is strategic selectivity, rather than comprehensiveness, that is, the identification of one or two critical environmental forces that affect the social product's marketing.

The plan also includes an assessment of opportunities and threats among which priorities must be set. Social marketers will take advantage of the highest priorities, monitor the median priorities, and discard the lowest priorities. Opportunities and threats that are the highest priorities define the critical social marketing issues.

Assessing opportunities and providing contingency plans for threats poses an early test of a campaign's capabilities and resources. The assessment will have to answer the following questions: How can each major opportunity be used to advantage in terms of staff, money, materials, activities, and time? How can each threat be countered in terms of staff, money, materials, activities, and time? Does the campaign have the required resources? Can resources be obtained in a reasonable time and at a reasonable cost?

Objectives for the Social Product

The preceding elements and assessments enable social marketers to set specific, measurable, and attainable social marketing objectives for the social product. A social product objective is equivalent to a targeted response from a target-adopter segment. Suppose a behavioral change is sought. If this change can result only after antecedent responses, then the objective at this stage may be to further the target adopters' awareness, knowledge, belief, attitude, intention, or trail adoption.

As an example, consider the information on the consumer segment in the marketing plan, as outlined in Case 16–1. At the level of the individual target adopter, a social change campaign to reduce dietary fat must motivate people to learn a new set of eating habits. Changing a habit is not easy and takes time. The change must be accomplished in stages. The planners of the campaign recognized that they must start at an antecedent stage and, therefore, decided to increase the consumer's recognition of the risky health effects of a high level of fat in the diet (a target-awareness response) and of the major sources of fat, identifying specific ways to reduce its intake (a target- knowledge response).

An alternative approach is to use a behavior modification perspective. In this approach, a target adopter's response is broken down into smaller behavioral elements. Specifically, eating behavior is disaggregated into its constituent elements, such as shopping, food preparation, selecting restaurants, choosing the time to eat, and so on. A campaign, then, might first target the easiest behaviors to modify and work up to the more difficult behaviors.

Social Marketing Strategies

The plan will include the social marketing strategy, that is, the mix of methods and tools by which the campaign seeks to achieve its objectives. This strategic mix consists of three components:

1. *Target-Adopter Segments.* The strategy spells out the target-adopter segments and the priorities to win their adoption of the social product. Different segments will have different needs and require specific marketing efforts. The rule is simple: one valid segment, one discrete marketing strategy.
2. *Social Marketing Mix.* The strategy defines the social marketing mix for each target segment. Each substrategy will be explained in relation to how it will respond to the opportunities, threats and key issues that the plan identified earlier.
3. *Social Marketing Budget.* The marketing strategy will specify the budgetary resources that are available to carry out the various elements and phases of the social change campaign.

Action Programs

This part of the marketing plan converts the broad marketing strategies into specific action programs. Each action program addresses four questions:

1. *What* will be done for this strategy?
2. *When* will it be done?
3. *Who* will do it?
4. *How* much will it cost?

For example, if the social marketer decides on an awareness-oriented social change campaign as the key element of a strategy for inducing the target-adopter population to change its habit of eating a high-fat diet, then the public action plan for promoting awareness will outline the specific activities of the campaign that are necessary to achieve awareness, the period in which these activities are to be started and completed, the people who will be responsible for implementation, and the necessary budgetary resources for materials, money, and personnel.

Different action plans can be coordinated in a timetable much like a Gantt chart of activities. The 52 weeks of the year occupy the columns, while the various campaign activities are listed in the rows. Dates inside the cells (the intersections of the time periods and the activities) will indicate when the activities with their expenditures will commence, when these will be reviewed, and when the activities will be completed. As a campaign proceeds, changes in the basic assumptions of the plan that may reflect changes in the social marketing environment will be noted by eliminating or reversing a cell in the chart.

Budgets

Action plans aim to achieve specific results. For each targeted activity, costs are estimated. The campaign budget is a statement of the monetary values of resources that the social marketing campaign must commit to achieve specific results.

Budgeting by Target Setting. The budget in the sample plan, outlined in Case 16-1, illustrates budgeting by target setting. The planner identified broad categories of activities, such as "the consumer target" and "the food organization target." The estimated cost of carrying out each activity is derived from the contractors who will supply the goods and services. These estimates of cost are the target costs to which the campaign will adhere.

Budgeting by Analysis. A superior alternative to the target-setting approach is one that analyzes how the plan's results are affected by different levels and mixes of social marketing elements. It then uses these predictive relationships to determine the corresponding required resources.

The adoption-response function is the relationship between the level of adoption and one or more elements of the social marketing mix. This function predicts the likely level of adoptions during a specified period, associated with different levels of one or more elements of the social marketing mix. Figure 16-1 shows a hypothetical adoption-response function with respect to expenditures for mass communication that assumes given levels of inputs of other elements of the marketing mix. This function is S shaped.

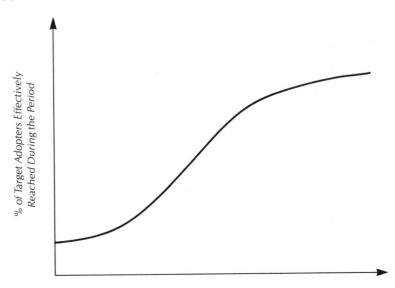

Mass Communication Expenditures During the Period
Figure 16-1 Adoption-Response Function

In general, higher expenditures for mass communication produce higher levels of responses from the target adopters. However, the response rate varies along a curve: few target adopters will be reached if the expenditures for mass communication are low; in the middle portion of the curve, higher levels of expenditures will yield higher proportions of target adopters; but at very high levels of expenditures, adoptions diminish and approach zero at some point.

Diminishing returns in a campaign will eventually occur because of two factors. First, there is an upper limit to the total reachable population of target adopters and second, those target adopters who do not respond initially tend to be more resistant to mass communication. As the upper limit is approached, it becomes ever more expensive to attract the remaining potential target adopters.

The practical question is how to estimate adoption-response functions. Two methods are available. One is to gather data on past responses of target adopters, and levels of the elements in the social marketing mix and then estimate the adoption-response functions through statistical techniques. The other method is judgmental; experts are chosen to supply intelligent guesses about the needed relationships. One such technique, known as the "decision calculus," consists of four steps.[1]

The first step calls for social marketers to describe their implicit model of the social marketing situation. They need to spell out the causal variables that influence the adoption response, together with the expected relationships among these causal variables.

In the second step, an outside consultant translates the social marketers' verbal description into a formal mathematical model. The adoption response is shown to be a function of the current influence of the causal variables that the social marketer wants to test and the lagged influences of previous social marketing efforts and the current influences of other variables.

In the third step, the model's parameters are estimated. The social marketer is asked for judgmental estimates of adoption-level outcomes if a social marketing variable were cut to zero, raised by 50 percent, maintained, and so on. These judgmental estimates are validated by comparing them against historical data. If the replication is poor, the judgmental estimates are revised.

In the fourth step, an interactive computer program incorporating the parameterized model is developed that enables the marketer to see what can happen with alternative decisions about the social marketing mix.

Once adoption-response functions have been estimated, the social marketer can use them to derive an optimal level of expenditures. The social marketer has to decide on the objective: whether to maximize the number of target adopters who are reached for a given level of expenditures or to minimize the cost for each target adopter who is reached.

Controls

In the plan's final section, the social marketer outlines the means by which progress will be monitored. Typically, the action plan's objectives and budgets are broken down into monthly or quarterly portions. The results are reviewed each period, and variances are spotted and interpreted. Unfavorable variances require corrective actions. Favorable variances also should be analyzed to discover ways to maintain or improve on the favorable outcomes.

A SOCIAL MARKETING PLAN
FOR MULTIPLE PRODUCTS AND MARKETS

Social marketers often manage several social-product adoptions simultaneously that are being targeted to multiple markets. Each product competes for a limited pool of resources. The problem of managing a multiple-product campaign is analogous to managing an investment portfolio in which one must decide which stocks and bonds to buy or sell and how much of one's resources should be devoted to each. In both cases, marketing multiple products involves issues related to the allocation of scarce resources. A satisfactory solution must deal with several issues:

1. Which social products or target-adopter segments should be given a higher level of resources?
2. Which ones should be given higher levels of specific types of resources?
3. From which social products or target-adopter segments can resources be withdrawn or reduced?

In managing any social change campaign, a perennial issue is one of allocating scarce resources. The two scarcest resources are technical resources, such as experts and specialists, machines, and materials, and the time and energy that staff devote to serving adopters. An approach to dealing with the allocation of scarce resources is the following. A first step is to rate each social product or adopter segment with respect to its requirements for the aforementioned resources. Ratings may be made along the following scale:

1 = extremely low or practically nil,
2 = quite low,
3 = somewhat low,
4 = somewhat high,
5 = quite high, and
6 = very high for this resource.

Next, the position of each social product or target-adopter segment should be plotted in the appropriate quadrant of the two resource-based portfolio matrix shown in Figure 16–2. Thus, each social product and target-adopter segment falls into one of four categories:

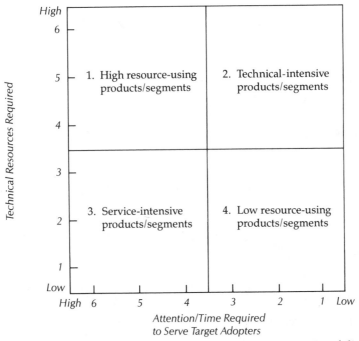

FIGURE 16-2 The Social Product–Target-Adopter Segment Portfolio Matrix

1. *High Resource-Using Products/Segments.* These products and segments fall into Quadrant 1 of the portfolio matrix. They demand high levels of technical resources and attention and time devoted to the target adopters for their effective diffusion or penetration.

2. *Technical-Intensive Products/Segments.* These products and segments require high technical resources but minimal attention and time to serve target adopters (Quadrant 2).

3. *Service-Intensive Products/Segments.* These products and segments require intensive attention and time to serve target adopters but minimal technical resources (Quadrant 3).

4. *Low Resource-Using Products/Segments.* These products and segments require only low levels of technical resources and attention and time devoted to serving target adopters.

The foregoing classification will provide solutions to the allocation of resources. For example, to the question, "Which social products or target-adopter segments should be given a higher level of resources?'' the answer is the high resource-using ones. To the question, ''Which ones should be given higher levels of specific resources?'' the answer is the technically intensive and service-intensive products and target-adopter segments. To the question, ''From which social products or target-adopter segments can resources be withdrawn or reduced?'' the answer is the low resource-using ones.

The social marketing plan outlined in Case 16–1 dealt with the managing of several segments of target adopters but it did not provide a system for allocating a campaign's resources to each segment. We can do so, using the matrix depicted in Figure 16–2. The seven target adopter segments, both individual and organizational, are first rated for the technical resources and attention and time required for services. Suppose the ratings were these:

Target-Adopter Segments	Technical Resources Demanded	Required Attention and Time for Services
Heavy meat-eating adults	4	2
Heavy junk-food-eating teenagers	6	4
Low-income black consumers	6	6
Working housewives who eat away from home	5	3
Food manufacturers	2	5
Food associations	5	4
Food providers	3	3

Accordingly, the high resource-using segments that should be given more total resources are the low-income black consumers, the heavy junk-food-eating teenagers, and the food associations. More technical resources should go to the often/regularly eating-out working housewives and the red-meat-eating adults. More service/time resources should go to the food manufacturing organizations. Finally, resources can be withdrawn or reduced from the food providers. This categorization helps the social marketer establish priorities for the target markets, according to the availability of resources.

An effective and efficient social change campaign will depend on developing a sound social marketing plan that systematically and comprehensively identifies all the elements and phases of the campaign and their coordination. Social marketing plans perform critical functions. They are useful in coordinating and integrating all roles in the campaign; enable staff to monitor, evaluate, and control the performance of the campaign; identify deviations from the standards of performance laid out in the plan; and allow staff to gather support from funding sources and influential support groups by presenting a blueprint of the campaign for their review.

CASE 16–1
A Social Marketing Plan for Project LEAN

A leading U.S. foundation is seeking to promote family health through a three-year campaign to encourage people to reduce the intake of fat in their diets.

Executive Summary

By means of mass communications, and community organization,the campaign will communicate to the American public the benefits and methods of adopting healthful food and dietary practices. The goal is to reduce morbidity and mortality from heart disease and cancer by encouraging the American public to reduce their intake of fat from 40 percent to 30 percent of their daily caloric intake.

The proposed approach summarized in this marketing plan has evolved from

1. A review of the relevant literature on social marketing and changing nutritional behavior.
2. An analysis of recent studies of consumers' attitudes and behaviors related to food.

SOURCE: This description of Project LEAN (Low Fat Eating for America Now) is taken from Sarah E. Samuels, A.R. Tarlov, and L.W. Green, *The Kaiser Family Foundation Health Promotion Program's Public Awareness and Education Campaign on Dietary Fat Reduction Strategic Plan*,1987, and subsequent documents through the first year of the timetable. Both Dr. Samuels and Dr. Green reviewed this case study.

3. In-depth interviews with nutrition-education experts and with representatives of constituency organizations that are concerned with dietary change.

4. An examination of existing national programs and community demonstration projects focused on diet and health.

The campaign will demonstrate how a public health media and marketing effort can help make the choice of lower-fat foods more attractive to the public and, as a result, stimulate a greater demand by consumers for more healthful foods. This marketing plan provides a rationale for the campaign and a description of the campaign's objectives and strategies, the components of the program, the action plans, the timeline, and the projected budget.

Current Social Marketing Situation

Profile of the target-adopter population. The campaign targets two segments of the target-adopter population: consumers and influential food organizations. The consumers are individuals who consume high-fat diets (over 40 percent) who need greater knowledge and skills to enable them to reduce their intake of fat and, thereby, to reduce the risk of disease. They consist of four high-risk segments: (1) heavy fat-eating adults, (2) heavy junk-food-eating teenagers, (3) low-income American consumers, and (4) working people who frequently eat at restaurants. The influential food organizations are (1) national organizations representing food and related industries, including producers, processors, and wholesalers, (2) professional associations that influence consumers' choice of foods, including groups representing chefs, dieticians, home economists, nutritionists, and consumer-affairs professionals, and (3) national and local food outlets and providers, including grocery stores, supermarkets, institutional food providers, restaurants, and school, governmental, and corporate cafeterias.

Review of the Social Product

The campaign's social product is an idea and a practice. The idea is this: Too much dietary fat is detrimental to one's health; it may lead to coronary heart disease, stroke, diabetes, arteriosclerosis, and cancers of the breast, colon, and prostate. The new practice to be disseminated is for consumers to identify the fat content of different foods and to purchase, prepare, and eat low-fat foods and for influential food organizations to develop and promote low-fat products and menu items.

Alternative Sources of Target Adopters' Satisfaction

The target adopters need to reduce morbidity and mortality from heart disease and cancer. Reducing the intake of fat, however, is only one among several alternatives for meeting this need. It is an alternative that places at least part of the solution in the consumers' hands.

The alternatives do not require the same level of initiative, sustained behavior modification, and participation in finding solutions by target adopters and are short term and interim. They include counseling and cholesterol-reducing medications, which address the symptoms, rather than dietary practices that contribute to the root cause of the problem. Furthermore, at least ten federal, voluntary, and scientific agencies already have recommended moderation or reduction in the consumption of fat as the prudent long-term measure to reduce the risk of heart disease and cancer.

Scan of the Environment

Of the ten leading causes of death in the United States, five have been associated with diets containing excessive amounts of fat and cholesterol. These five are coronary heart disease, stroke, diabetes, arteriosclerosis, and cancers of the breast, colon, and prostate. Coronary heart disease is responsible for one in every three deaths in the United States. High levels of dietary fat and cholesterol are correlated with elevated plasma cholesterol and coronary artery disease. These high levels of plasma cholesterol increase the risk of coronary heart disease, arteriosclerosis, and stroke. Obesity contributes to hypertension, diabetes, and elevated cholesterol, all major risk factors for heart disease. Trials of the restriction of fats have been shown to reduce coronary heart disease. In fact, projections show that the reduced consumption of fat from current levels (37 percent of calories from fat) to 30 percent would cut in half the prevalence of heart disease and cancers of the breast, colon, and prostate.

Opportunities and Threats

Target-adopter population. Among target adopters, patterns of consuming and preparing food have arisen that represent a combination of opportunities and threats. The major ones include these:

1. Fat intake by Americans increased from 32 percent of caloric intake in 1919 to 41 percent in 1982. Although the total intake of calories did not change during this period, threat of the increased intake of fat has increased because many Americans are increasingly sedentary and thus require fewer calories to maintain their ideal weight. Recent reversals of the trend have reduced fat intake in the American diet from its peak of 41 percent to 37 percent in the late 1980's.

2. Dietary levels of fat and cholesterol are slightly higher for men than for women, and the intake of foods containing cholesterol is higher for black Americans than white Americans. An opportunity exists to segment the target-adopter population according to the degree of risk.

3. Americans are increasingly eating outside the home. In 1965, they spent 83 percent of their food dollars in the home, but in 1984, that proportion was only 58 percent. Between 25 percent and 30 percent of all meals are now eaten away from home. By 1986, two out of every five dollars that were spent in restaurants went to fast-food restaurants that serve food that is highest in fat, cholesterol, and calories. Data from the National Restaurant Association show that families with working wives ate 28 percent of their lunches and 19 percent of their dinners in restaurants. With more working women, the trend toward purchasing "convenience" foods and eating out will rise. The Nationwide Food Consumption Survey reports that 75 percent of Americans do "regular snacking," which is associated with the increased consumption of fat and cholesterol. This picture sums up the threat that the campaign aims to minimize.

Among influential food organizations, particularly processed-food manufacturers and fast-food retailers, it is well known that advertising is the major form of promotion. The food industry spends $15 billion a year on advertising, which represents an opportunity for the campaign. Advertising has effectively promoted current eating trends; similarly, it can be used to foster more healthful eating habits. Counteradvertising is called for. The successful experiences of the Stanford community projects in California and the North Karelia Project in Finland in significantly reducing the consumption and production of high-fat foods through comprehensive media, marketing, and community organization campaigns can be used to guide the plan of this campaign.

The social product. Three food groups provide approximately 90 percent of the fat in the American food supply: (1) fats and oils, (2) meats, poultry, and fish, and (3) dairy products. In the fats-and-oils group, the use of butter has declined while the use of margarine has risen—a welcome trend. A large-scale shift from animal to vegetable sources of fat has taken place. These trends have helped reduce cholesterol, but not necessarily other fats. In the dairy-products group, since 1980, cheese has replaced whole milk as the chief source of fat—an unwelcome trend. The higher intake of cholesterol from the increased use of cheese, low-fat milks, and frozen desserts has offset the decline from the decreased use of whole milk. Overall, the long-term trend is toward the increasing intake of fat in this food area.

Alternative sources of satisfaction. Many people resort to diet pills and drugs, weight-reducing salons, or cosmetic surgery for weight loss, but these measure are not pertinent to reduction of dietary fat. The appeal of these products to target adopters is considerable: ease and convenience. It is far more convenient to use cholesterol-reducing medications than to acquire the know-how to identify the fat content of different foods and to exercise discipline in eating only low-fat products and menu items. Available alternative fat-reducing social products will continue to threaten the campaign's success.

Opportunities and threats in the marketing environment. In the future, food manufacturers are likely to produce tasty, low-fat forms of popular foods. When they do, these foods will constitute a real opportunity for the campaign. In fact, this marketing plan explicitly provides for steps to encourage the technological development of low-fat foods.

Objectives for the Social Product and the Campaign

1. For consumers, to reduce dietary fat intake by 1 percent each year, from current levels to 30 percent of calories by 1998.
2. For influential food organizations, (1) to increase the availability and accessibility of low-fat foods through supermarkets, restaurants, and workplace and school cafeterias and (2) to promote collaboration among appropriate national and local food organizations to achieve the fat-reduction goals.

Social Marketing Strategies

Social Marketing Mix for Target Consumers

- *Market Research.* Research into the knowledge, attitudes and practices of different segments was undertaken to identify the high-fat consumer groups and the ways to influence them to change their behavior.
- *Targeting.* On the basis of the market research, target segments were identified. High-risk segments for specific campaign strategies will be further specified and refined. The target segment for the initial mass-media promotions is the middle majority in the diffusion curve (from the 20th to the 80th percentile of adopters on the normal curve of adoption).
- *Positioning.* Communication and advertising messages will be positioned to fit each target segment. Campaign themes will be tailored to each segment.
- *Communication Channels.* A variety of media channels will be used. High-income target adopters—though not a primary target audience because most have already made significant changes—can be reached effectively through print media, such as newspapers and magazines; low-income consumers can be reached more effectively through television and radio.
- *Distribution Channels.* Target adopters will be provided with the means of carrying out their intentions to adopt a low-fat diet. Campaign information will be accessible. Low-fat food alternatives will be available. Food manufacturers will be encouraged to take advantage of the business opportunities in developing and providing tasty low-fat foods. Low-fat foods will be enthusiastically marketed in supermarkets and restaurants.

- *Publicity.* Advertising and informational messages, as well as promotional events, will be produced that will attract attention to the cause of better health through low-fat diets.

Social Marketing Mix for Target Influential Food Organizations

Some influential food organizations will be hostile to the campaign for a low-fat diet, others will be indifferent, and still others will be supportive. For hostile groups, the campaign will reveal the business opportunities inherent in producing, selling, and serving low-fat foods and, at the least, make an effort to reduce their perceptions of the threat of this campaign and to minimize their active opposition. For organizational allies, the campaign will facilitate their active cooperation in the campaign and their collaboration with other organizations, including members of Partners for Better Health, in cosponsoring the campaign. For neutral influential groups, the campaign will identify the groups with the greatest potential influence on target adopters and convert them to supporting the campaign.

Social Marketing Budget

The estimated three-year budget for the campaign is $3.5 million; $1.5 million was required for the initial phase of the public awareness campaign during the first year. Estimates for the second and third years, each at $1 million, are based on projected costs for production and distribution for the communications program. The expenses incurred in the first year's planning and start-up will not arise in the second and third years.

Action Programs

The campaign's entire first year was devoted to planning, developing, and producing campaign materials and organizational partnerships. A technical advisory committee, campaign staff, Partners for Better Health (consisting of 30 collaborating national organizations), and scientific and industry panels were organized; a distribution network established; and test markets prepared for start-up. Market research was conducted during the first year, and evaluation planning was done. In the second and third years, the campaign will operate through the distribution channels, media products will be developed and produced, and the campaign will be implemented in specific localities and test markets. The preliminary timetable of the campaign's activities is as follows:

November 1987	Meeting of foundation's Board of Trustees; approval of the final plan and budget.
December 1987	Ad agency assigned.
April 1988	Consumer/market research launched; scientific advisory panels to meet.
May 1988	Begin to develop the campaign, select contractors, and construct the organizational blueprint.
	Ad agency conducts research via focus groups, communication messages are developed, and printed materials are designed. Initial meetings of advisory panels held.
March 1989	The Food and Nutrition Board releases the *Diet and Health Report* highlighting the risks of high-fat diets.
May 1989	Plans for test markets are developed through grants to ten communities, and evaluation procedures are set.
September 1989	All materials, products, and systems in place for the official launching of the campaign.
November 1989	The public awareness campaign is launched nationwide, and grants are made to ten communities (media markets).
May 1990	The Food and Nutrition Board

releases its follow-up report on recommended actions to reduce the intake of fat in diets, and the media campaign is launched, linking its messages to the report of the Food and Nutrition Board.

Budgets

The projected three-year budget for the Campaign to Reduce Dietary Fat is as follows:

Year 1 (1989)

Consumer targets		
Advertising campaign	Ad Council	$ 500,000
Public relations and publicity	A public relations agency	225,000
Food influential targets:	A public relations agency	80,000
Food organization targets:	A public relations agency	111,000
Test markets	10 unidentified communities	350,000 (Year 2)
Research	1 or more unidentified firms	350,000 (Year 3)
Consumer research		60,000
Tracking campaign's reach		90,000 (Years 2 and 3)
Test-market evaluation		50,000 (Years 2 and 3)
Analyses of other national surveys		10,000
Administration	Foundation staff	130,000
Additional projected expenditures for years 2 and 3		2,000,000
	Grand Total	$3,956,000

Controls

The campaign will carry out ongoing evaluation. During the planning year, quantitative and qualitative research will contribute to a thorough understanding of the target audience. This research will aid in the development of media messages and will complement existing national consumer research studies.

Quantitative research will provide direction for the program, while qualitative research will examine consumers' attitudes, knowledge, and behaviors. The latter will reveal not only what people think but why they think that way. Research will utilize focus groups and will be conducted by an advertising agency to develop public-service advertising concepts. Evaluation studies will be generated to measure how well the campaign is accomplishing its goals and objectives.

17

Organizing and Implementing Social Marketing Programs

Not even the most carefully formulated social marketing plan can succeed in winning adoptions of its social product if it is not effectively implemented. Putting a plan into practice means two things: structuring the organization and implementing the programs. Structuring the organization takes place at three levels: the headquarters level, the local field-operations level, and the program-support level (coordination among departments).

STRUCTURING THE ORGANIZATION

Often a social marketing campaign is organized within an existing organization, as was the campaign to reduce dietary fat ("Project LEAN") spearheaded by the Kaiser Family Foundation. Other examples are oral rehydration and family planning campaigns that are administered through health ministries in Third-World countries, and antismoking campaigns, launched by the American Cancer Society and the American Medical Association.

A social change program that operates within a broad and existing organization confronts the issue of being integrated into that organization as a legitimate organizational unit. Kotler and Andreasen argued that such integration evolves in three stages: an initial "resistance" stage, a growth and "acceptance" stage, and a mature or "established" stage.[1] Specific organizing strategies are available for each stage.

This chapter focuses on organizing and implementing a social marketing plan that is starting up whole. Several organizational issues will arise:

1. Who in the organization will be involved directly or indirectly in implementation?
2. What specific work responsibilities will each perform?
3. How will these various responsibilities be related to one another?

We began to address the first issue by delineating three levels of organization.

Headquarters Level

Program management at the headquarters level involves carrying out a set of specific tasks. A management team is established. Its tasks have to be specified in detail, appropriate team members have to be assigned, and evaluation has to be undertaken so that each task is related to the others.

How detailed should the task specification be? The answer is, the level of detail that is required for effective action by each team member. Organizational elements should be detailed enough to allow each team manager to disaggregate each assigned task at the field-operations level as well.

Consider Project LEAN. Advertising is a critical activity in the social marketing plan. It can be broken down into the following tasks for an advertising manager:

1. Determining the advertising message and execution.
2. Formulating the media plan and getting it approved.
3. Executing the media plan.

These tasks can be further disaggregated into several subtasks that an advertising manager can assign to subordinates. Executing the media plan has such subtasks as planning a media buy, negotiating with the media, deciding to purchase a media slot, and monitoring placement of advertising in the media. In this context, each task or combination of tasks is assignable to a lower-level staff aide who reports to the advertising manager.

The allocation of specified tasks and their coordination and relationship is accomplished by developing an organizational structure. Social marketers have several options; they can organize by social marketing functions, by social products, by target-adopter segments, or by a mix of the latter two.

Functional-organization design. When a campaign involves a relatively simple social product for adoption by a single target-adopter segment or several small target-adopter segments, then a functional-organization design is called for. The components of this design are shown in Figure 17–1a.

A relatively simple social product is one that has a clearly defined social marketing objective, strategy, and tasks. Consider the 1976 Swine Flu Immunization Program of the Centers for Disease Control of the U.S. Department of Health, Education and Welfare (HEW). Case 17–1 summarizes the elements of this program. The program's objectives was relatively simple: to vaccinate at least 60 percent of the general American population between July 1976 to January 1977. The strategy was likewise clear-cut: create the serum needed and establish a mass vaccination program quickly. The tasks were straightforward:

1. Study the severity of the problem and the likelihood of an outbreak leading to an epidemic.
2. In the likelihood of an epidemic, prepare a mass-inoculation program with the necessary funding and other resources.

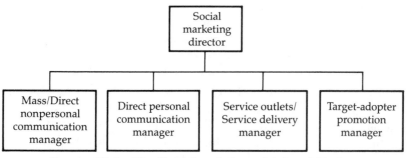

FIGURE 17–1a The Functional-Organizational Design

3. Have the president propose the program to Congress by the first quarter of 1976.

4. Get Congress to provide the funds for the program by the second quarter.

5. Have the president sign it into law.

6. Prepare implementation plans and secure the cooperation of federal departments and agencies.

7. Launch clinical trials of the vaccine by the start of the third quarter and complete negotiations with vaccine manufacturers.

8. Contract with vaccine manufacturers to produce 200 million doses of the vaccine between July and October 1976.

9. Organize and get public and private health care systems at the state and local levels to deliver the vaccine to 215 million Americans between July 1976 and January 1977.

For this type of campaign, a functional organization design is the optimal one.

Product-management design. When social marketers have to manage multiple social products that are diverse and too numerous for a functional setup, then it makes sense to organize by social products. Figure 17–1b, illustrating this structure, shows that the design does not dispense with functional management, but adds a layer to it. Those assigned as product managers take charge of the social marketing functions. Here is how a product manager's job is defined in a business context, at the General Foods Corporation.

Product managers at General Foods acted as both marketing and business managers for their brands. On the marketing side, they had the mission of planning and executing all advertising, promotion, pricing, and merchandising strategies for their brands. More generally, they had to compete for and coordinate all their division's functional resources for their respective brands, which include technical inputs, marketing research, sales force programs, processing, and packaging. On the operations side, they were responsible for their brands' financial contribution through volume attainment, marketing spending, and pricing decisions. On the planning side, they worked with top

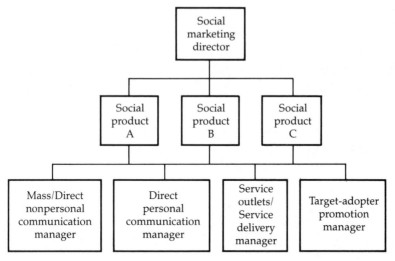

FIGURE 17–1b The Product-Management Design

management on setting current fiscal objectives and longer-range expectations (five-year strategic plans).[2]

Managers of a social product also have both planning and operating responsibilities. They are "middle managers" who must function in the roles of superiors, equals, and subordinates all at the same time. As middle managers, they are "both delegators and doers, both strategists and operators, . . . both coaches and players."[3]

A situation calling for a product-management design is the U.S. organization Common Cause, a citizen-action group described in Case 17–2. Common Cause's social products were categorized as short term and long term. When it was founded in 1971, the organization determined that it had to "establish a record of success" early. The short-term product line included winning the right of 18 year olds to vote. Its longer-term social products included (1) withdrawal of all U.S. forces from Indochina, (2) campaign-finance reform in federal elections, (3) reform of the U.S. Congress, including an end to the committee seniority system and to closed congressional hearings, and (4) equal rights for women. To ensure effective implementation of each social product, Common Cause appointed several product managers.

Segment-management design. As Case 17–2 describes, when Common Cause reached a plateau in its membership, it became strategically critical to think of its work from the perspective of segmenting the target-adopter population. Thus, the organizational emphasis shifted to membership development. For this purpose, Common Cause divided the voting-age American population into several segments of target adopters:

1. The better educated, higher income, generally white middle-class segment, which formed the core of its loyal supporters.
2. Disadvantaged groups.
3. Retired people.
4. Blue-collar laborers.
5. Civil service workers.
6. Military personnel.
7. Youths.
8. Academics.

Segment 1 was targeted for what Common Cause called "membership renewal." Among the remaining segments, Common Cause decided to place top priority on Segment 7. At this stage, it was more strategic for Common Cause to think of target-adopter segments than of social products in organizing its efforts and staff. Because organization follows strategy, the appropriate organizational design was by target-adopter segment, or segment management, as depicted in Figure 17–1c.

The segment/product-management design. Once Common Cause succeeded in its target-adopter segmentation strategy, it reached the point when the development of social products and membership renewal were equally important objectives. Then, it decided to set up a "matrix organization structure," or segment/product management design, as described in Figure 17–1d.

This design aims to combine the merits of both product management and segment management without incorporating their respective shortcomings. However, in practice, it has its own set of problems. Under it, people work under two chains of command. One chain of command is the vertical flow shown in Figure 17–1d. People at the bottom are responsible to those at the top who function as the respective segment managers. The second chain of command is a horizontal flow in which the same

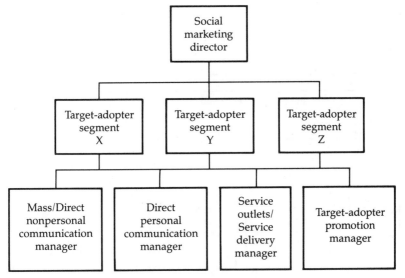

FIGURE 17–1c The Segment-Management Design

people work as members of several project teams, each of which is focused on a particular social product. As members of a project team, these same people are responsible to the leader of the team.

Experience has shown that it takes a long time to make the "matrix" structure work efficiently. Flexibility and continuing co-operation among people at all levels of the organization are needed. Open and direct lines of communication along and across both chains of command are necessary and require a level of interpersonal skills that few people can be assumed to have. This type of organizational structure depends on intensive training of staff in interpersonal-oriented skills.

Field-Operations Level

The field-operations level of a social campaign or program is in closest contact with the target adopters. Therefore, the successful implementation of a campaign or program depends on the performance of staff members at the local level. In Common Cause, district liaison and volunteer activists and staff of local chapters constitute the field operations. In the Swine Flu Immunization Program, the field level included the staffs of public and private health care facilities, medical staffs, and volunteer aides.

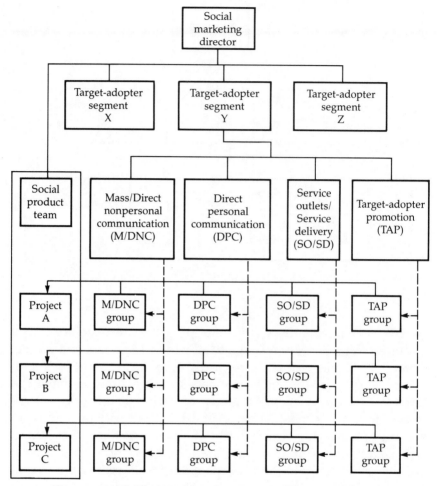

FIGURE 17–1d The Segment/Product-Management Design

Designing field operations. In designing the marketing tasks of the field operations, one must consider the nature of the target-adopter segments, together with the campaign's objectives for each segment, to be uppermost. The primary marketing tasks are as follows:

1. Prospecting: Identifying prospective target adopters.
2. Communicating: Informing and persuading them about the social products.
3. Triggering adoption: Drawing prospective target adopters to act on their intentions.

4. Servicing: Providing services to prospective and existing target adopters.
5. Research: Conducting field research and intelligence work.
6. Allocating: Evaluating the relative importance of each prospective group of target adopters and allocating the campaign's resources accordingly.

What about the structure of the field operations? The organizational structure at the headquarters level will influence the structure of the field operations. This structure is relatively simple if a functional-organization design is used. In this case, field operations will follow a territorial structure, with each field-operations worker assigned to a territory that is defined by the smallest local administrative unit. One or more of these units will constitute a territory. The field-operations worker is the program's representative in the assigned territory.

When the headquarters structure is organized along product-management lines, then the field operations typically is organized along social product lines. If a segmented structure is adopted at the top, field operations will be structured according to the several segments of target adopters. Once the marketing tasks and field operations structure are determined, the question arises, How many field workers should a campaign have? The basic consideration is output in relation to costs. The output question is, "How many staff wouuld it take to achieve the desired results, given the marketing tasks that are assigned to field operations?" In business marketing, a popular approach to determining the size of staff is known as the "workload approach."

1. Target adopters are grouped into size classes according to their priority in the campaign.
2. The number of necessary field visits to a target adopter during a given campaign period is established for each class, reflecting estimates of the number and length of visits that are likely to produce the desired results.
3. The number of prospective and existing target adopters in each size class is multiplied by the corresponding "call frequency" to arrive at the total workload required for the coverage of a specific territory.
4. The average number of visits a field-operations worker can make per program or campaign period is determined.
5. The number of field-operations workers who are needed is

then determined by dividing the total annual visits required by the average annual visits a field-operations worker can make.

This formula for estimating the size of a field-operations staff can be illustrated by a campaign, waged by Common Cause, that was targeted mainly to influence congressional policy. The campaign involved an effort to halt funding of a supersonic transport aircraft requested by the U.S. Department of Defense. The Common Cause campaign targeted approximately 500 members of Congress and legislative staff, along with 1,000 influential media representatives. Congressmen and staff required 14 calls during the campaign's duration, while media representatives required five calls during the same period. The Common Cause campaign, therefore, required a field operations staff that could make 12,000 calls or visits [(500 × 14) + (1,000 × 5)] during the campaign. Suppose that the average field worker in this campaign could make 120 calls in that period. Then, the Common Cause campaign would need 100 full-time field-operations workers.

How are these workers to be compensated? The field operations of some campaigns do not have to deal with compensation when the campaign is basically staffed by volunteers, as was the case with Common Cause. For field operations that have to hire a work force, the issue of compensation involves the following considerations.

1. The compensation's fixed component, or "basic pay," and its variable component, or commissions and bonuses.
2. The expense allowances that cover travel, lodging, and dining.
3. The fringe benefits, including paid vacations, sickness or accident benefits, life and health insurance, moving allowances, professional dues, and pension plans.

When added up, these items can total a substantial amount. Field operations are expensive, typically accounting for the largest proportion of a marketing campaign's budget for promotion. When field activities are not properly executed (for example, when lobbying visits are unsuccessful and adoptions are low or nonexistent), then much of a campaign's funds for promotion can be wasted.

How should social marketers determine the components of

compensation? They have at least two bases. One is to decide by means of the going market price, in which case a compensation package is based on prevailing industry practice. An alternative basis is the ability to pay. Most social campaigns have limitations on funding, some of which are severe. Under these circumstances, many campaigns actually have little choice but to base compensation packages on what they can afford. Furthermore, each component of a compensation package serves a particular objective. Fixed basic pay and fringe benefits are compensation as a means of livelihood. Expense allowances along with basic pay are compensation that reflect a worker's normal productivity. Commissions and bonuses are payment for workers' extra efforts and greater-than-expected results.

Managing field operations. The social marketer's task of managing field operations begins with the recruitment and retention of necessary field staff. These tasks can be critical for social marketing campaigns that depend heavily on volunteers, as is the case with Common Cause. Because it failed to develop a system of managing volunteers, Common Cause encountered considerable problems, including those of internal communications and staff turnover. On-the-job training was minimal, and work assignments were casually based on personal preferences.[4] The Swine Flu Immunization Program faced an even more basic problem, that of attracting an adequate number of medical volunteers. The evaluation report stated that "participation of volunteers was less than expected."[5]

Kotler and Andreasen noted that it is becoming increasingly difficult to obtain volunteers. "The pool of those who come forward with little or no encouragement is shrinking. Those who might come forward are more hard-headed about their choices," they concluded.[6] Social marketers must carefully plan the recruitment and management of volunteers by first defining the pool of target volunteers and then by selecting an appropriate recruitment appeal. To retain recruited volunteers, marketers should study volunteer dropouts to find out why they left and survey current volunteers about their satisfactions and dissatisfactions on the job.

What about the management of the effort and quality of work, particularly of volunteers? Kotler and Andreasen called for "running a tighter ship."[7] Recruitment should not be dominated by feelings of gratitude toward individuals who have volunteered their services, and the leadership should not refrain from criticizing the performance of volunteers when that is warranted because it can only encourage the predilection of volunteers to undisciplined performance. The better approach is to treat volunteers like professional full-time workers: establish performance standards, train personnel, supervise them, and hold them accountable to standards of performance.

Program-Support Level

Implementing a social marketing plan involves the coordination of several tasks and departments in a campaign organization. Staff support covers the disbursement of funds, training, research, supplies and materials, properties and facilities, and transportation, among others. Because support personnel operate at the same level, cooperation, rather than authority from above, is the rule. Support staff must persuade colleagues who are equals, which places a premium on interpersonal skills that are in short supply.

The tasks of coordination and cooperation are rendered even more difficult by conflicts that arise between the objectives and concerns of one department and another and between the social marketer and the support staff. Table 17–1 summarizes some of these potential conflicts.

What kind of cooperative effort would work? Let's consider the situation more carefully, taking into account several features of a marketing organization:

1. Conflicts arise between two departments or among several ones.
2. Interests conflict on one or more issues.
3. Departments are related together voluntarily in a single setting.
4. Relationships are built around a division of labor and an exchange of one or more resources.
5. Campaign activities are sequential: One department proposes and another evaluates and responds with a counter proposal, and so on.

These are the features of a negotiation or bargaining situation. Managing it effectively requires negotiation skills. What are the

TABLE 17-1 Summary of Contrasting Viewpoints of Social
Marketing and Other Departments
in an Organization

Other Departments	Their Emphasis	Social Marketing's Emphasis
Operations	Standardized service	Custom service
	Average quality control	Tight quality control
	Narrow service line	Broad service line
	Noninterference from target adopters during the service	Participation of target adopters
Research	Long lead time for design and implementation	Short lead time for both
	Intrinsic scientifically esthetic design	Utilitarian design
	Analysis	Implications
Personnel/Human Resources	Complete papers and forms before starting	Immediate start, irrespective of papers and forms
	Long preparation and training	On-the-job training
	Systematic written evaluation of job performance	On-the-spot subjective evaluation
Procurement	Standard supplies and materials	Nonstandard supplies and materials
	Concern about price	Concern about quality
	Economic lot sizes to minimize expenditures	Large lot sizes to avoid stockouts
Finance	Hard and fast budgets	Flexible budgets to meet changing needs
	Organization-wide reports	Specific reports on a project or target-adopter segment
	Control of expenditures	Release of expenditures
Legal	Documentation	Action
	Restrictions/limitations	Possibilities/actionables
	Letter of the law	Spirit of the law

SOURCE: Philip Kotler, *Marketing Management: Analysis, Planning, Implementation and Control*, 6th ed., © 1988, p. 717. Adapted by permission of Prentice-Hall, Inc., Englewood Cliffs, NJ.

appropriate negotiation skills? They are well summarized in a strategy called "principled negotiation,"[8] which has four basic rules:

- *Separate the People From the Problem.* First, understand the forcefulness of the other group's viewpoint and imagine the level of emotion with which they hold it. Second, openly discuss the feelings of members of both groups but without rancor or emotional outburst, so the negotiation does not degenerate into unproductive name-calling. Third, listen actively and acknowledge what is being said; communicate about problems and solutions, rather than about one or another group's shortcomings; and move toward articulating objective interests rather than subjective feelings.

- *Focus on Interests, Not Positions.* An interest is what causes someone or some group to take a position. Make certain that everyone understands the groups' interests. Then be flexible about the means for achieving them.

- *Invent Options for Mutual Gain.* Use brainstorming and other creative idea-generating methods to search for options. These methods can facilitate "side-by-side" bargaining as against the typically unproductive "face-to-face" bargaining. Options can help identify and shape joint interests.

- *Insist on Objective Criteria.* When the other group is insisting on its position and wants to impose its will, insist that the agreement must reflect some fair objective criteria that are independent of either group's position. This way, agreement is reached on principle, rather than by pressure.

IMPLEMENTATION OF THE SOCIAL MARKETING PROGRAM

Having examined how social marketers set up organizational structures to implement a marketing plan from within, below, and outside their own level in an organization, we now turn to an assessment of how an organization itself can effectively implement a social marketing plan. In this context, implementation is treated both as a process and as a set of skills.

Implementation as a Process

The process of implementation consists of a series of steps. This process is illustrated, using Hosmer's four-step definition, by the

Common Cause campaign to monitor violations of the campaign-financing disclosure law.[9] Table 17–2 summarizes this campaign with hypothetically generated data. Hosmer's four steps of implementation are as follows:

1. Specify functional or task objectives.
2. Develop functional policies and standard procedures.
3. Design functional programs and their supporting budgetary plans.
4. Take immediate, appropriate actions to start and maintain the program toward the specified functional objectives.

Functional objectives. Using the qualifier "functional" or "task" is a way of clarifying the particular level in a campaign in which a given step is taken. Objectives are the results "where the functional and technical units are expected to be at a specific time in the future."[10] The statements, as outlined in Table 17–2, provide direction and purpose to the social marketer's department, as well as to the other departments. They also constitute the standards for evaluating each department's performance. As shown in Table 17–2, a hypothetical social marketing director spells out five sets of objectives: four for program-support departments and one for the top leader, chairperson of the governing board of the campaign.

Functional policies and standard procedures. Social marketers must set clear functional policies and standard procedures. The functional policies inform planners how to decide on the means to attain the functional objectives. Standard procedures tell them how to take actions on those decisions. These two elements specify the conventional management wisdom about how to react to certain recurring situations at the field level. These policies and procedures also help social marketers coordinate their field-operations efforts with those of other departments.

Functional programs and budgetary plans. In this step, social marketers carefully describe the specific activities that the social marketing unit and each department must undertake to attain their respective functional objectives within the designated policy guidelines. These sets of activities constitute the different functional programs. Then, social marketers can move to specify and allocate the resources required to carry out the proposed activi-

TABLE 17-2 Sample Implementation Work Plan for the Common Cause Project to Monitor the Disclosure of Election Campaign Financing

Departments	Functional Objectives	Policies and Standard Procedures	Programs and Budgetary Plans	Initiating/Sustaining Actions
Field unit, state volunteer team (SVT), and SVT leader District liaison volunteers (DLVs)	Complete investigation of 240 law violators by end 1st quarter of 1972. Sue all "provable" cases including "guilty" donors by second quarter of 1972. Sue CRP to make public list of contributors by April 7, 1972.	No investigation will use nonlegal means/procedures. Drop any case with less than a winning chance. Give priority and full complement of field, network support staff, membership personnel/funding to a major case.	Add 8 volunteer lawyers at current per diem rate. Transfer to this project 24 deputy SVT leaders from the Congressional Reform Project and State Issues Project, including 48 of their DLVs at same per diem rates.	Inform SVT leaders and DLVs concerned of changes in the project assignments and arrange for briefing. Requisition Membership for needed volunteer lawyers.

310

Unit	Tasks	Policies	Budget Allocations	Actions
Network Support Staff and Communication Unit	Supply legal/other research data to 240 investigations by start first quarter. Provide telephone/other communication support to all sued cases. Monitor CRP reactions/moves and phone in significant ones.	All research must have approved research request and accompanying brief. No telephone/other communication facilities may be used for personal purposes. All monitoring reports must be written, including those already given orally.	Get legal/other research allocation—$36,000 for first 2 quarters of 1972. Add 25 volunteer phone operators at usual per diem rate. Get CRP monitoring allocations—$5,000.	Obtain research briefs on all research requests. Requisition Membership for needed volunteer phone operators. Prepare training programs for volunteers. Hold meeting of CRP monitoring team and CRP field team.
Membership Development Unit	Recruit 8 new volunteer lawyers by mid January 1972. Hire them as consultants if not recruitable as volunteers. Recruit 25 new volunteer phone operators by end January 1972. Arrange for smooth transfer of 24 deputy SVT leaders and 48 DLVs to this project by end January 1972.	All volunteers must be screened for minimum qualifications. All qualified volunteers must sign project term commitment. No currently working volunteer may be transferred to another project without his or her prior consent.	Get legal consultant contingency allocations—$1,500 per month each. Get volunteer recruitment allocation—$150 each.	Mail out and follow up by phone on volunteer sourcing from local chapters. Hold meeting and individual sessions with designated transferees.

(continued)

TABLE 17-2 Continued

Departments	Functional Objectives	Policies and Standard Procedures	Programs and Budgetary Plans	Initiating/Sustaining Actions
Finance/Administrative Unit	Fund allocation and availability to this project of $140,000 over first 2 quarters. Release funds at most 5 days after request. Obtain expense liquidation every tenth of the month.	A statement of allocated funds and expenses for every project will be prepared quarterly. The prepared statement will compare actual allocated funds and expenses versus the plan. Variances from the plan will be analyzed and reported.	Add 2 volunteer accounting clerks at usual per diem rate. Obtain additional standby funding for $40,000 from the bank.	Modify project planning and control procedures to allow for contingencies. Inform all concerned of modifications. Apply for $40,000 loan at bank.
Governing board chair	Approve all quarterly plans within 10 days of submission. Accomplish all quarterly plans.	All quarterly forecasts of activities must be submitted 30 days before the effective date. All quarterly results must be reviewed with the project director concerned within 10 days of submission.		Look for potential replacements for current field director and network support chief legal counsel.

ties. These specifications constitute the budgetary plans for each functional unit.

Presenting the specific activities with the required budgetary level has a way of driving home an important point: Activities are the means to achieve the objectives, but they cost money. Another point of emphasis is that one set of activities has to be carried through by another set of activities involving another department. The concept and practice of coordination face an acid test in this step.

Initiating and sustaining actions. The last step in the implementing process, strictly speaking, is not a step but a continuous chain of actions. It involves taking the appropriate starting action, followed by reinforcing and sustaining ones. The starting action or actions relate to the set of activities designated in the previous step. They "start off" these activities and thereby also kick off the task of implementation.

Implementation as a Skill

Implementation also depends on leadership skills. These skills have been examined from several perspectives. For example, Bonoma identified four primary skills that are critical for effective implementation:[11]

- *Allocating Skills.* Knowing where or to what activities, functions, and program the resources (time, money, and personnel) should be allocated.
- *Monitoring Skills.* Knowing the ways to obtain feedback on the outcomes of social marketing actions and the ways to do something about them.
- *Organizing Skills.* Knowing what should be done by whom and how these different assignments and responsibilities relate to one another in achieving the program's objectives.
- *Interacting Skills.* Knowing how to get things done through others by means of power, coordination, or the prudent use of divisions and conflicts.

To Kanter, the middle manager is the personification of the implementor.[12] Obviously, the innovative middle manager is the effective implementor. In a study of 165 middle managers in five companies, Kanter noted that when these managers geared up for "moving-into-action" (the implementing phase), their effectiveness reflected the exercise of five skills:

- *The Persuasion Skill:* Getting things done by "persuading more than ordering, though [they] sometimes use pressure as a last resort."
- *The Collaborative Skill.* Getting things done by "building a team, which entails among other things frequent staff meetings and considerable sharing of information."
- *The Participative Skill.* Getting things done by "seeking inputs from others—that is, asking for ideas about users' needs, soliciting suggestions from subordinates, welcoming peer review, and so forth."
- *The Political Skill.* Getting things done through "acknowledging others' stake or potential stake in the project—in other words, being politically sensitive."
- *The Motivating Skill.* Getting things done by "sharing rewards and recognition willingly."[13]

Like Kanter, Uyterhoeven is concerned with middle managers, the individuals most responsible for the implementation of strategy.[14] He identified five implementation skills:

- *Subordinate-Peer-Superior Role-Playing Skills.* Implementors or administrators relate to their bosses as subordinates, to their colleagues as peers, and to their project team members as superiors. To be effective, they must meet the multiple and conflicting demands arising from this triple set of relationships. Thus, they must be able "to shift quickly and frequently from one to another."
- *The "Playing Coach" Skill.* Effective implementors are both "delegators and doers, both strategists and operators, or . . . both coaches and players." The roles require different skills, but to be effective, implementors must possess and combine them.
- *The "Bilingual" Skill.* Effective implementors have the role of translating the strategic language of their superiors into the operational language of their subordinates to achieve results. This role requires the performance of two sequential tasks: figuring out what has to be done to translate the strategy into practice and then determining how to get it done.

- *The Political Skill.* Good administrators have the "political sensitivity [and] the constitution to stomach pressures and conflicts." Implementation involves reconciling "different interests and interest groups, conflicting goals and ambitions, and positions of power and weakness."
- *The Coordinative Skill.* Implementation cannot move forward without the cooperation of many departments. Thus getting things done involves knowing how to coordinate mutual activities and build cooperation.

Social marketers may easily get the impression that the implementor or administrative role requires superhuman skills. But studies have shown that these skills are not the result of heroism but of hard work, experience, and active learning behaviors. This analysis suggests that social marketers would be well advised to acquire these skills and if they are delegating responsibilities for implementation, they should seek these skills in people they choose.

CASE 17–1

The 1976 Swine Flu Immunization Program

In February 1976, six U.S. Army recruits at Fort Dix, New Jersey, were hospitalized for swine flu. One recruit died. The report on these cases reached the Centers for Disease Control (CDC) in Atlanta, which maintains an early warning system for monitoring infectious diseases. The Fort Dix cases were noteworthy because CDC believed that the swine flu strain was the cause of a pandemic that swept the world in 1918–19, resulting in an estimated 21.6 million deaths, or 1 percent of the world population at that time.

Upon learning of the Fort Dix cases, the CDC director consulted with other U.S. government agencies, as well as outside consultants, and asked the army to study the cases at Fort Dix. On February 19, 1976, the CDC director sent a memorandum to U.S.

SOURCE: Myron D. Fottler, "Improving Health Care Planning: Some Lessons from Immunization," *Long Range Planning*, 17 (5) (1984), pp. 88–95. Quotations are from this article.

Department of Health, Education, and Welfare (HEW) recommending that if an immunization program were set up, (1) it should combine input from the public and private sectors, (2) the federal government should advise vaccine manufacturers to produce and contract through HEW for 200 million doses of vaccine, and (3) the vaccine should be made available at no cost to state health agencies that would distribute it through public, private, and volunteer channels.

Less than one month later, CDC, HEW, and the U.S. Army consulted on the Fort Dix results of the study. The study concluded and projected that "there could be small outbreaks occurring in other areas but [which will go] undetected." The report implied that the swine flu virus had already spread, could break into an epidemic in the United States, and spread to the rest of the world.

A poll of experts in the areas of influenza and immunization produced an estimate that over 60 percent of the American population would accept a vaccine as part of an anti-swine flu campaign. CDC determined that an immunization program that would reach 60 percent of the population was preferable to one that focused on high-risk groups alone. CDC estimated that the epidemic had a 10 percent probability of occurring; if it occurred without a preventive immunization program in place, the cost of the resulting epidemic would be over $6 billion. CDC calculated that the cost of producing and administering a swine-flu-immunization program at $1.00 per person, or $210 million for the entire U.S. population. With these calculations and projections, CDC recommended a mass inoculation program and won the approval of the other key governmental agencies.

On March 24, 1976, President Gerald Ford dramatically announced he was proposing to Congress a swine flu immunization program: "No one knows exactly how serious this threat could be, nevertheless, we cannot afford to take a chance." Congress acted swiftly. By the first week of April, the House of Representatives and the Senate passed Public Law 94-266, which provided over $135 million for a comprehensive, nationwide flu-immunization program.

Between April and July 1976, HEW initiated and completed clinical trials of the vaccine, which furnished the data for the development of the vaccine serum. Negotiations with vaccine manufacturers were undertaken, and HEW selected four major pharmaceutical companies. The industry's annual production of flu vaccine at that time was 20 million doses; this program required the four companies to produce over five times that amount within a five-month period. The major flu outbreak was predicted to take place in mid-October, and manufacturers were contracted to produce and deliver the vaccine according to this timetable: 8 million doses by July 9, 20 million doses by September 3, and 200 million doses by October 29.

How did these plans work out? The record shows that the immunization campaign encountered serious problems. The production of the vaccine took two months longer than planned. Deliveries of the vaccine did not come on schedule, and these delays resulted in slowdowns throughout the campaign. Delivery of the first vaccine supplies occurred in October instead of the preceding July, as planned. As a result the organization of state, local, and private vaccination programs also was delayed.

What were the major causes of the delays? A postmortem analysis of the program indicated that the vaccine manufacturers' concern about legal liability was the biggest cause of the delays. Insurance companies had initially refused to include swine flu vaccine in the manufacturers' normal product-liability coverage, anticipating numerous legal suits and injury claims that could amount to $9.5 billion–$25 billion. Without adequate product-liability insurance, manufacturers threatened to stop producing the vaccine and withhold delivery of their vaccine from their inventories. To deal with the liability issue, Congress enacted a law providing that "all claims for injury or death resulting from the program have to be filed against the Federal Government and decided through procedures of the Federal Tort Claims Act." Lawyers for the U.S. Department of Justice estimated that the damages filed under this act could very well exceed $1 billion. Errors and mishaps in manufacturing the vaccine did result in injuries and legal claims. For example, one drug company accidentally mixed up strains of the vaccine and discovered the error only after two million doses had been produced and delivered. Cases of adverse reactions to the vaccine in children occurred, prompting HEW to instruct vaccination centers to stop vaccinating children and teenagers until further tests warranted a resumption. Not enough medical volunteers materialized to administer the program, and many physicians refused to participate after learning about the controversies over product liability and safety.

Reports of fatalities from the vaccine were aired. CDC investigated 35 reported deaths from the vaccine but concluded that the deaths could not be linked to the vaccine or to the vaccination procedure. Yet the adverse publicity had taken its toll on the program, shaking public confidence while health officials failed to respond adequately to the adverse publicity. Ten states suspended the inoculation program. Monitoring surveys, however, indicated that practically every American was aware of the immunization program and that the percentage of people who did not intend to get vaccinated rose from 20 percent when the program began to 58 percent when the program was terminated. Reports of more than 50 cases of a rare form of paralysis, known as Guillian-Barre, or French polio, that were traceable to the vaccinations ultimately led to the permanent suspension of the campaign. Ironically, the epidemic never materialized.

CASE 17–2
Common Cause: An American Citizen Action Group

John W. Gardner, former secretary of the U.S. Department of Health, Education, and Welfare, organized Common Cause in July 1970. Gardner's goal was to create a wide-ranging "citizen's lobby" to deal with "the basic issue that underlies all others, whether citizens will have access to their own government and whether we can call our government to account."

Gardner, a highly respected public figure identified with conservative politics, proceeded to build a broad-based campaign of diverse political backgrounds when he selected to serve on Common Cause's Board of Governors big-city mayors; black American political leaders; representatives of labor unions, civil rights groups, and consumer-protection-organization figures; and corporate and business leaders. Skeptics in Washington, D.C., had predicted the demise of Gardner's campaign, despite the high-powered supporters.

SOURCE: Christopher Gale and L. E. Grayson, "Common Cause," L. E. Grayson and C. J. Tompkins, eds., *Management of Public Sector and Nonprofit Organizations* (Reston, Va.: Reston Publishing Co., 1984), pp. 150–168. Quotations are from this source.

The prevailing skepticism toward the campaign influenced the planning. A first-year membership-recruitment goal of 100,000 was targeted. The mail responses, however, averaged 1,000 letters a day, and after 20 weeks of operation, Common Cause realized it would greatly exceed its goal. At the end of its first year, Common Cause had 218,523 members, a figure that surpassed the 155,000 members of the other highly regarded citizen group, the League of Women Voters.

In organizing Common Cause, Gardner built a small staff of trained lobbyists and public relations experts. Field operations were placed in the hands of volunteers. The local-level organization took the form of local chapters staffed by volunteers. However, local chapters could not initiate their own "agendas for action." Agenda setting would be done at national headquarters.

Common Cause set its reform agenda by soliciting advice from its membership within 15 categories of action that the campaign leaders recommended. Results of the membership referendum led to seven priorities that more than 50 percent favored: "overhaul and revitalize government" (95 percent), "protect and enhance the environment" (90 percent), "improve criminal justice system" (89 percent), "withdraw all U.S. forces from Indochina" (85 percent), "help eliminate poverty" (80 percent), "fight sex and race discrimination" (75 percent), and "make government accountable" (53 percent).

Common Cause then selected a more specific subissue within each cluster of priorities and decided to test a few of these issues in its initial phase. In the first year, issues were selected that leaders believed would likely establish "a record of success" for the organization. Two were chosen: the right of 18 year olds to vote in federal elections and defeat of a costly new program, the Supersonic Transport aircraft. Common Cause proved to be successful in its lobbying campaign, and these initial victories were utilized to recruit an even larger membership.

With the short-term victories, Common Cause decided to tackle more ambitious governmental and political reform issues: (1) the war in Indochina, (2) the reform of financing of federal election campaigns, (3) congressional reform, in particular, the elimination of the seniority system and closed congressional hearings, and (4) equal rights for women. The first priority was the monitoring and reform of the financing of election campaigns. In 1972, Common Cause sued both national political parties to restrain them from violating a law that limited individual contributions to political campaigns to under $5,000 per political candidate. It successfully lobbied Congress to enact a stronger campaign financing law. With the stronger law in place, Common Cause launched investigations of over 200 violations of campaign financing.

In a 1973 interview, Gardner reflected on Common Cause's "success" and identified five principal factors:

1. A social change campaign must have stamina and be prepared to commit itself over a long period.
2. Any campaign depends on an informed public that can counteract the activities of special-interest groups. Political figures are highly responsive to informed, alert citizens.
3. Campaigns have to target and focus their activities. Indignation and outrage by a few is not enough. A campaign has to choose its targets and mobilize strength, numbers, and money behind its efforts.
4. Alliances have to be created between governmental leaders and other influential groups.
5. A campaign must be run professionally. Gardner observed: "Citizens must be prepared to match the professional skill and knowledge of their opponents."

How was Gardner's formula for success put into practice? Common Cause organized a professional lobbying system that focused on Washington, D.C., operated through a telephone-based activist hot line. It partitioned the country by states and the states by congressional districts, operationally speaking. Statewide volunteer teams were headed by a team leader for each state. These teams, known as district liaison volunteers, were the primary contacts between headquarters and members of the chapters. In effect, an efficient telephone-based communication and distribution network was established between headquarters and membership. Common Cause could then quickly trigger members' actions in the form of rallies, letters, and telephone calls to legislative representatives; generate broad-based citizen action; and ultimately arouse the attention of the mass media. To support the efforts of the state teams, the system also created a second smaller action network at the headquarters. This network consisted of a staff group of two managers, who assisted with procedures and operations problems, and four area supervisors who were each responsible for supporting the network's activities in ten states.

In its second year, Common Cause became increasingly concerned about its membership. Although membership-building activities received 33 percent of the total budgetary resources, there were signs of slippage. Common Cause's penetration of "the better educated, higher income, generally middle-class white" segment of American society had reached saturation. Furthermore, recruitment efforts through extensive mailings had not generated the desired level of new members. The organization then decided on a plan for a broader-based growth in membership by recruiting "other major segments in American life such as the disadvantaged groups, retired people, blue-collar laborers, civil service workers, military personnel, youth groups, and academics." To accomplish this goal, Common Cause established a new Development Division to oversee the recruitment and maintenance of members.

18

Controlling
Social Marketing
Programs

Social marketers cannot achieve timely and efficient implementation if they lack an appropriate control system. Although campaign management can be categorized into planning, implementing, and controlling functions, managing, in practice, is a continuous process. Social marketers do their work by continually assessing, planning, implementing, controlling, evaluating, and replanning their programs.

THE NATURE OF SOCIAL MARKETING CONTROL

In implementing a social marketing campaign, social marketers will work on the day-to-day activities and tasks. Many things can affect the day-to-day activities and tasks and cause deviations from what the work plan specified. If these deviations take an unfavorable course, then a campaign can fall short of its objectives. The basic idea of social marketing control is to keep activity-driven and people-driven deviations within tolerable limits so that the campaign as a whole has a high probability of achieving its objectives.

It follows that social marketing control has two related aspects: the control of activities or the performance of tasks and the con-

322

trol of the staff's performance in implementing activities and tasks. These aspects are referred to here as "controlling performance" and "controlling performers," respectively. These terms reflect the following definition of control:

Management control is primarily a process for motivating and inspiring people to perform organization activities that will further the organization's goal. It is also a process for detecting and correcting unintentional performance errors and intentional irregularities.[1]

The Process

Thinking of control as a process makes it easier to do it. Figure 18-1 shows the control of performance (activities, tasks, programs, and the like) and of performers (staff roles) as a process. According to this model, social marketers must begin by establishing specific, measurable standards of performance and performers. If the standards are unmeasurable or if they are unacceptable to the staff involved, effective control cannot be achieved.

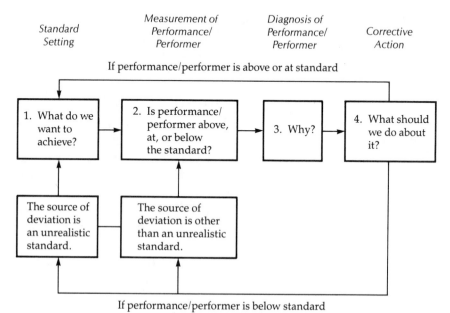

FIGURE 18-1 The Performance/Performer Control Process

Consider, for example, Project Head Start, described in Case 18-1. No explicit standards were developed to measure the performance of the staff and the program either at the planners' level or at the local community level. Everyone in this social change campaign seems to have been carried away by the emotionally charged rhetoric of President Johnson: "We have taken up the age-old challenge of poverty. . . ." and cannot afford to lose "generations of our children to this enemy of the human race. . . ." and "the bread that is cast upon these waters will surely return many thousandfold."[2]

The same intoxication pervaded the minds of staff at the field-operations level. One study reported:

> The potential and promise of Head Start in the spring days of 1965 were overwhelmingly exciting. The chance to work with low-income children and parents in a nursery school project that was well funded was a dream come true for many of us who had been scrounging and scraping to develop a sensitive program in ghetto areas of Los Angeles.[3]

Management-control problems arise in numerous social marketing campaigns. Fired by a sense of accomplishing tasks of high redeeming social value and inspired by deep emotional attachment, many social change campaigns are run as if they are self-controlling and self-correcting. Sadly, this usually is not the case. Emotionalism runs counter to the first step in the control process—planning and plotting feasible and measurable objectives and developing measurable inputs and outputs of the campaign.

The second step in the control process is to measure and compare performance against definable standards. This step is meaningless unless measurable standards of performance are in place. The experience of Project Head Start clearly illustrates this problem. In most instances, the staff did not undertake a meaningful measurement of performance, and the result was confusion.

The third step in the control process is to diagnose why the results of the measurement of performance and performers came out the way they did. Social marketers must always diagnose the results even if the results match or exceed the standards. Such a diagnosis enables them to understand whether credit belongs to the performers or to outside factors and whether these favorable factors will continue to operate.

When the results fall short of the standards, diagnosis can then reveal the likely source or sources. This diagnosis is the basis for the final step in the control process—taking corrective actions. The outcome of this final step feeds back into the second step if the diagnosis reveals that the deviation was due to other than an unrealistic standard. It feeds back into the first step if the diagnosis shows that the source of the deviation is an unrealistic objective. Social marketers must take all the steps if they are to exercise control over a campaign. If they complete only one or a few of the steps, they are not fully exercising control; they are just monitoring. Falling short of even the first step is, in effect, abdicating control.

What about timing? When should social marketers check on performance and performers? There are three timing options: before, during, and after the actual performance of a campaign activity. Controlling before the performance is really a form of pretesting. It is practiced in aircraft manufacturing and construction projects because the consequences of not doing so can be disastrous. A case can be made that a set of controls should have been developed for screening the teaching materials in the Head Start Preschool Education Program before they were used (see Case 18-1).

Controlling the performance during an activity is equivalent to midstream correction. It may have to be done when early signs indicate that an activity, although not fully carried out, may not be leading to the desired results. Suppose that in the Head Start situation, the Los Angeles program manager found that during the summer quarter of the program, head teachers were not properly consulting with parents. Then, corrective actions should not have waited until the end of the quarter, but should be instituted immediately to steer the nonperforming head teachers back on course. Controlling after the performance is the common understanding of management control: checking on results of completed activities to improve subsequent similar types of activities.

PERFORMANCE-CONTROL DEVICES

To check if the performance of a planned activity is meeting standards and attaining the objective, social marketers can use several devices. A control device can measure how the performance compares with standards or objectives, or it can measure how the performance compares with the inputs or the resources used.

Adoption-based Control Devices

Roberto proposed the use of a set of performance-control tools that reflect the relationships of effectiveness and efficiency together, as depicted in Figure 18–2.[4] These tools result in both effectiveness analysis and efficiency analysis.

Effectiveness analysis compares the program's performance to two "standards": the relevant program objective and the total potential target adopters' need for a social product. The first comparison produces the program's goal-effectiveness control index; the second produces the program's potency-effectiveness control index.

Efficiency analysis measures and compares the program's performance in relation to two other standards: the total resources that the program used to generate an outcome and the estimated

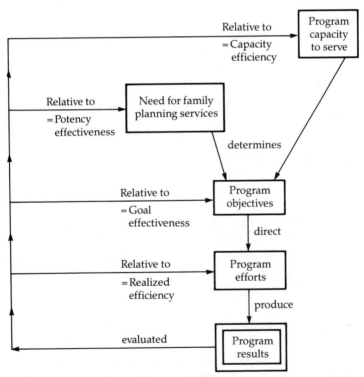

FIGURE 18–2 A Framework for Identifying Performance-Control Devices
SOURCE: Eduardo L. Roberto, *Strategic Decision Making in a Social Program* (Lexington, Mass.: Lexington Books, 1975), p. 114.

capacity of the program that is needed to generate the outcome. The first comparison produces the program's realized-efficiency control index, and the second produces the program's capacity-efficiency control index.

How will these two sets of tools help social marketers in their control objectives? Consider once again the Los Angeles County Head Start program. Suppose the standards for the satisfactory levels of the control indices were set. Then suppose that the measurements of the indices were similar to the ones shown in Table 18-1. The control process now moves into the diagnostic stage. The following are examples of diagnoses of the Head Start program.

Goal-effectiveness diagnosis. In the 1965 summer Head Start program, the administrators recognized they were short 16 students in relation to the target, but this was not worrisome. The

TABLE 18-1 Summary of a Hypothetical Performance-Control Analysis of the Summer 1965 Los Angeles County Head Start Program

Performance-Control Index	Estimated Value of the Index	Chosen Satisfactory Level	Tentative Conclusion about the Performance
Goal effectiveness	784 enrolled pre-schoolers: 800 target enrollees = 0.98	1.10	Neither satisfactory nor dissatisfactory
Potency effectiveness	784 enrolled pre-schoolers: 5,227 total potential enrollees = 0.15	0.20	Unsatisfactory
Realized efficiency	$494,960 total direct costs: 784 enrolled preschoolers = $631 per preschooler	$600	Unsatisfactory
Capacity efficiency	784 enrolled pre-schoolers: capacity for serving 1,005 = 0.78	0.80	Neither satisfactory nor dissatisfactory

deficiency was equal to the number of students served by a single teaching team in the program. The program was new, and there was an opportunity to improve future enrollments. The program, after all, still served 784 preschoolers. The leaders concluded that goal effectiveness was satisfactory for the short term and that the target would have to be modified in the next phase of the program. Goal-effectiveness diagnosis was useful in setting the program's standards and objectives. One program manager observed that they came to appreciate the significance of being as operational as they could about selecting and specifying program objectives. He said the program administrators realized that if they got too general and broad there was no way they could link the results to the planning.

Potency-effectiveness diagnosis. In estimating the need for the Head Start form of preschool education, the program managers came to appreciate the importance of distinguishing low-income segments, or specifying potential target adopters, including low-income whites, blacks, Hispanics, and American Indians. The highest poverty rate was experienced by the American Indians, as many as 40 percent of whom were poor in Los Angeles. Adopter segmentation would also have identified the working poor and the nonworking poor, as well as big families and small families. The program managers eventually asked themselves, Whose need should we serve first? The neediest of the poor households or those at the margin who are "easier to manage" and, therefore, who have a better chance of "succeeding"? The managers concluded that the size of the potential population of target adopters depended on the definition and measurement of the poor. If the measures of the U.S. Social Security Administration were used, all families with annual incomes below $8,400 would have been included in the program, or 13 percent of the population of Los Angeles. However, if the measures of the U.S. Bureau of Labor Statistics were used, the target-adopter population would have been 25 percent because the bureau's poverty line was an annual income of $14,200.[5]

Realized-efficiency diagnosis. A diagnosis of the data for measuring the program's realized-efficiency index indicated that a special cost-accounting system was needed that would capture the program's costs relative to alternative spending decisions. For example, fixed expenditures, such as electricity and rent, were incurred that were not related to the number of preschoolers served. Some expenditures pertained to an extraneous segment of target adopters, such as the parents of the preschoolers. Some expenditures, such as accountant's fees and training costs, did not relate to the adoption objectives.

Capacity-efficiency diagnosis. In the program-control diagnosis, managers discovered that it was important to define carefully the program's "potential capacity" to generate the desired performance. For example, the potential capacity of the head teachers is not equivalent to the number of head teachers who potentially are available for teaching at the development centers. It is an absolute supply concept. What was needed was an effective concept of supply equivalent to the idea of effective demand. The managers realized they could count only those potential head teachers who were qualified and available. When they adjusted for this change, they found that the capacity-efficiency index value was closer to the designated level.

Given the several performance-control devices, which should social marketers apply? They should choose the tools that are most useful in helping them bring the performance up to the program's objectives and in furnishing insights on improving all aspects of the program's activities.

PERFORMER-CONTROL TOOLS

In addressing the management-control issue, Drucker asserted that the "ultimate control of the organization . . . lies in its people decisions." He observed that "even the most powerful 'instrument board,' complete with computers, operations research, and simulation, is secondary to the invisible, qualitative control of any human organization, its systems of rewards and punishments, of values and taboos."[6] Tools for controlling performers or the staff, therefore, are a powerful system for controlling a social marketing campaign. Rewards and punishments are tools to *motivate* performers, and values and taboos are leadership tools for controlling performers.

Motivation

The motivation of performers can be influenced and controlled in two ways: with behavior modification and with goal setting. The latter depends on a performer's self-control; the former on external controls that affect him or her.

Shaping a performer's motivation with a behavior modification program relies on the use of positive reinforcements. The first principle is that positive reinforcers are more lasting motivators than are negative reinforcers, although the latter can be effective in stopping undesirable behavior. A second principle is that whatever the reinforcer (a reward or a punishment), the closer it follows the target behavior, the more likely it is to be effective.

Industrial organizations that apply these principles have reported impressive results in increased productivity, cost savings, and improved services. Table 18–2 presents a list of these organizations, together with a brief description of their behavior modification programs and the results that have been obtained. Although critics of these programs have sounded an alarm over their indiscriminate application, these examples are useful lessons for social marketers.

A goal-setting program defines a goal that an individual is trying to accomplish.[7] The basic concept is that conscious, tough, and specific goals are more effective motivators than are implicit, easy-to-achieve, and generalized goals. Staff who understand clearly and are challenged by what a social program seeks will be more motivated and productive than will those who are merely told to do "what you're supposed to do" and to "do your best."

Goal setting has to reflect the needs of the performer or staff and realistic outcomes to provide a foundation for effective behavioral reinforcement. It may be regarded as a version of behavior modification. Szilegyi and Wallace[8] differentiated the two:

1. Because of their timing requirements, behavioral modification programs are immediately implementable and show immediate results. In contrast, goal-setting programs focus on overall performance relative to performance standards; therefore, they take longer to implement and their results are not seen immediately.

2. Goal-setting programs emphasize the establishment of goals, while behavior modification programs focus on reinforcers and the contingencies of behavioral reinforcement.

3. Goal-setting programs consider the performer's needs as being important and basic factors to deal with. Behavior modification programs are oriented to measurable objectives and ignore such less-measurable factors as human needs. When social marketers are seeking immediate control over performers, behavior modification is more effective. However, the goal-setting approach is likely to bring about more lasting control.

Leadership

According to studies of the accounts of business and government leaders, "the core problem for leaders in organizations involves getting others to do what is necessary to accomplish the organization's goals."[9] Therefore, leadership is critical to management control, since it is responsible for ensuring that an organization's goals are being achieved. Social marketers are well advised to incorporate the following leadership rules into their planning:

- Effective leadership is grounded in specific tasks and objectives. The more routine a subordinate's tasks, the greater the need for the leader to exercise tight control, be explicit about the requirements of the tasks, and standardize the performance of the tasks. The more stressful a subordinate's tasks, the greater the need for a leader to show concern and sensitivity.
- A leader's expertise is a factor in controlling the program. Specifically, the greater the expertise, the greater the effectiveness of the control tools.
- The attitudes and needs of the staff affect control. The greater a subordinate's need for independence and the higher his or her ability and intrinsic motivation, the less appropriate is tight control. The more routine the work and the less threatened staff feel in performing it, the greater the need for leaders to focus on the tasks and on concern and sensitivity to the staff's needs.
- A leader's influence with superiors also has to be considered. Specifically, the greater the leader's influence, the less the need to share control with subordinates. Leaders who are authoritative and firm in dealing with subordinates tend to be highly effective.

TABLE 18-2 Behavior Modification Programs in Selected Industrial Organizations

Organization	Type of Employee	Specific Program Goals	Reinforcers	Results
Emery Air Freight (1969–76)	Cross section of total work force (500 out of 2,800)	1. Increase productivity 2. Improve service quality	Frequent use of praise and recognition	1. Estimated savings of $3 million over 3 years 2. Attainment of performance goals increased from 30 percent to 95 percent of the time
Michigan Bell: Maintenance Service (1974–76)	Supervisors, mechanics, and maintenance workers (200 out of 5,500)	1. Improve productivity 2. Improve quality 3. Improve safety 4. Improve customer relations	Daily, weekly, and quarterly self- and supervisory feedback	1. Improved costs and efficiency 2. Improved service quality and safety 3. No change in absenteeism, but a decrease in pay satisfaction

General Electric (1973–76)	Employees at all levels (1,000)	1. Increase productivity 2. Decrease turnover and absenteeism 3. Approve timing 4. Meet EEOC objectives	Frequent use of praise, feedback, and other reinforcers	1. Increased productivity 2. Decreased direct labor costs 3. Improved training of minority workers
B. F. Goodrich Chemicals (1972–76)	Manufacturing workers at all levels (100 out of 420)	1. Increase productivity 2. Improved meeting of scheduled deadlines	1. Weekly use of praise and recognition 2. Freedom to choose one's work activity	Production increased 300 percent

SOURCE: Andrew W. Szilagyi and Marc J. Wallace, *Organizational Behavior and Performance*, 3rd ed. (Glenview, Ill.: Scott, Foresman & Co.,' 1987), Exhibit 5–9, p. 120. First printed in W. Clay Hamner and Ellen P. Hamner, "Behavior Modification on the Bottom Line," *Organization Dynamics*, Spring 1976, © 1976. Reprinted by permission of the publisher, American Management Association, New York. All rights reserved.

- Another factor to consider is the need for the staff's commitment to a decision. The more the staff are unconcerned about or unaffected by decisions involving activities and tasks, the less control should be shared with them. The greater the need to involve staff in decisions by virtue of their knowledge and commitment, the greater should be the sharing of control and influence with them.
- The shorter the time available for doing or completing an activity, the more dominant and controlling a leadership style should be.
- Some staff roles require intensive training and development. The greater the need for staff development, the less controlling a leadership style should be.

The reader will notice that this list of rules contains some incompatible or contradictory advice. For example, imagine the director of the Head Start program in Los Angeles applying these rules. Table 18–3 summarizes the possible outcomes. Five of the aforementioned rules called for a leader to take firm control and to share it, and two rules advised the opposite. Given the conflicting rules, how should a campaign leader behave in terms of the control function? Some theorists recommend that leadership be "situational."[10] This approach is reflected in the following rules:

- Determine if your usual leadership style fits the situations you are in.
- Some situations call for a different style from your usual one. Therefore, you may have to adjust your style when these situations arise.
- Sometimes a situation calls for a leadership style that you are not comfortable with. In such a case, you will have to acquire new skills and behaviors.
- You may want to get out of situations that demand a leadership style you cannot accept or are unwilling to learn.

In effect, social marketers are advised to recognize the situations that call for specific styles of leadership and choose the one that is appropriate.

TABLE 18-3 Analysis of a Hypothetical Leadership Style of the Director of the Los Angeles County Head Start Program

Question Asked by Leadership Proposition	Program Situation versus the Question Asked	Proposition's Prescribed Leadership Style
Are the subordinates' tasks routine?	No	Adopt loose controls, flexible requirements for tasks, and nonstandardized performance of tasks. Be participative.
Are the subordinates' tasks stressful?	Yes	Be a high person-concern leader.
Do you have much expertise?	Yes	Exercise greater control.
Do the subordinates need independence?	A whole lot	Avoid tight controls; be participative.
What is the subordinates' ability?	High	Avoid tight controls; be participative.
Is the subordinates' work challenging?	Yes	Be a high person-concern leader.
Do the subordinates feel threatened about survival?	No	Be a high task-concern leader.
What is your influence with your superiors?	Not so great	Share control with subordinates; be participative.
What level of power do you have over your subordinates?	Neither high nor low	Be a person-concern leader.
What is your relationship with your subordinates?	Good	Be a task-concern leader.
Are your subordinates affected/concerned by decisions about activities?	Yes	Share control; be participative.
Is your subordinates' support, cooperation, knowledge and commitment needed?	Yes	Share control; be participative.
Are there time pressures on the program activities?	Yes	Exercise tight control; be less participative.
Is the development of your subordinates important or unimportant?	Important	Be less controlling and more participative.

Case 18–1
Project Head Start: A Program in the U.S. War on Poverty

On May 18, 1965, the White House released the following announcement:

> President Johnson announced today that 2,500 Head Start projects which will reach about 530,000 children of the poor this summer in 11,000 Child Development Centers will be operated as part of the War on Poverty in every state in the Union. The program will cost $112 million.[11]

Initially, 1,676 Head Start projects were approved, involving 9,508 centers and 375,942 children at a total cost of $65,686,741. The centers were mandated to provide preschool training to prepare youngsters to enter regular school. The Head Start projects were designed to use the services of 41,000 professionals, including teachers, physicians, dentists, and nurses, and more than 47,000 low-income people would be employed. As many as 500,000 part-time volunteers would be enlisted. The projects also were directed at "assisting parents as well as the children . . . and treating health defects in the half-million children, including 100,000 with eye difficulties, 50,000 with partial deafness, 30,000 with nutritional deficiencies, and 75,000 lacking important immunizations."[12] Projects were to be operated in both rural and urban areas in 261 of the nation's 300 counties.

Background

Sociologists noted that poverty was historically one of the country's most "persistent and intractable problems," despite serious governmental efforts to reduce poverty since the New Deal pro-

SOURCES: George Brain, "The Early Planners," Julius B. Richmond, "The Early Administrators," J. B. Richmond, D. J. Stipek, and E. Zigler, "A Decade of Head Start," June Solnit Sale, "Implementation of a Head Start Preschool Education Program," and E. Zigler and J. Valentine, "Speeches by Lyndon B. Johnson," all in E. Zigler and J. Valentine, eds., *Project Head Start: A Legacy of the War on Poverty* (New York: Free Press, 1979); Michael Harrington, *The Other America: Poverty in the United States* (New York: Macmillan Co., 1962); and Robert A. Rosenbaum, *The Public Issues Handbook* (Westport, Conn.: Greenwood Press, 1983), pp. 303–315.

grams of the 1930s.[13] Estimates of the number of poor people from 1940 to 1970 are as follows:

Year	In Millions of People	As a Percentage of the Total Population
1940	45.0	33.3
1960	39.9	22.2
1970	25.4	12.6

A major study of poverty, entitled *The Other America,* shocked Americans into recognizing the depth of the problem.[14] This recognition led to the establishment of antipoverty programs by the Kennedy administration in the early 1960s. In the Kennedy years, the attack on poverty was modest. President Johnson increased and accelerated these programs, winning approval of Congress for the Economic Opportunity Act (1964), which created a new governmental agency, the Office of Economic Opportunity (OEO).

The Head Start program grew out of OEO's mandate. The idea of Head Start came from a recognition of the need to bring together local and national resources targeted to education.

Mission, Objectives, and Beneficiaries

Project Head Start's mission was depicted in a planning report that identified deficient early childhood development as a root cause of poverty.

> There is considerable evidence that the early years of childhood are the most critical point in the poverty cycle. . . . For the child of poverty there are clearly observable deficiencies in the processes which lay the foundation for a pattern of failure—and thus a pattern of poverty—throughout the child's entire life . . . . There is adequate evidence to support the view that special programs can be devised for these [children] which will improve both the child's opportunities and achievements.[15]

The project's planners defined program objectives that would affect seven areas of child development:

1. Improving a child's physical health and abilities.
2. Fostering emotional and social development by encouraging self-confidence, spontaneity, curiosity, and self-discipline.

3. Improving a child's mental processes and skills.

4. Establishing patterns and expectations of success for the child that will create a climate of confidence for future learning.

5. Increasing a child's capacity to relate positively to family members and others and strengthening the family's ability to relate positively to the child.

6. Developing in children and their families a responsible attitude toward society.

7. Increasing the sense of dignity and self-worth within children and their families.[16]

The project's planners recognize they were not dealing with a uniform population of children and families. They viewed the target-adopted population as consisting of "a variety of subpopulations differing in age, ethnic origin, family stability, degree of socio-cultural impoverishment, physical health, and other dimensions."[17]

Components of the Program

Head Start planners conceptualized the project as having five components: (1) health, (2) education, (3) parental involvement, (4) nutrition, and (5) social and psychological services. The health component included the provision of "medical examinations, including visual acuity and hearing tests, dental examinations, and immunizations" and the wherewithal to correct the health problems.[18] The education component specified a teacher-student ratio of one teacher with two aides to each group of 15 children, or a 1:5 ratio. This ratio was designed to enable teachers to offer special attention to individual problems and innovative teaching methods tailored to the needs of individual children.

The goal of the parental-involvement component was to get parents to participate in the project. Parents could serve as aides to teachers, nurses, and social workers; cooks; clerks; storytellers; or recreational supervisors. Classes were provided in home economics and in child-rearing practices. The nutrition component was carried out by providing at least one hot meal and one snack each day for the children. The social and psychological services component set up a referral service, psychologists and social workers would identify cases that required counseling or participation in mental health clinic programs. Numerous changes in these components were made over the course of the program.[19] A summary of these program changes is contained in Table 18–A.

Implementation of the Program

The implementation of the program in Los Angeles County, California, illustrates the scope of the implementation issues. The project's education component was the focus.[20] The following account was developed by the administrator of the Los Angeles Center for Early Education.

Planning Programming Activities: early April to May 1965

1. Defined the program's objectives—a focus on child development or a focus on preparation for later schooling.
2. Begin recruitment of teachers, assistant teachers, teachers' aides, and suitable sites for 800 children. Formed a support group to provide educational and art materials for the child development center.

Recruitment of Teachers: May 1965

1. Developed job descriptions and performance standards for teachers.
2. Conducted interviews and hired 64 teachers.

Teacher Training: June 1965

1. Conducted a 6-day training program for 75 teachers, led by scholars, educators, parents, and community representatives.

Finding Sites for Child Development Centers: May to June 1965

1. Identified and selected sites throughout Los Angeles County, consisting of churches, schools, parks, housing projects, community recreational centers, settlement houses, and nursery schools.
2. Won approvals of sites from local and state agencies.

Summer Program Start-up: June to August 1965

1. Staff worked with parents and people in the community for the start-up, with a major emphasis on language and cultural differences.

2. Head teachers initiated home visits.

3. Conducted field trips and outings for the children to broaden their experiences.

4. Forced to close the centers for a few days because of the eruption of race riots in the Watts neighborhood of Los Angeles and the imposition of curfews by the police.

TABLE 18–A Summary of Project Head Start
and Related Programs

Period and Program	Description
1965–present: Summer Head Start	Comprehensive summer program to include nutritional, health, social, educational, and mental health services for poor preschool children.
1966–present: Full-year Head Start	Offered Head Start services as a year-round program.
1967–present: Follow Through	An Office of Education-administered program extending Head Start services to Head Start children when entering kindergarten and elementary school.
1967–present: Parent and Child Centers	Demonstration program for families with children up to age 3, offering Head Start-type services to the children and the entire family.
1969: Head Start and Follow Through Planned Variations	A program providing Head Start centers with the choice of an educational curriculum that would best meet the needs of the children and community.
1969: Head Start Supplementary Training Program	A program giving aid to parents of Head Start children to pursue higher education degrees.
1971–74: Health Start	Demonstration program providing medical and dental services and health education to Head Start children and other children from low-income families.

Period and Program	Description
1972–present: Head Start Services to Handicapped Children	A program carrying out the 1972 Congressional mandate requiring at least 10 percent of Head Start enrollees to be handicapped children.
1972–present: Child Development Associate Program	Training program for workers in Head Start and day care centers to provide professional credentials in the child care field.
1972–75: Home Start	A three-year demonstration program providing Head Start health and educational services to children and parents in their homes.
1972–present: Education for Parenthood Program	A program sponsored by the Office of Child Development and the Office of Education to prepare teenagers for parenthood through working with young children in Head Start and other centers.
1973–present: Child and Family Resource Program	A program using Head Start centers as a base for community services to families with children from birth through age 8 and prenatal services for pregnant women.
1973–present: Head Start Improvement and Innovation Program	An evaluation and improvement program for local Head Start programs aimed also at encouraging the development of programs more responsive to local community needs.
1974–76: Head Start collaboration with the Medicaid Early and Periodic Screening, Diagnosis, and Treatment Program	A joint program with the Social and Rehabilitation Service to make early and periodic screening, diagnosis, and treatment services available to Medicaid-eligible Head Start and non-Head Start children.
1974–present: Project Developmental Continuity	Cooperative program with the public school systems to assure greater continuity of child development services for Head Start children as they move from preschool to elementary school.

SOURCE: Adapted with permission of The Free Press, a Division of Macmillan, Inc., from *Project Head Start: A Legacy of the War on Poverty*, Edward Zigler and Jeanette Valentine, Editors. Copyright © 1979 by The Free Press.

19

◆

Evaluating
Social Marketing
Programs

The final stage of managing a social marketing campaign involves evaluation. Two issues are foremost: (1) Has the campaign brought about the changes intended and have other factors led to change? (2) Has it brought about changes that are desirable from a societal and ethical point of view, employing the right means to achieve the desired ends? Although these evaluations are framed from a postimplementation viewpoint, social marketers have to be concerned with them not only after implementation but from the beginning of the campaign, in its planning phase, and throughout the campaign.

The first issue, impact evaluation, is relatively easy to deal with. In fact, support organizations, such as donors, require evaluation studies. The idea that social marketing campaigns also have to incorporate ethical questions and pursue ethical evaluations is a newer concept. There are two compelling reasons for ethical concern. First, to command respect, a profession must acknowledge the need for responsibility, discipline, and accountability. Second, with regard to the social marketing profession, the acknowledgment of ethical concerns is humanizing, obligating marketers to work on behalf of their clients' or adopters' long-term well-being and satisfaction.[1]

IMPACT EVALUATION

In evaluating the impact of a social marketing campaign or program, the task is to assess whether and how social marketing brought about the observable outcomes. In other words, evaluation research looks at causal links. Suchman identified several components of impact evaluation:[2]

1. A campaign or program must demonstrate performance. It must be established that target clients and adopters actually received the intended social product.
2. The program must demonstrate the effectiveness of its performance. This component directly examines causal links. It will determine whether statistically significant effects were obtained, and whether these effects are clearly traceable to the program.
3. The program must also demonstrate the significance of its performance—its outcomes, or targeted effects, from a societal point of view.
4. The program must demonstrate efficiency, whether its benefits outweigh the costs and whether the outcomes reflected an efficient utilization of the available resources.
5. The program must determine the social and psychological processes that led it to obtain its effects.
6. The program must demonstrate its value.

Several of these criteria have already been covered or will be covered in a subsequent section. Therefore, here, the focus will be on evaluation tasks 2 and 5.

Cause-Effect Evaluation

Two basic steps underlie cause-effect evaluation: identifying a program's intended effect or effects and designing and implementing cause-effect evaluation research.

Identifying Intended Effects

This first step may sound easy. After all, the intended effects should be found in a program's objectives. However, many social change campaigns describe their objectives exclusively in qualitative terms, failing to operationalize such effects so they are measurable and researchable.

Consider the case of the Sesame Street Project—education of preschoolers by way of television—described in Case 19-1. Sesame Street's stated objective is "to promote the intellectual and cultural growth of preschoolers, particularly disadvantaged preschoolers."[3] Thus, there are three sets of target effects to operationalize:

1. intellectual and cultural growth effects;
2. intellectual and cultural growth effects on *all* preschoolers;
3. intellectual and cultural growth effects on *disadvantaged preschoolers.*

Four extensive impact-evaluation studies were performed on the Sesame Street Project.[4] These studies, however, had difficulty operationalizing the aforementioned effects. Intellectual growth can be operationalized as "learning scores." The issue arose, however, whether to employ "absolute" scores or "comparative" scores (a comparison of the scores between high-income and low-income preschoolers, the gap in which was a principal target to be closed). Furthermore, none of the four evaluation studies incorporated a measure of cultural growth; it was merely assumed that increases in intellectual growth would carry over to cultural growth.

Using learning scores to measure the intellectual growth of all preschoolers would seem relatively easy to do. Yet, given the limited evaluation resources and the fact that public television is not available everywhere in the United States, "all" could not mean 100 percent of the potential preschoolers. However, defining "all" as the number of preschoolers that the project's resources can reach limits "all" to a considerably fewer number of potential preschoolers.

The third effect, the intellectual and cultural growth of disadvantaged preschoolers, poses two measurement problems. The first is whether to consider the learning scores of disadvantaged preschoolers as absolute or comparative scores. When the Sesame Street project referred to "disadvantaged preschoolers" in its objectives, it did so in the context of the "national problem of a widening academic achievement gap" between high-income and low-income preschool children. Narrowing this gap, therefore, was an intended effect of the project and yielded a comparative learning score.

Settling on the measure of a comparative score, however, raises an additional problem. As an objective, "narrowing the gap in academic achievement" contradicts another objective of the project, namely, the intellectual growth of all preschoolers. Program objectives, as has been discussed, must be specific, quantifiable, and attainable. The Sesame Street project's two objectives, of narrowing the gap in the academic achievement of disadvantaged and advantaged preschoolers and of raising the achievement of all preschoolers are incompatible. In fact, one evaluation study found "an inevitable negative relationship between the . . . means for stimulating the growth of all children and narrowing the academic achievement gap."[5] A lesson to be drawn is that the more the program objectives are explicit, the easier it is to discern inconsistent objectives.

Cause-Effect Evaluation Research

Once it is agreed how a program's intended effects should be measured, social marketers can move to determine the extent to which a program and its components "caused" the intended effect and whether other plausible causes may have led to the outcome. There are three basic types of cause-effect evaluation research: experimental methods, quasi-experimental methods, and ex post facto methods. Table 19–1 describes and compares the three. Tables 19–2 through 19–4 summarize the questions that social marketers will ask of evaluation research undertaken by any one of the three methods. At this point, two concepts come into play: randomization in determining the research design and the appropriate method of analysis to apply to the data.

Randomization. To obtain an accurate cause-effect evaluation of large-scale programs and campaigns, Campbell and Boruch argued, a randomization-based design of both the program and the evaluation research is necessary.[6] Randomization calls for randomly assigning prospective target adopters to different "treatment" groups, representing different configurations or manipulations of the program variables (elements of the social marketing mix). It offers the advantage of rendering the different treatment groups equivalent to one another on most background variables. When background variables, such as age, economic status, sex,

TABLE 19-1 The Three Kinds of Cause-Effect Evaluation Research Methods

Comparison Points	Experimental Methods	Quasi-Experimental Methods	Ex Post Facto Methods
1. Control over the manipulation of the independent variables	Complete	Partial	Least/none
2. Control over the random assignment of respondents to independent variables (treatment conditions)	Complete	Incomplete; assignment to levels (or treatment conditions) not at random	None: self-selection into levels
3. Control over the extraneous variables	In the laboratory experiment, almost complete; in the field experiment, incomplete.	Almost none	None
4. Control over when and how the dependent variable or variables are measured	Complete	Partial	Least

TABLE 19-2 Questions to Ask When Using the Experimental Research Methods

1. Are the methods for selecting respondents (or subjects) clearly specified? If random selection is not to be used, are the sample, accessible population, and target-adopter population sufficiently described so the user of the research can judge to what population the results can be generalized?

2. Are the methods for assigning subjects to levels of the social marketing mix (treatment conditions) well described so the user of the research can judge whether the methods are random or, if not, how serious the problem of nonequivalence of the initial groups is?

3. Are the levels of the social marketing or treatment conditions, adequately described so another researcher can replicate the study? Does the description include the setting, tasks, service deliverers, and procedures and operations of the study itself?

4. Is the social marketing mix, or treatment conditions, of sufficient intensity and duration that an effect can reasonably be expected? Is the size of the sample large enough to reveal statistically significant effects?

5. Is there likely to be an attrition of respondents/subjects from the study? If so, what plans have been made to control for the effects of the resulting differential withdrawal from different groups?

6. Is it likely that the independent variable will be diffused to the untreated or placebo groups?

7. What control is in place over whether the independent variable will actually be implemented as the researcher has specified?

8. Is the dependent variable being reliably and validly measured? Are threats to instrumentation being controlled? Are different measures of the dependent variable being used and are measurements being taken at any time other than immediately after the end of the treatment period?

9. Are demand characteristics, novelty, disruption, Hawthorne, experimenter, placebo, and task effects, and pretest sensitization being controlled or adequately described so the user of the research can judge the limitations on generalizability?

SOURCE: M. L. Smith and G. V. Glass, *Research and Evaluation in Education and the Social Sciences,* © 1987, p. 513. Adapted by permission of Prentice-Hall, Inc., Englewood Cliffs, NJ. Chapter 6 of this reference also provides details of the threats to validity cited in Item 9 of this table.

Table 19-3 Questions to Ask When Using Quasi-
Experimental Methods

---

1. Are the methods for selecting the respondents or subjects clearly described? Are the sample, accessible population, and target population fully described so the user of the research can judge to what population the findings will apply?

2. For nonequivalent comparison-group designs, are the methods of assigning respondents to the levels of the social marketing mix (treatment conditions) fully described? Are enough characteristics of the respondents' identified so the user of the research can judge to what extent the groups are nonequivalent? Are matching or statistical-adjustment procedures described and justified?

3. For interrupted time-series designs, are sufficient pretreatment measures being taken to ensure a stable baseline of the dependent variable?

4. For regression-discontinuity designs, are the assumptions of the design met? For example, is the relationship between pretest and criterion variables linear? Is the cut-off selection procedure compromised in any way?

5. Are the levels of the social marketing or treatment conditions, including characteristics of setting, tasks, service deliverers, and procedures, adequately described, so other people can thoroughly understand how to apply the social marketing mix or treatment in their own setting?

6. Is the social marketing mix, or treatment conditions, of sufficient intensity and duration that an effect is reasonable to expect? Is the social marketing mix or treatment actually going to be implemented as specified? Is the size of the sample large enough?

7. How is attrition going to be controlled?

8. Is a good measure of the dependent variable available? How are threats to instrumentation being controlled?

9. Are the limitations in the design and its execution acknowledged and described for the user of the research to consider in subsequent uses of the research findings?

SOURCE: M. L. Smith and G. V. Glass (1987), *Research and Evaluation in Education and the Social Sciences,* © 1987, p. 175. Adapted by permission of Prentice-Hall, Inc., Englewood Cliffs, NJ. Chapter 7 of this reference also provides details of the three quasi-experimental designs cited in Items 2, 3, and 4 of this table.

TABLE 19-4 Questions to Ask When Using the Causal-
Comparative or Ex Post Facto Research Methods

1. Is the sampling procedure adequate for establishing generalizability? Are the individuals and their environment sufficiently described so the user of the research can judge to what population and settings the research findings will apply?
2. In between-groups designs, is the basis for group membership well justified? Are the groups internally homogeneous?
3. If matching is to be done, is regression a threat to the finding's internal validity? How closely are the groups being matched? Are appropriate statistics being chosen to depict the difference among groups?
4. In path models, is the theory presented before the analysis, or is it to be made post hoc and based on the data? Is the theory sufficiently complete, or are influential variables not specified in it? Are the variables being measured with high levels of reliability?
5. In archival time-series designs, what controls over threats to internal validity from history, maturation, and attrition does the design provide? Is there a likelihood of a threat to instrumentation when a change in the dependent variable's measurement is coming from a reaction to the social marketing program or intervention? Are the form, quantity, and standardization of the archival records sufficient and compatible with the purposes of the study?
6. For all three designs, are the reliability and validity of the measurement adequate?
7. How is the planned analysis going to handle the plausible explanation of results from extraneous variables? How does it plan to avoid the correlation-causation fallacy or the post hoc fallacy?
8. Are the limitations in the design and analysis of the study properly acknowledged to guard against the overgeneralization and overinterpretation of results?

SOURCE: M. L. Smith and G. V. Glass, *Research and Evaluation in Education and the Social Sciences*, © 1987, p. 194. Adapted by permission of Prentice Hall, Inc., Englewood Cliffs, NJ. Chapter 8 of this reference also provides details of the three ex post facto designs cited in items 2, 4, and 5 of this table.

and education, are not randomized, they give rise to alternative plausible hypotheses to explain the observed effects. However, in rendering the different groups uniform on program variables, randomization permits a relatively clear assignment of cause and effect.

Figure 19-1 illustrates how randomization is accomplished in terms of age, a background variable. When a large sample of

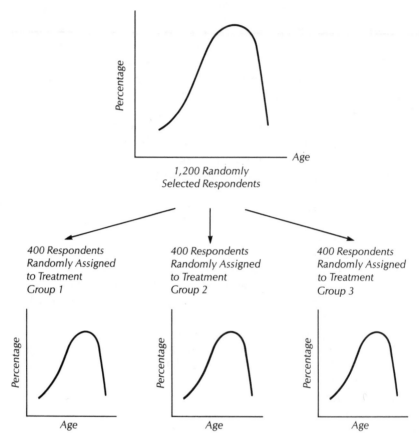

FIGURE 19-1 The *Ceteris Paribus* Effect of Randomization on the Background Variable of Age

SOURCE: Eduardo L. Roberto, *Applied Marketing Research* (Metro Manila: Ateneo de Manila University Press, 1987), Figure 4-2, p. 101.

1,200 respondents is randomly drawn from the target-adopter population and then randomly assigned to, say, three different treatment groups (for example, two experimental groups and a control group), the resulting three subsamples are likely to be similar to the original 1,200 sample as well as to one another. Differences among subsamples on background variables such as age can be statistically tested. The results will normally show no statistically significant differences. With randomization, the results of testing different program effects are comparable, and one can infer a cause with a high degree of confidence.

Pertinent Applicable Data Analysis. When it is not feasible to incorporate randomization, then the task of rendering the different treatment groups equivalent on background variables is handled by the pertinent-data-analysis method. This method adjusts for preexisting differences so that remaining differences among groups on program effects can be clearly traced to the program. Because it is technical, the reader should refer to Rindskopf for further details.[7]

What do social marketers do when evaluation studies yield conflicting results on program outcomes, as happened with the data on Sesame Street and Project Head Start? Social marketers can do two things. First, they can determine which technique to favor, adopting the technique that offers the best approximation of the randomization effect. Second, they should take a long-term view, "to search for convergence over time."[8] If the results of many experiments over time converge, then social marketers can confidently say that a true average effect exists. If the variation in results persists, it may mean that the program will work under certain conditions but not under others. Then the task of social marketers and evaluation researchers is to identify those conditions and focus the program where it works.

Process Evaluation

Process evaluation extends cause-effect evaluation to determine two additional things:

1. How much did each element of the program contribute to the effects?
2. What is it in the situation and the behavior of target adopters that facilitated or hindered the obtained effects?

The first question probes whether the program process leading to the effects was shaped more by the distinctiveness of the social product, the program's communication efforts, the presentation of the social product's adoption costs, the social product's ready and convenient availability, adoption promotion, service delivery, or some combination of these elements. In other words, process evaluation treats each element in the social marketing mix discretely. The second question shifts the evaluator's attention to the target adopter's behavior and situational determinants. Cook et al.'s evaluation of the Sesame Street Project illustrates this shift.

Cook et al. found a set of facilitative influences operating on the target preschoolers in addition to the project's intended learning effects.[9] Preschoolers with higher learning scores (both absolute and comparative) learned more and learned faster because their parents encouraged them to discuss what they learned and watched the television programs. This process of discussing, however, occurred more often with high-income than with low-income families. The implications of these two evaluation findings are that (1) a major objective of the Sesame Street program should be to involve the parents of all preschoolers and (2) parental participation in low-income households should be given special emphasis.

Cook et al. also identified, but did not confirm, some possible hindering influences:

> In the context of stimulating the growth of all children, television at an early age might facilitate the passive acquisition of knowledge and might make the child less able to ask questions and discover answers for himself. Such an active questioning frame of mind might be particularly useful as our world becomes increasingly more complex.[10]

The emphasis on students' initiative also was a goal of Project Head Start. When Project Head Start came under heavy criticisms, one of its defenders stated frankly that although a "basic requirement for any social program is that its goals be explicitly stated and widely recognized throughout the life of the program" [this] has not been the case with Head Start, and its image has suffered as a result."[11] He went on to say that what "the creators of Head Start hoped to bring about [was] greater *social competence* (i.e., initiative) in disadvantaged children. By social competence, we meant an individual's everyday effectiveness in dealing with his environment."[12]

In process evaluation, analytical techniques and theories must be combined to uncover underlying causal variables and processes. Social marketers should become familiar with these techniques and theories or find expert sources of assistance.

ETHICAL EVALUATION

Ethical evaluation seeks to determine a program's ethical character. In doing so, social marketers must apply three different ethical criteria, which are implied in the ethical evaluation question, "Did the program ethically cause a right or desirable change in a right or desirable way?" The first criterion concerns the ethical consequence of a program's impact. The second criterion, "right change," refers to the rightness or desirability of the program's objectives, for example, the ethical character of the segmentation and targeting of target adopters. The third criterion, "the right way," refers to the ethical issue of selecting proper means to achieve the program's objectives (the means-end ethical issue).

Impact Ethics

Every social marketing program will produce changes and consequences that are unintended, or side effects of the intended effects. Social marketers will raise value questions about first-order and higher-order effects and then make a conscious choice about which values are priorities.

First-order Effects and Consequences

Kelman and Warwick provided an example of how to frame value questions regarding a program's direct consequences and how to make a conscious choice of values in the context of two contrasting policies on the control of population.[13] One is a "voluntarist" policy that promotes free contraceptive information and devices. The other is a "coercive" policy that denies families with "too many" children social benefits, such as subsidized maternity care, free education, and welfare.

The American Institute of Society, Ethics, and the Life Sciences studied these policy options in 1971 for the U.S. Commission on Population, Growth and the American Future. The basic values of freedom, justice, security and survival, and welfare were identified as constituting the core values for evaluating the ethical consequences of the two policies on population. The institute concluded that promoting free access to contraceptive information and methods enhances or at least maintains the values of freedom and general welfare. A reservation was noted, however: Uncontrolled population growth can . . . "jeopardize the general welfare if one group in society grows at a faster rate than others."[14] If families are denied social benefits because they are larger than the officially approved size, then an injustice will have been committed in ostracizing particular groups.

Given these conflicting values, what conclusions regarding evaluation can be drawn? Social marketers have to weigh diverse and often conflicting values. To illustrate this fact, consider the Sesame Street Project again. Here the values to weigh were those of academic achievement and intellectual and cultural growth in children. In the 1960s and early 1970s, American social critics questioned the inherent worth of these values. They asked, Were these ultimate values or instrumental values for achieving other goods or values? Cook et al., for example, pointed out that parents and teachers often regard a child's academic achievement and intellectual growth ''merely as means to gaining better jobs and economic security, as means of raising one's social status by virtue of a diploma or a degree, or as means of pleasing parents.''[15] In this analysis, the value priority of end-values (ultimate values) has to be weighed against the priority of instrumental values, such as jobs, security, and achieving high social status. Or are the latter values the ultimate values, which should be treated on an equal basis with the Sesame Street project's explicit values of academic achievement and intellectual growth?

In this situation, the social marketer's responsibility is to examine carefully the following issues:

1. Do the objectives of the social marketing program or social change campaign serve the values that it intends to serve and achieve?

2. Are these values end-values (intrinsically meritorious in themselves) or instrumental values (lower-order values that are the means to achieve the end- or ultimate value)?

3. Is there a conflict of values that is built into the very program and its objectives?

The goal of analyzing values in the context of evaluation is to determine whether a program is rooted in ethical criteria, whether the values being served are desirable ones, and if a conflict in values arises, which values should be given priority in the program.

Unintended Consequences

What about the side effects and unintended consequences of a program? Kelman and Warwick observed that side effects and unintended consequences are criteria to be considered in an evaluation.[16] The practical task for social marketers is to find some way to predict or anticipate these side-effects and consequences.

This can be done by taking a system's view of a program and treating the system being affected as a set of interrelated subsystems. Consider, for example, how a target adopter's values will be affected by a program. The often-heard objection to the use of incentives in family planning programs is a reflection of this issue. In Third-World countries, in particular, incentives that essentially pay couples to limit the size of their families may have the long-term consequence of encouraging a materialistic, "do-for-pay" value perspective.

Another consideration that affects target adopters is their aspirations and the means of achieving their aspirations. Many social change programs motivate adopters with high aspirations to effect the targeted change. This was the case, for example, in Project Head Start. After the summer project in Los Angeles was completed, one staff aide stated: "Charlie Brown was right: 'There is no heavier burden than a great potential'. . . . Great changes did not occur in neighborhoods, the schools did not change, parents still had to struggle to bring up their children in less than desirable housing situations, and low-income people remained unemployed or underemployed."[17] Yet this staff aide found one redeeming value: The lives of the few parents who volunteered their time to the project were changed and improved.

The Teacher Corps provides a dramatic example of what can happen when aspirations generated by a program far outstrip the means available to satisfy them. The Teacher Corps promoted an expectation that conventional school systems and colleges and universities would operate creatively and competently in the program. Teacher-interns looked forward to "more innovation and experimentation and, particularly, a community-centered curriculum . . . more oriented toward local low-income black pupils."[18] They wanted change, and they wanted to participate in it. In the course of their training, however, interns in one southern university found that about half the faculty had no experience with the poor and professors had little inclination to work effectively with the interns or lacked the know-how to do so.

Corwin found at the end of the program that many teacher-interns became pessimistic, disillusioned, and cynical; three-fourths expressed a lower level of commitment to teaching at the end of the program than they had expressed during the first month.[19] Nearly half were more alienated from schools, and more than half were alienated from the Teacher Corps.

Kelman and Warwick identified the reasons for these negative consequences. The raising of expectations and aspirations without providing the necessary supportive environment and resources can produce depressing frustration. When aspirations are not matched by attainment, "the net effect may be short-term enthusiasm followed by long-term depression. In fact, the experience of having been stimulated and then frustrated may lead to a lower probability of future action than existed before the intervention."[20] At a minimum, social marketers should ask, How acceptable is it, ethically, to raise aspirations without some reasonable assurance that the opportunities and resources for achieving them will be forthcoming.

Ethical Criteria for Selecting Target Adopters

The choice of a program's objectives will determine the choice of the target adopters. For example, when the Sesame Street Project decided that one of its objectives is to "narrow the academic achievement gap," it decided, in effect, that it must target low-income preschoolers. Poor children score lower on academic achievement tests than do children from higher economic classes when they start school. Each year of formal schooling increases this gap. This gap is at its narrowest at before children enter school. Therefore, the key is a preschool education project focused on economically disadvantaged preschoolers.

In another program, a feminist on the U.S. Commission on Civil Rights argued that in defining the population problem as a fertility-control problem, population planners must focus on the woman because it is "only she [who] can have babies. The highest ethical priority in any intervention dealing with fertility is to give women control over their own bodies and reproduction."[21] Again, the definition of the problem leads to the selection of the target group.

Ethical Considerations of Social Marketing Research

Ethical issues involving social marketing research typically involve the core values of justice and freedom. This is particularly the case when research methods entail some form of dissembling and deception or the withholding of information. An example is a social experiment that is set up to request a small donation from persons without telling them that they will be approached again for a larger donation. The researcher's aim is to test whether seeming to want a small donation opens persons to giving larger donations later.

Users of deceptive research procedures have long justified them by arguing that without such procedures, data are likely to be contaminated or distorted by respondents' awareness of what the research is trying to accomplish. Respondents may give answers they feel the researchers want or give socially acceptable responses. Respondents may also offer answers that aim deliberately to undermine the researchers' task. As Kelman observed:

> Deception violates the respect to which all fellow humans are entitled and the trust that is basic to all interpersonal relationships. Such violations are doubly disturbing since they contribute, in this age of mass society, to the already powerful tendencies to manufacture realities and manipulate populations. Furthermore, by undermining the basis of trust in the relationship between investigator and subject, deception makes it increasingly difficult for social scientists to carry out their work in the future.[22]

Should respondents be expected to give their consent to the release of information that is required for evaluating a program? Consent is obtained by informing respondents of the types of question they will be asked, the effort required in responding to the questions, and the use to which the data will be put. This full disclosure of the aims of a research program has elicited strong negative reactions from marketing researchers.[23] At a minimum, social marketing research should take into account these ethical issues.

Ethical Criteria in Determining a Social Marketing Mix

Since a social marketing mix represents the set of means that marketers select to achieve the objectives of a program, ethical criteria should inform the choices of the means of carrying out a social marketing program or campaign. Two programs with different sets of social marketing mixes will illustrate this type of ethical issue: the New Jersey Negative Income Tax Experiment[24] and the Preschooler Nutrition and Education Experiment in Cali, Colombia.[25] Table 19-5 summarizes the negative income tax program, and Table 19-6, the preschooler nutrition program.

TABLE 19-5 The Social Marketing Mix in the New Jersey Negative Income Tax Program

Elements of Social Marketing Mix		Treatment Groups[b]								
		1	2	3	4	5	6	7	8	9
Social Product Monthly cash payments determined by an income guarantee and a "tax" rate combination (percentage)[a]										
Guarantee	"Tax" Rate									
1. 50	30	x								
2. 50	50		x							
3. 75	30			x						
4. 75	50				x					
5. 75	70					x				
6. 100	50						x			
7. 100	70							x		
8. 125	50								x	
Direct Nonpersonal Communication (such as pamphlets)		x	x	x	x	x	x	x	x	
Direct Personal Communication (recruitment visit to explain social product and conditions for participation)		x	x	x	x	x	x	x	x	
Adoption Promotion 1. Cash payment income received is tax exempt		x	x	x	x	x	x	x	x	
2. Each monthly income report filed gets paid		x	x	x	x	x	x	x	x	

[a]The income guarantee is expressed as a percentage of the poverty level, and the tax rate is the reduction in payments exceeding the guaranteed level. The combination of these two determines the cash payment or cash-transfer amount that an individual or a family gets. For example, consider combination (or social product) 2. Suppose the income guarantee of 50 percent equals $3,000. Given the 50 percent tax rate, a person/family earning $4,000 would be taxed $2,000

These tables illustrate how different social marketing mixes raise ethical issues. Here, we will just examine the preschooler nutrition program. In August 1970, the program conducted a house-to-house canvass of some 7,500 households in the poor district of Union de Vivenda Popular in the Colombian city of Cali. The canvass sought to identify families whose children were born between June and November 1967. The canvassers ensured that qualified respondents were willing to participate and that the children involved in the study did not have serious neurological dysfunctions. They found 333 nutritionally deprived children who met these criteria. The children were placed into seven treatment groups. Groups 1 to 4 received the combination nutrition and education social marketing mix for different lengths of time. Groups 5 to 7 received only the nutrition component for various periods and received the educational component only in the fourth year of the program.

Children were assigned to the several treatment groups according to a "randomized block" design. This design divided the target district into 20 sectors. For each sector, it computed an index derived from the scores on mean height, weight, and per capita family income. The design then used the obtained index to rank the 20 sectors and randomly assigned each of the first 5 sectors to either groups 1-4 or 5-7. There were 13-19 children in a sector. The design repeated this random assignment process for the next 3 sets of 5 sectors. Then the program designers tested the 7 treat-

---

and would receive a cash transfer or payment of $1,000 ($2,000, which is what was left of the $4,000 after the tax plus $1,000 to raise the $2,000 to the $3,000 guaranteed level). This produces for the recipient a total income of $5,000.

The different combinations were given to people in 3 income strata. This constituted, in effect, 24 treatment groups. Target-adopter segment 9 is obviously the control group, also in 3 incomes strata and, therefore, in effect, 3 control groups.

[b]"x" means presence of the social marketing mix element. Measures of the effects of the social marketing mixes were defined as work effort or work response. These were operationalized as family earnings and hours worked. Family income was measured monthly through monthly income reports, while hours worked as measured from quarterly interviews.

SOURCES: H. Watts and A. Rees, eds., *Studies Relating to the Validity and Generalizablity of the Results: Part C of the Final Report of the New Jersey Graduated Work Incentive Experiment* (Madison: Institute for Research on Poverty, University of Wisconsin, 1974); and H. Watts and A. Rees, eds., *The New Jersey Income Maintenance Experiment*, vol. 2 (New York: Academic Press, 1978).

TABLE 19-6 The Social Marketing Mix in the Cali, Colombia, Preschool Nutrition and Education Program

Elements in the Social Marketing Mix	Treatment Groups[a]						
	1	2	3	4	5	6	7
Social Products							
1. Nutritional services (satisfying 75 percent of the recommended calorie and protein intake)	x	x	x	x	x	x	x
2. Educational services							
a. Developing cognitive processes, language, social abilities, & psychomotor skills	x	x	x	x			
b. Instructions on personal hygiene	x	x	x	x			
Distribution							
At school	x	x	x	x			
At home					x	x	x
Direct Personal Communication							
Periodic visits to make sure food was consumed, not sold					x	x	x
Service Delivery (four hours a day)							
Nutrition: Year 1	x	x	x	x	x	x	x
Year 2	x	x	x		x	x	x
Year 3	x	x			x	x	
Year 4	x				x		
Education: Year 1	x	x	x	x			
Year 2	x	x	x				
Year 3	x	x					
Year 4	x				x	x	x

[a] "x" means presence of the social marketing mix element. Measures of the social marketing mixes: (1) nutritional effects were in height and weight and (2) educational effects were by adapted versions of several well-known cognitive tests like the Wechsler Intelligence Scale For Children (WISC). These were taken before and at the end of each service delivery year plus midway through Year 3.

SOURCE: H. McKay, A. McKay, and L. Sinisterra, *Stimulation of Intellectual and Social Competence in Colombian Preschool Age Children Affected by the Multiple Deprivations of Depressed Urban Environments: Second Progress Report* (Cali, Colombia: Human Ecology Research Station, 1973).

ment groups for equivalence and found that randomized blocking yielded similar groups.

The New Jersey Negative Income Experiment Tax was similarly constituted, with eight treatment groups and one control group involving 1,374 lower-income households. Households were selected by random sampling of poverty tracts in 3 New Jersey communities—Trenton, Patterson-Passaic, and Jersey City—and 1 community in Pennsylvania—Scranton. The program design randomly assigned the families to 1 of the 8 treatment groups or the control group. However, before this random assignment, the design selected the families first for 3 income strata. Thus, the total number of effective groups (both treatment and control) was not 9 (8 treatment groups plus 1 control group) but 27 (8 treatment groups times 3 income strata plus 1 control group times 3 income strata). In any case, a test of the equivalence of the initial groups confirmed the similarity of all the groups.

The ethical issue raised by both cases is this: What right do the program designers have to treat people differently who had similar needs? The Colombian nutrition program did not inform the families which children would receive both nutrition and education and which would receive just nutrition. The program planners were conscious of the ethical values implicit in their decisions. The director of the New Jersey program, David N. Kershaw, justified the selection of people for that program as follows:

> Its virtues include simplicity of administration (it is a self-administered program which makes use of forms similar to those used by the Internal Revenue Service), equity (it is paid to all whose incomes fall below a prescribed level), dignity (there are no indiscriminate or compulsory "services" provided), and the creation of conditions conducive to individual initiative (the negative tax grant is not taken away from a recipient dollar for dollar as his earned income increases).[26]

But the values addressed were not the critical ones. The value of individual freedom received no mention in Kershaw's brief operational and ethical appraisal of the New Jersey program.[27]

How much was individual freedom disregarded? Kelman and Warwick specified that individuals are free when the following conditions hold:

1. The structure of the environment provides them with options for choice.
2. They are not coerced by others or forced by circumstances to elect only certain possibilities among those of which they are aware.
3. They are, in fact, aware of the options in the environment and possess knowledge about the characteristics and consequences of each. Though such knowledge may be less than complete, there must be enough to permit rational deliberation.
4. They are psychologically able to weigh the alternatives and their consequences. . . . [T]his means not only possessing information but being able to use it in coming to a decision.
5. Having weighed the relative merits of the alternatives, they can choose among them. . . . [There is no] deficiency of will [because] . . . a person who cannot pass from deliberation to choice must be considered less than free.
6. Having chosen an alternative, they are able to act on it . . . [because they have] knowledge about how to implement the choice, [no] anxiety about acting at all, or . . . confidence in their abilities.[28]

As more and more of these conditions are violated, the less free the person becomes. The elements of the social marketing mix in the New Jersey and the Cali programs failed the test of all six conditions. These programs make it clear that the demands of cause-effect impact evaluation can be at odds with the demands of ethical evaluation. In a later publication, Kershaw recognized the conflict over values: "There is often a direct conflict between ethics and experimental efficacy which creates a considerable strain on social experimenters." This concern led him to stress the need for setting up standards: "The characteristics of social experiments make the development and application of a set of ethical principles not only more difficult but, because of the large number of individuals simultaneously affected by a given decision in the experiment, in some ways even more compelling than the adoption of medical ethics has been."[29]

So what are social marketers to do? Kelman and Warwick made two suggestions:

1. Social-marketing-mix "manipulation would seem more acceptable to the extent that the people affected participate in

the process, are free to enter and leave the program, and find their range of choices broadened rather than narrowed.''

2. Social-marketing-mix "manipulation also seems more acceptable if the manipulators are not the primary beneficiaries of the manipulation, are reciprocally vulnerable in the situation, and are accountable to public agencies.''[30]

Ethics and Social Marketing

Like any profession, social marketing is bound by ethical rules, ethical criteria in its work, and ethical evaluation of its products and programs. Drucker referred to these rules as the "ethics of responsibility.''[31] The first ethical rule is, Do no harm.

Social marketers must regard themselves as being ethically responsible for all aspects of their social marketing efforts—determining the objectives of the program, segmenting target adopters, research, communications and promotion, distribution channels, and the design of the social marketing mix. We cannot overemphasize the importance of this responsibility, especially since an increasing number of social marketers are getting involved in the planning, implementation, control, and evaluation of diverse social change programs and campaigns in many countries. It will be a sad and unfortunate event if social marketing programs are judged to have neglected ethical criteria and rules.

CASE 19-1
The 'Sesame Street' Television Project

Social Marketing Environment

In 1967, during the decade of the War on Poverty in the United States, Joan Ganz Cooney gained insight into the national poverty problem in connection with her work in television. She had been a public affairs producer for a New York City television station. She believed that the key to breaking the "vicious cycle of poverty" was the lack of decent education among poor people.

SOURCE: Thomas D. Cook, et al., *"Sesame Street" Revisited* (New York: Russell Sage Foundation, 1975), chaps. 1–3, 5. All quotations are from this source.

The world is fast changing and complex. To survive, not only must young people have intellectual capacities to solve problems, but these capacities have to keep pace with the changes.

Cooney concluded that an antipoverty effort must seek to raise the intellectual capabilities and educational achievement of poor people. Children, she determined, should be the principal targets of reform. But the question arose, Which poor children should be targeted?

At that time, two important books were published: J. McV. Hunt's *Intelligence and Experience* and Benjamin Bloom's *Stability and Change in Human Characteristics*. These books concluded that intellectual capacity develops most and fastest during a child's first few years and that intellectual development can be influenced by envionmental factors.

As a result of these studies, Cooney narrowed the problem to that of building sound and effective preschool education. In her grant proposal, she noted that to create new forms of preschool education that allow or encourage preschoolers to spend their day merely in play activities without formal instruction is the equivalent of an "educational wasteland." Cooney called for a new experiment in preschool education utilizing television. Thus, the "Sesame Street" project was born.

Objectives and Target Adopters

Cooney initially defined the objectives as follows: "The general aim is to promote the intellectual and cultural growth of pre-schoolers, particularly disadvantaged preschoolers." At a later stage, the target adopters were broadened to all preschoolers but with an emphasis on disadvantaged and low-income preschool-ers. Besides intellectual development, a second key objective was to foster awareness of cultural and ethnic-group differences.

Social Marketing Mix

As planned and implemented, the "Sesame Street" project sought a social marketing mix that consisted of (1) pretesting the preschool educational product, (2) selecting effective distribution, and (3) direct personal communication.

The social product. In March 1968, Cooney created a nonprofit organization, the Children's Television Workshop (CTW), to produce the "Sesame Street" television series. Each one-hour show is fast moving and action packed. The actors and actresses, both people and puppets, skillfully interact to provide instruction in the alphabet, arithmetic, body parts, and problem solving. Each show is self-contained, so a child does not have to watch every show in a particular sequence.

The series portrays actions that take place in an inner-city ghetto among low-income people. Most of the adult actors and many of the children in the shows were black Americans. Other actors are carefully chosen to represent diverse social and cultural groups in the United States. The intent of their roles and friendly interactions is to foster "cultural awareness."

In developing the design of the social product, CTW planners devoted 18 months to pretesting each television show before it was broadcast. The test respondents were the target adopters—economically disadvantaged children—and the pretest material was a portion of a show. The product design that was tested was the attention-holding qualities of the show and the learning effects achieved. Only those shows that passed these two indicators of effectiveness were incorporated into the television series; those that failed were either modified or rejected.

Product distribution. The corporation for Public Broadcasting (CPB, the U.S. public television network) distributed the "Sesame Street" series. However, the series could not be made available to all households with television sets because at that time, public television reached areas in which only 75 percent of Americans lived. CPB broadcast the series every school day for one hour at times when children could view it either at home or at nursery school. In planning the distribution, CTW anticipated that children would miss some of the shows in the series; therefore, each show would be broadcast several times during a season.

After a successful first year of operation, CTW and CPB decided to rebroadcast the weekday shows on Saturdays to ensure that children had yet another day to view them. In the second year, CPB aired the series once in the morning and once in the afternoon each school day. In subsequent years, the broadcasts were even more frequent. During 1972, for example, children in Chicago could watch the shows four times a day, Monday through Saturday, and then twice on Sunday. By this time, "Sesame

Street'' had established its reputation as a popular means of distributing preschool education.

Personal communication. Educational Testing Service (ETS), the evaluators of ''Sesame Street,'' referred to the project's personal communication-component as an ''encouragement-to-view treatment.'' Personal communication consisted of home visits to randomly selected households before the 1970 and 1971 viewing seasons. These home visits included promotional material, such as buttons, balloons, magazines, and other children's souvenirs. During a visit, the program communicator impressed on parents and children the importance of viewing the Sesame Street shows. During the 1971 season, these efforts consisted of monthly visits and telephone calls to households. Personal communications were accomplished by neighbors of the households that were visited or called. Personal communication reached two-thirds of the households surveyed during the first evaluation study in 1970.

Managing Influence Groups

One notable feature of ''Sesame Street's'' social marketing was its success in winning support from a wide range of influence groups. One indicator of this support is the financial backing it received, as noted in Table 19–A. Several U.S. governmental agencies, business corporations, and foundations were major donors. Governmental support also took the form of endorsements from high-level U.S. governmental officials. For example, in 1970 testimony before Congress, Sidney Marland, then U.S. commissioner of education, stated:

> I would like to have a Sesame-type creativity going on in drug abuse, or a Sesame-type creativity going on in vocational education for maybe as many as 20 or 30 of the crafts and technologies to draw young people in at 14, 16, and 18, the way they draw in the three-, four-, and five-year-olds into ''Sesame Street.'' We need persons with the same kind of exquisite talent and creative leadership as Joan Ganz Cooney who is the creative force behind ''Sesame Street.''

The social marketers of ''Sesame Street'' attracted a great deal of attention from the mass media. *Time* published a major story on ''Sesame Street'' in November 1970, which said: ''Sesame

TABLE 19-A Funding Received by the Children's Television Workshop for "Sesame Street" (For Fiscal Years 1968–71)

Sources	Amount
Federal	
Office of Education	$ 6,225,000
Office of Economic Opportunity	350,000
Office of Child Development	300,000
National Institute of Child Health and Human Development	15,000
National Foundation on the Arts and Humanities	10,000
Total federal support	$ 6,900,000
Private	
Carnegie Corporation	$ 2,100,000
Ford Foundation	2,025,000
Corporation for Public Broadcasting	1,650,000
Public Broadcasting Service	600,000
Markle Foundation	237,800
Learning Resource Institute	150,000
3M Company	37,200
Total private support	$ 6,800,000
Grand Total	$13,700,000

SOURCE: Taken from *"Sesame Street" Revisited* by Thomas D. Cook, et al., © Russell Sage Foundation, 1975. Used with permission of the Russell Sage Foundation.

Street has earned straight A's"; it also featured the program in subsequent issues. The favorable press endorsement created a highly positive public attitude toward the television series that no public official involved with education or business leaders could afford to ignore. Sesame Street's ongoing success is in demonstrating that television can be used as a mass instructional technology to improve the quality of education.

Epilogue

We have examined a great variety of social change programs and campaigns, worldwide, pinpointing their strengths and weaknesses. Social change programs can be large scale or small scale in their funding; have as their scope local communities, regions, or entire national populations; be sponsored only by private organizations, by governments, or by a combination of both; be implemented over a long period or a short period; involve single or multiple social products, with or without a tangible-product base; and aim to generate diverse types of responses from target adopters, including changes in ideas, practices, behaviors, and values.

The objectives, responses, and characteristics of a particular social change program will influence the design and implementation of the program and the emphases that social marketers place on the various elements and tools of the social marketing mix. For example, the global campaign to detect, prevent, and control the spread of the AIDS virus is understandably mass-communication driven, reflecting the need to disseminate information on AIDS rapidly to as many people in as many countries as possible. However, family planning programs in developing countries are compelled to assign a high priority to distribution channels for the dissemination of contraceptives. Other campaigns, such as the Head Start preschool education program, relied heavily on the use of training and counseling services.

The science of social marketing is relatively new as an approach to changing public behavior in socially desirable ways. Many of its tools have proven themselves in commercial applications and are on the way to proving themselves in social applications. There is, however, one significant caveat that social change agents confront. Given the vast and profound changes that governments and private organizations, worldwide, are seeking to produce, and given the limited resources for social change programs, social change agents must strive to develop the most effective and efficient programs. They can do so by utilizing scientific knowledge and technology, rather than relying simply on ad hoc, intuitive, scattershot hunches and approaches.

Great changes and opportunities exist to produce desirable changes in the ways that individuals and groups think and behave and in meeting human needs. The balance of the scales of social change, we hope, will shift away from the use of force and violence to the use of persuasion and voluntary action. We trust that this book will be useful in highlighting the strategies and means of peaceful, planned social change designed to elevate the quality of life throughout the world.

◆

Notes

CHAPTER 1
The Nature and Role of Social Campaigns
to Change Public Behavior

1. Ronald Kotulak, "Minorities Target of New AIDS Education," *Chicago Tribune,* July 26, 1987, p. 1.

2. Shirley A. Star and Helen MacGill Hughes, "A Report on an Educational Campaign: The Cincinnati Plan for the United Nations," *American Journal of Sociology,* 55 (1950), pp. 389–400.

3. Herbert H. Hyman and Paul B. Sheatsley, "Some Reasons Why Information Campaigns Fail," *Public Opinion Quarterly,* 2 (1947), pp. 412–423.

4. L. S. Robertson, B. O'Neill, and C. W. Wixom, "Factors Associated with Observed Safety Belt Use," *Journal of Health and Social Behavior,* 13 (March 1972), pp. 18–24.

5. M. Ray and S. Ward, "Experimentation for Pretesting Public Health Programs: The Case of the Anti–Drug Abuse Campaign," *Advances in Consumer Research,* 3 (1976), pp. 278–286.

6. P. Feingold and M. Knapp, "Anti–Drug Abuse Commercials," *Journal of Communication,* 27 (1977), pp. 20–28.

7. M. T. O'Keefe, "The Anti-Smoking Commercials: A Study of Television's Impact on Behavior," *Public Opinion Quarterly,* 35 (1972), pp. 242–248.

8. H. Mendelsohn, "Some Reasons Why Information Campaigns Can Succeed," *Public Opinion Quarterly,* 37 (1973), pp. 50–61.

9. R. I. Evans, "Planning Public Service Advertising Messages: An

Application of the Fishbein Model and Path Analysis," *Journal of Advertising*, 7 (1978), pp. 28–34.

10. D. Douglas, B. Westley, and S. H. Chaffee, "An Information Campaign That Changes Community Attitudes," *Journalism Quarterly*, 47 (1970), pp. 479–487.

11. N. Maccoby et al., "Reducing the Risk of Cardiovascular Disease: Effects of a Community-Based Campaign on Knowledge and Behavior," *Journal of Community Health*, 3 (1977), pp. 100–114.

12. *Progress*, 53 (March 1968), published by Unilever, pp. 26–32.

13. Paul F. Lazarsfeld and Robert K. Merton, "Mass Communication, Popular Taste, and Organized Social Action," in William Schramm, ed., *Mass Communications* (Urbana: University of Illinois Press, 1949).

14. G. D. Wiebe, "Merchandising Commodities and Citizenship on Television," *Public Opinion Quarterly*, 15 (Winter 1951–52), pp. 679–691.

15. Ibid., p. 633.

16. Michael L. Rothschild, "Marketing Communications in Nonbusiness Situations or Why It's So Hard to Sell Brotherhood Like Soap," *Journal of Marketing*, 43 (Spring 1979), pp. 11–20.

17. Neil J. Smelser, *Theory of Collective Behavior* (New York: Free Press, 1963).

18. Philip Kotler, "What Consumerism Means for Marketing," *Harvard Business Review*, 50 (May–June 1972), pp. 48–57.

19. W. B. Cameron, *Modern Social Movements* (New York: Random House, 1966), pp. 27–28.

20. Philip Kotler, "The Elements of Social Action," *American Behavioral Scientist* (May–June 1971), pp. 691–717.

21. Karen Fox and Philip Kotler, "Reducing Cigarette Smoking: An Opportunity for Social Marketing?" *Journal of Health Care Marketing*, 1 (Winter 1981), pp. 8–17.

22. W. L. Weiss, "Improve Productivity Overnight," *The Collegiate Forum* (Fall 1980), p. 2.

23. Bureau of Health Education, Centers for Disease Control, U.S. Public Health Service, *Adult Use of Tobacco, 1975* (Washington, D.C.: U.S. Public Health Service, 1976).

24. Eduardo L. Roberto, "Profile: The Filipino Consumer," *Occasional Paper No. 4* (Metro Manila: Asian Institute of Management, 1982).

CHAPTER 2
The Social Marketing Approach to Social Change

1. Philip Kotler and Gerald Zaltman, "Social Marketing: An Approach to Planned Social Change," *Journal of Marketing*, 35 (July 1971), pp. 3–12.

2. Milton Rokeach, *Beliefs, Attitudes and Values* (San Francisco: Jossey-Bass, 1968).

3. Philip Kotler, "Megamarketing, or Breaking Into Blocked Markets," *Harvard Business Review,* 64 (March–April 1986), pp. 117–124.

4. Philip Kotler, *Principles of Marketing,* 2nd ed. (Englewood Cliffs, N.J.: Prentice-Hall, 1983), p. 17.

5. Karen Fox and Philip Kotler, "Reducing Cigarette Smoking: An Opportunity for Social Marketing?" *Journal of Health Care Marketing,* 1 (Winter 1981), pp. 8–17.

6. Sandra Wallman, *Perceptions of Development* (Cambridge, England: Cambridge University Press, 1977).

7. A. J. Meyers, C. H. Block, and D. C. E. Ferguson, "Teaching Mothers Oral Rehydration," *Horizons,* 2 (April 1983), p. 14.

8. John T. Gardiner, "John F. Kennedy Family Service Center," in R. E. Hardy and J. G. Cull, eds., *Organization and Administration of Service Programs for the Older Americans* (Springfield, Ill.: Charles C. Thomas, 1975), pp. 145–153.

9. Philip Kotler, *Marketing Management,* 6th ed. (Englewood Cliffs, N.J.: Prentice-Hall, 1988).

10. Eduardo L. Roberto, "Profile: The Filipino Consumer," *Occasional Paper No. 4* (Metro Manila: Asian Institute of Management, 1982).

11. James M. Mintz and Colin May, "Action on Drug Abuse: 'Really Me,' Canada's Social Marketing Program on Alcohol and Other Drugs." Paper presented at the 35th International Congress on Alcoholism and Drug Dependence, Oslo, 1988.

12. Ronald G. Corwin, *Reform and Organizational Survival* (New York: John Wiley & Sons, 1973).

13. John Samuels, "Evaluating Social Persuasion Advertising Campaigns—An Overview of Recent C.O.I. Experience." Paper presented at a seminar on communication and social research, organized by ESOMAR (European Society for Marketing and Opinion Research), London, 1977.

14. *Amnesty International Handbook* (London: Amnesty International, 1983).

15. Westinghouse Population Center, *Contraception Distribution in the Commercial Sector of the Philipines.* (Columbia, Md.: Health System Division, Westinghouse Population Center, 1973).

16. Cited in Mintz and May, "Action on Drug Abuse."

CHAPTER 3
Social Marketing Research

1. Eduardo L. Roberto, *Strategic Decision Making in a Social Program* (Lexington, Mass.: Lexington Books, 1975); and Eduardo L. Roberto and E. S. Valbuena, "Deciding on the Appeal for a Family Planning Cam-

paign with the Use of a Consumer Attitude-Behavior Model," *Philippine Review of Business and Economics*, 13 (December 1976), pp. 1–28.

2. J. Rohde and S. Fabricant, *ORT Country Assessment Report* (Manila: U.S. Agency for International Development, 1984), p. 1.

3. Manuel Ylanan, *Final Report on the Condom Marketing Research Project* (Metro Manila: Population Center Foundation, 1978).

4. G. A. Churchill, *Marketing Research: Methodological Foundations*, 4th ed. (Hinsdale, Ill.: Dryden Press, 1987).

5. Ibid.

CHAPTER 4
Mapping the Social Marketing Environment

1. S. T. Maidlow and H. Berman, "The Economics of Heroin Treatment," *American Journal of Public Health*, 62 (October 1972), pp. 1397–1406.

2. Ibid., p. 1397.

3. N. E. Zinberg and J. A. Robertson, *Drugs and the Public* (New York: Simon & Schuster, 1972).

4. Alan Gartner and Frank Riessman, *Self-Help in the Human Services* (San Francisco: Jossey-Bass, 1977).

5. G. Levin, G. Horsch, and E. Roberts, "Narcotics and the Community: A System Simulation," *American Journal of Public Health*, 62 (June 1972), p. 867.

6. Maidlow and Berman, "The Economics of Heroin Treatment," p. 1317.

7. C. D. Basil and C. W. Cook, *The Management of Change* (New York: McGraw-Hill Book Co., 1974).

8. W. Howard Chase, *Issue Management: Origins of the Future* (Stamford, Conn.: Issue Action Publications, 1984).

9. H. A. Linstone and M. Turoff, *The Delphi Method: Techniques and Applications* (Reading, Mass.: Addison-Wesley, 1975).

10. John Naisbitt, *Megatrends* (New York: Warner Books, 1982).

11. Chase, *Issue Management*, p. 52.

12. W. L. Miller, *The Survey Method in the Social and Political Sciences: Achievements, Failures, Prospects* (New York: St. Martin's Press, 1983).

13. Eduardo L. Roberto, *Applied Marketing Research* (Quezon City, Philippines: Ateneo University Press, 1987).

14. A. J. Rowe, R. O. Mason, and K. E. Dickel, *Strategic Management and Business Policy* (Reading, Mass.: Addison-Wesley, 1982).

15. Chase, *Issue Management*, p. 38.

CHAPTER 5
Analyzing the Behavior of Target Adopters

1. Milton Rokeach, *Beliefs, Attitudes and Values* (San Francisco: Jossey-Bass, 1966).

2. Daniel Katz, "The Functional Approach to the Study of Attitudes," *Public Opinion Quarterly*, 24 (Summer 1960), pp. 163–204. H. C. Kelman, "Three Processes of Social Influence," *Public Opinion Quarterly*, 25 (1961), pp. 57–58.

3. M. L. Ray, *Advertising and Communication Management* (Englewood Cliffs, N.J.: Prentice-Hall, 1982).

4. M. L. Ray, "Marketing Communications and the Hierarchy of Effects," in P. Clarke, ed., *New Models for Mass Communication Research* (Beverly Hills, Calif.: Sage Publishing Co., 1973), pp. 147–176. T. S. Robertson, J. Zielinski, and Scott Ward, *Consumer Behavior* (Glenview, Ill.: Scott Foresman & Co., 1984).

5. Canadian Facts, *A Survey of the Public's Attitudes toward the Energy Situation*. Report presented to the Department of Energy, Mines and Resources, Ottawa, Ontario, 1979; and J. S. Milstein, *Energy Consumers' Awareness, Attitudes, and Behavior* (Oak Ridge, Tenn.: Office of Conservation and Solar Energy, U.S. Department of Energy, 1979).

6. B. M. Morrison, "Impacts on Household Energy Consumption: An Empirical Study of Michigan Families," in *Sociopolitical Impacts of Energy Uses and Policy Contents* (Washington, D.C.: National Research Council, National Academy of Sciences, 1978).

7. J. McGuire, "Theoretical Foundations of Campaigns," in R. E. Rice and W. J. Paisley, eds., *Public Communication Campaigns* (Beverly Hills, Calif.: Sage Publications, 1981), pp. 41–70.

8. J. N. Sheth and S. Sudman (1976), "Malnutrition and Marketing," discussion paper (Champaign-Urbana: University of Illinois, 1976).

9. R. E. Smith and W. R. Swinyard, "Information Response Models: An Integrated Approach," *Journal of Marketing*, 46 (Winter 1982), p. 80.

10. Ibid., p. 85.

11. Ibid., p. 86.

12. Elihu Katz and Paul Lazarsfeld, *Personal Influence: The Part Played by People in the Flow of Mass Communication* (Glencoe, Ill.: Free Press, 1955).

13. Robertson, Zielinski, and Ward, *Consumer Behavior*.

14. T. G. Williams, *Consumer Behavior* (St. Paul, Minn.: West Publishers, 1982).

15. See, for example, J. R. Moncuso, "Why Not Create Opinion Leaders for New Product Introduction?" *Journal of Marketing*, 33 (July 1969), pp. 20–25.

16. G. M. Armstrong and L. P. Feldman, "Exposure and Sources of Opinion Leaders," *Journal of Advertising Research*, 16 (August 1976), pp. 21–27.

17. Ernest Dichter, "How Word-of-Mouth Advertising Works," *Harvard Business Review*, 44 (November–December 1966), pp. 147–166.

18. Robertson, Zielinski, and Ward, *Consumer Behavior.*

19. J. Deutsch and Y. Liebermann, "Effects of a Public Advertising Campaign on Consumer Behavior in a Demarketing Situation," *International Journal of Research in Marketing*, 2 (1985), pp. 287–290.

20. B. F. Pilgrim and F. F. Shoemaker, "Campaigns to Affect Energy Behavior," in R. E. Rice and W. J. Paisley, eds., *Public Communication Campaigns* (Beverly Hills, Calif.: Sage Publications, 1981), p. 171.

21. Ibid., p. 175.

22. M. Fishbein and I. Ajzen, *Belief, Attitude, Intention and Behavior: An Introduction to Theory and Research* (Reading, Mass.: Addison-Wesley, 1975).

23. Eduardo L. Roberto and E. S. Valbuena, "Deciding on the Advertising Appeal with the Use of a Consumer Attitude-Behavior Model," *Philippine Review of Business and Economics*, 2 (December 1976), pp. 1–28.

24. B. Sternthal and C. S. Craig, *Consumer Behavior: An Information Processing Perspective* (Englewood Cliffs, N.J.: Prentice-Hall, 1982), p. 65.

25. R. W. Belk, "Situational Variables and Consumer Behavior," *Journal of Consumer Research*, 2 (December 1975), pp. 157–164.

26. A. J. Meyer et al., "Skills Training in a Cardiovascular Health Education Campaign," *Journal of Consulting and Clinical Psychology*, 48 (1980), pp. 129–142.

27. L. S. Robertson, B. O'Neill, and C. W. Wixom, "Factors Associated with Observed Safety Belt Use," *Journal of Health and Social Behavior*, 13 (March 1972), pp. 18–24.

28. S. G. Philliber and W. W. Philliber, "Social and Psychological Perspectives on Voluntary Sterilization: A Review," *Studies in Family Planning*, 16 (January–February 1985), pp. 1–28.

29. R. G. Geen and M. B. Quanty, "The Catharsis of Aggression," in L. Berkowitz, ed., *Advances in Experimental Social Psychology*, vol. 10 (New York: Academic Press, 1976).

30. P. C. Feingold and M. L. Knapp, "Anti–Drug Abuse Commercials," *Journal of Communication*, 27 (Winter 1977), pp. 20–28.

31. McGuire, "Theoretical Foundations of Campaigns," p. 62.

32. P. A. Stevens, J. G. Greene, and L. H. Primavera, "Predicting Successful Smoking Cessation," *Journal of Social Psychology,* 118 (1982), p. 235.

33. Philliber and Philliber, "Social and Psychological Perspectives on Voluntary Sterilization."

34. Ted Roselius, "Consumer Rankings of Risk Reduction Methods," *Journal of Marketing,* 35 (January 1971), pp. 56–61.

35. H. G. Gemunden, "Perceived Risk and Information Search: A Systematic Meta-Analysis of the Empirical Evidence," *International Journal of Research in Marketing,* 2 (1985), pp. 79–100.

CHAPTER 6
Analyzing the Diffusion of Social Products

1. Philip Kotler, *Marketing Decision Making: A Model-Building Approach* (New York: Holt, Rinehart & Winston, 1971).

2. The rapid penetration model is expressed by

$$Q_t = r\overline{Q}(1-r)^{t-1}$$

where Q_t = increment in cumulative target adopters (the number of target adopters at time t) as a fraction of the potential volume of target adopters,

r = rate of penetration of untapped potential (a constant),

$\overline{Q}$ = total potential of target adopters as a fraction of the total population, and

t = time period.

Assume that the survey indicated that 40 percent of all households will eventually adopt the social product ($\overline{Q}$ = 0.4). Also assume that in each time period, 30 percent of the remaining target-adopter population is penetrated. Therefore, the increment in the penetration of new target adopters in the first period is

$$Q_1 = r\overline{Q}(1-r)^{1-1} = r\overline{Q} = .3(.4) = .12$$

In the second period, this increment is

$$Q = r\overline{Q}(1-r)^{2-1} = r\overline{Q}(1-r) = r(\overline{Q}-r\overline{Q}) = .3[.4 - .3(.4)] = 0.084$$

and so on, as shown in Figure 6–1.

The resulting forecasts can be refined as data from monitoring the results of the diffusion program become available. Once the adoption campaign has been launched, and two time periods have passed, the penetration rate (*r*) can be updated by finding the ratio of the second period's increment in new target adopters to the difference between the ceiling level and the increment of new target adopters in the first period. Another updated estimate of *r* can be made when the third period's results are in. The social marketer can average the past estimates of *r* as the data come in to determine a current *r* to use in the prediction equation.

3. L. A. Fourt and J. N. Woodlock, "Early Prediction of Market Success for New Grocery Products," *Journal of Marketing*, 2 (October 1960), pp. 31–38.

4. In the S-curve model, the rate of penetration is proportional to the rate of penetration already achieved and to the distance from the ceiling level. Any point in it is defined in the equation:

$$Q_T = \overline{Q} \, [1 + e^{-(a+bt)}]^{-1}$$

where Q_T = cumulative percentage of adoption by the time *T*,
   t = time,
   $\overline{Q}$ = the ceiling level of adoption,
   a = a constant that positions the curve on the time scale,
   b = the adoption rate or rate of penetration.

5. Mathematically, this model is specified by the equation:

$$Q_t = rQ_T(\overline{Q} - Q_T) + p\,(\overline{Q} - Q_T)$$

where Q_t = the number of new target adopters in the current period,
   Q_T = the cumulative number of target adopters to date,
   r = the effect of each target adopter on each nonadopter,
   $\overline{Q}$ = the total possible number of potential target adopters,
   p = the individual conversion rate in the absence of the target adopters' influence.

6. F. M. Bass, "A New Product Growth Model for Consumer Durables," *Management Science*, 15 (January 1969), pp. 215–227.

7. Eduardo L. Roberto, *Strategic Decision-Making in a Social Program* (Lexington, Mass.: Lexington Books, 1975).

8. T. S. Robertson, J. Zielinski, and S. Ward, *Consumer Behavior* (Glencoe, Ill: Scott Foresman & Co., 1984).

9. L. A. Brown, *Innovation Diffusion: A New Perspective* (New York: Methuen, 1981).

10. E. M. Rogers, *Diffusion of Innovations* (New York: Free Press, 1962).

11. M. S. Alba, ''Microanalysis of the Socio-Dynamics of Diffusion of Innovation,'' unpublished doctoral dissertation, Northwestern University, 1967.

12. Rogers, *Diffusion of Innovations;* and E. M. Rogers and F. F. Shoemaker, *Communication of Innovations: A Cross-Cultural Approach* (New York: Free Press, 1971).

13. P. B. Horton and C. L. Hunt, *Sociology,* 6th ed. (New York: McGraw-Hill Book Co., 1984), p. 524.

14. A. Apodaca, ''Corn and Custom: The Introduction of Hybrid Corn to Spanish American Farmers in New Mexico,'' in E. H. Spicer, ed., *Human Problems in Technological Change* (New York: Russell Sage Foundation, 1952), pp. 35–39.

15. Horton and Hunt, *Sociology.*

16. W. F. Wertheim, ''Resistance to Change: From Whom?'' in H. D. Evers, ed., *Modernization in South-East Asia* (London: Oxford University Press, 1973), pp. 97–107.

17. J. S. Coleman, ''Conflicting Theories of Social Change,'' *American Behavioral Scientist,* 14 (May–June 1971), p. 637.

18. Robertson, Zielinski, and Ward, *Consumer Behavior,* p. 380.

19. Kotler, *Marketing Decision Making.*

20. *Amnesty International Handbook* (London: Amnesty International Publications, 1983), p. 15.

21. Rogers and Shoemaker, *Communication of Innovations.*

CHAPTER 7
Designing the Social Product

1. Eduardo L. Roberto, *Applied Marketing Research* (Metro Manila: Ateneo de Manila University Press, 1987).

2. Eduardo L. Roberto, ''Operasyon Walang Lagay, Inc.,'' social marketing case prepared for the Program for Development Managers, Asian Institute of Management (Manila, Philippines, 1987), p. 1.

3. Ibid., p. 3.

4. R. L. Prosterman, *The Decline in Hunger-Related Deaths* (San Francisco: Hunger Project, 1984), p. 20.

5. Roberto, ''Operasyon Walang Lagay, Inc.,'' p. 20.

6. B. F. Pilgrim and F. F. Shoemaker, ''Campaigns to Affect Energy

Behavior," in R. E. Rice and W. J. Paisley, eds., *Public Communication Campaigns* (Beverly Hills, Calif.: Sage Publications, 1981).

7. W. J. McGuire, "Theoretical Foundations of Campaigns," in R. E. Rice and W. J. Paisley, eds., *Public Communication Campaigns* (Beverly Hills, Calif.: Sage Publications, 1981), p. 62.

8. C. S. Craig and J. M. McCaan, "Assessing Communication Effects on Energy Conservation," *Journal of Consumer Research,* 5 (September 1978), pp. 82–88.

9. H. Assael, *Consumer Behavior and Marketing Action* (Boston: Kent, 1981).

10. C. E. Osgood and P. H. Tannenbaum, "The Principles of Congruity in the Prediction of Attitude Change," *Psychological Review,* 62 (1955), pp. 42–55.

11. Leonard L. Berry, "Services Marketing is Different," in C. H. Lovelock, ed., *Services Marketing: Text, Cases and Readings* (Englewood Cliffs, N.J.: Prentice-Hall, 1984).

12. W. Earl Sasser, "Match Supply and Demand in Service Industries," *Harvard Business Review,* 53 (July–August 1975), pp. 98–106.

CHAPTER 8
Making the Social Product Available

1. L. W. Stern and A. I. El-Ansary, *Marketing Channels* (Englewood Cliffs, N.J.: Prentice-Hall, 1988).

2. Philip Kotler, *Marketing Management,* 6th ed. (Englewood Cliffs, N.J.: Prentice-Hall, 1988), p. 530.

3. A. Ghosh and C. S. Craig, "An Approach to Determining Optimal Locations for New Services," *Journal of Marketing Research,* 23 (November 1986), pp. 354–362.

4. W. C. Black, "Choice-Set Definition in Patronage Modeling," *Journal of Retailing,* 60 (Summer 1984), pp. 63–85; and D. A. Gautshi, "Specifications of Patronage Models for Retail Center Choice," *Journal of Marketing Research,* 18 (May 1981), pp. 162–174.

5. Stern and El-Ansary, *Marketing Channels.*

6. Jeffrey Pfeffer, *Power in Organization* (Marshfield, Mass.: Pitman Publishing Co., 1981).

CHAPTER 9
Managing the Costs of Adoption

1. Adam Smith, *An Inquiry into the Nature and Causes of the Wealth of Nations* (1776; reprint New York: P. F. Collier & Sons, 1909), p. 36.

2. Philip Kotler and Sidney Levy, "Demarketing, Yes, Demarketing," *Harvard Business Review* (November–December 1971), pp. 74–80.

3. E. J. Dunfee, "Dying for a Little Thrill," *Asia Magazine,* May 31, 1987, p. 14.

4. Philip Kotler and Alan Andreasen, *Strategic Marketing for Nonprofit Organizations* (Englewood Cliffs, N.J.: Prentice-Hall, 1987).

5. John L. Crompton and Charles W. Lamb, Jr., *Marketing Government and Social Services* (New York: John Wiley & Sons, 1986).

6. Thomas T. Nagle, *The Strategy and Tactics of Pricing* (Englewood Cliffs, N.J.: Prentice-Hall, 1987), p. 2.

7. Ibid.

8. Karen F. A. Fox, "Time as a Component of Price in Social Marketing," in Richard P. Bagozzi et al., eds., *Marketing in the 1980s* (Chicago: American Marketing Association, 1980), pp. 464–467, quotation on p. 465.

9. H. G. Gemunden, "Perceived Risk and Information Search: A Systematic Meta-Analysis of the Empirical Evidence," *International Journal of Research in Marketing,* 2 (1985), pp. 79–100.

10. Ted Roselius, "Consumer Rankings of Risk Reduction Methods," *Journal of Marketing,* 35 (January 1971), pp. 56–61.

11. P. J. Robinson, "Applications of Conjoint Analysis to Pricing Problems," in D. B. Montgomery and D. R. Wittink, eds., *Market Measurement and Analysis* (Cambridge, Mass.: Marketing Science Institute, 1980), pp. 183–205.

CHAPTER 10
Promoting Through Mass Communication

1. N. Philipps and E. Nelson, "Energy Savings in Private Households: An Integrated Research Program," in Christopher H. Lovelock and Charles B. Weinberg, *Readings in Public and Nonprofit Marketing* (New York: Scientific Press, 1978), p. 293.

2. Anders Englund, "Changing Behavior Patterns: Sweden's Traffic Switch," in Christopher H. Lovelock and Charles B. Weinberg, *Readings in Public and Nonprofit Marketing* (New York: Scientific Press, 1978), pp. 225–230.

3. Vilstrup Kasper, *The Bornhelm Experiment: Summary Report on an Anti-Smoking Education Experiment in Denmark, 1973–74* (Copenhagen: Vilstrup Research, 1974), p. 3.

4. B. Zeigarnik, "On the Retention of Completed and Uncompleted Activities," *Psychologische Forschung,* 9 (1927), pp. 1–85.

5. J. C. Maloney, "Is Advertising Believability Really Important?", *Journal of Marketing,* 27 (1986), pp. 1–8.

6. Michael Ray, *Advertising and Communication Management* (Englewood Cliffs, N.J.: Prentice-Hall, 1982).

7. Ibid., p. 254.

8. Brian Sternthal and C. S. Craig, "Fear Appeals; Revisited and Revised," *Journal of Consumer Research*, 3 (December 1974), pp. 23–34.

9. Ray, *Advertising and Communication Management*.

9a. Ibid.

10. A. Mehrabian, *Nonverbal Communication* (Chicago: Aldine Publishing Co., 1972).

11. M. W. DeLozier, *The Marketing Communication Process* (New York: McGraw-Hill Book Co., 1976).

12. P. Ekman, W. V. Friesen, and S. Ancoli, "Facial Signs of Emotional Experience," *Journal of Personality and Social Psychology*, 39 (1980), pp. 1125–1134.

13. D. Druckman, R. M. Rozelle, and J. C. Baxter, *Nonverbal Communication: Survey, Theory and Research* (Beverly Hills, Calif.: Sage Publications, 1982).

14. Eduardo L. Roberto, *Applied Marketing Research* (Metro Manila: Ateneo University Press, 1987), and *Strategic Decision-Making in a Social Program* (Lexington, Mass.: Lexington Books, 1975).

15. Renée Sabatier, "AIDS in the Developing World," *International Family Planning Perspectives*, 13 (September 1987), pp. 96–103.

16. L. Liskin and R. Blackburn, "AIDS: A Public Health Crisis," *Population Reports*, 14 (July–August 1986), p. 207.

17. Ibid., p. 209.

18. Bill Hewitt, "The Politics of AIDS," *Newsweek*, August 10, 1987, p. 12.

19. "Locking Up AIDS," *Asiaweek*, October 9, 1987, p. 20.

20. Warren J. Keegan, *Global Marketing Management*, 4th ed. (Englewood Cliffs, N.J.: Prentice-Hall, 1988), p. 501.

21. Greg Harris, "The Globalization of Advertising," *International Journal of Advertising*, 3 (1984), pp. 223–234; and Yoram Wind, "The Myth of Globalization," *Journal of Consumer Marketing*, 3 (Spring 1986), pp. 23–26.

22. Keegan, *Global Marketing Management*.

23. Hewitt, "The Politics of AIDS," p. 13.

CHAPTER 11
Promoting Through Selective Communication

1. Michael Ray, *Advertising and Communication Management* (Englewood Cliffs, N.J.: Prentice-Hall, 1982).

2. Murray Roman, *Telemarketing Campaigns* (New York: McGraw-Hill Book Co., 1983), pp. 248–251.

3. Bill Abrams, "More Firms Use '800' Numbers to Keep Customers Satisfied," *Wall Street Journal,* April 7, 1983, p. 31.

4. H. Katzenstein and W. S. Sachs, *Direct Marketing* (Columbus, Ohio: Charles E. Merrill Publishing Co., 1986), p. 240.

5. A. Mehrabian and M. Williams, "Nonverbal Concomitants of Perceived and Intended Persuasiveness," *Journal of Personality and Social Psychology,* 13 (1969), pp. 37–58.

6. W. T. Packwood, "Loudness as a Variable in Persuasion," *Journal of Counseling Psychology,* 21 (1974), pp. 1–2.

7. D. W. Addington, "The Effects of Vocal Verification on Rating of Source Credibility," *Speech Monographs,* 38 (1971), pp. 242–247.

8. *Guidelines for Telephone Marketing* (Washington, D.C.: Direct Marketing Association, April 1984).

CHAPTER 12
Promoting Through Personal Communication

1. Eduardo L. Roberto, *Strategic Decision Making in a Social Program* (Lexington, Mass.: Lexington Books, 1975), p. 87.

2. R. R. Blake and J. S. Moulton, *The Grid for Sales Excellence: Benchmarks for Effective Salesmanship* (New York: McGraw-Hill Book Co., 1970).

3. H. C. Cash and W. J. E. Crissy, *Psychology of Selling* (Flushing, N.Y.: Personnel Development Associates, 1958).

4. W. R. Swinyard and M. L. Ray, "Advertising-Selling Interactions: An Attribution Theory Experiment," *Journal of Marketing Research,* 14 (November 1977), pp. 509–516.

5. Ibid, p. 511.

CHAPTER 13
Triggering Target Adopters' Actions

1. J. H. Mintz, "National Program to Reduce Tobacco Use," paper presented at the 6th World Conference on Smoking and Health, Keidanren Kaikan, Tokyo, Japan, November 10, 1987.

2. Heidi Liepold, "Break Free: The National Program to Reduce Smoking," *Health Promotion,* 24 (Spring 1986), pp. 9–10, 25.

3. J. F. Bunker, M. P. Eriksen, and J. Kinsey, "AIDS in the Workplace: The Role of Employee Assistance Programs," *The Almacan,* 17 (September 1987), pp. 18–26.

4. N. Govoni, R. Eng, and M. Galper, *Promotional Management* (Englewood Cliffs, N.J.: Prentice-Hall, 1986).

5. F. Korten, "Community Participation: A Management Perspective

on Obstacles and Options," in D. C. Korten and F. B. Alfonso, eds., *Bureaucracy and the Poor: Closing the Gap* (Singapore: McGraw-Hill International Book Co., 1981), p. 181.

6. Samuel Paul, *Community Participation in Development Projects: The World Bank Experience* (Washington, D.C.: World Bank, 1987), p. 2.

7. H. C. Kelman, "Compliance, Identification and Internalization: Three Processes of Attitude Change," *Journal of Conflict Resolution,* 2 (1958), pp. 51–60.

8. W. R. Brieger, J. Ramakrishna, and J. D. Adeniyi, "Community Involvement in Social Marketing; Guineaworm Control," *International Quarterly of Community Health Education,* 7 (1986–87), pp. 19–31.

9. Charles de Weck, "The Practicalities of Participation: Some Problems Facing the Advisor Employed by an Integrated System of Cooperatives in Peru," in J. Nash, J. Dandler, and N. S. Hopskins, eds., *Popular Participation in Social Change* (Paris: Mouton Publishers, 1976), pp. 431–438.

10. Ibid., p. 437.

11. Ibid., p. 434.

CHAPTER 14

Managing Service Delivery and Target Adopters' Satisfaction

1. A. Parasuraman, V. A. Zeithaml, and L. L. Berry, "A Conceptual Model of Service Quality and Its Implications for Future Research," *Journal of Marketing,* 49 (Fall 1985), pp. 41–50.

2. Valarie Zeithaml, "How Consumers' Evaluation Processes Differ Between Goods and Services," in James H. Donnelly and William R. George, eds., *Marketing of Services* (Chicago: American Marketing Association, 1981).

3. Parasuraman, Zeithaml, and Berry, "A Conceptual Model of Service Quality."

4. D. W. Cowell, *The Marketing of Services* (London: William Heinemann, 1984), pp. 204–206.

5. T. R. Mitchell, *People in Organizations,* 2nd ed. (Tokyo: McGraw-Hill International, 1983), chap. 17.

6. Ralph M. Barnes, *Motion and Time Study,* 4th ed. (New York: John Wiley & Sons, 1973), chap. 4.

7. Philip Kotler, *Marketing for Nonprofit Organizations* (Englewood Cliffs, N.J.: Prentice-Hall, 1975).

8. Philip Kotler, "Atmospherics as a Marketing Tool," *Journal of Retailing,* 49 (Winter 1974), pp. 48–64.

9. G. Lynn Shostack, "Designing Services that Deliver," *Harvard Business Review*, 62 (January–February 1984), pp. 133–139.

10. Eduardo L. Roberto, *Strategic Decision Making in a Social Program* (Lexington, Mass.: Lexington Book, 1975).

11. C. H. Kepner and B. B. Tregoe, *The Rational Manager: A Systematic Approach to Problem Solving and Decision Making* (New York: McGraw-Hill Book Co., 1965), chap. 11.

12. Shostack, "Designing Services that Deliver."

13. Erving Goffman, *The Presentation of Self in Everyday Life* (Garden City, N.Y.: Doubleday, 1959).

CHAPTER 15
Mobilizing Influence Groups

1. Philip Kotler and A. R. Andreasen, *Strategic Marketing for Nonprofit Organizations*, 3rd ed. (Englewood Cliffs, N.J.: Prentice-Hall, 1987), p. 327.

2. "Curb 'Junk Foods' in Schools?", *U.S. News and World Report*, September 24, 1979, p. 59.

3. Richard R. Nelson, "Organizational Responses to Public Policy Issues: The Case of Day Care," in D. C. Korten and R. Klause, eds., *People-Centered Development* (West Hartford, Conn.: Kumarian Press, 1986), p. 266.

4. D'Vera Cohn, "Fairfax PTAs, Students Support AIDS Education," *Washington Post*, December 2, 1987, p. C8.

5. J. F. Bunker, M. P. Eriksen, and J. Kinsey, "AIDS in the Workplace: The Role of the EAPs," *The Almacan*, 17 (September 1987), p. 21.

6. Cohn, "Fairfax PTAs, Students Support AIDS Education."

7. Graham T. Allison, *Essence of Decision: Explaining the Cuban Missile Crisis* (Boston, Mass.: Little, Brown & Co., 1971).

8. John R. P. French and Bertram Raven, "The Basis of Social Power," in Dorwin Cartwright, ed., *Studies in Social Power* (Ann Arbor: University of Michigan Press, 1959).

9. Philip Kotler, "Megamarketing," *Harvard Business Review*, 64 (March-April 1986), pp. 117–124.

10. Jeffrey Pfeffer, *Power in Organizations* (Marshfield, Mass.: Pitman Publishing Corp., 1981), pp. 153–154.

CHAPTER 16
Developing the Social Marketing Plan

1. J. D. C. Little, "Models and Managers: The Concept of a Decision Calculus," *Management Science*, 16 (April 1970), pp. B466–B485.

CHAPTER 17
Organizing and Implementing Social Marketing Programs

1. Philip Kotler and A. R. Andreasen, *Strategic Marketing for Nonprofit Organizations,* 3rd ed. (Englewood Cliffs, N.J.: Prentice-Hall, 1987).
2. F. Stewart DeBruiker and D. J. Reibstein, eds., *Cases in Marketing Research* (Englewood Cliffs, N.J.: Prentice-Hall, 1983), pp. 325–326.
3. Hugo E. R. Uyterhoeven, "General Manager in the Middle," in Richard G. Hamermesh, ed., *Strategic Management* (New York: John Wiley and Sons, 1983), pp. 410–411.
4. Christopher Gale and L. E. Grayson, "Common Cause," in L. E. Grayson and C. J. Tompkins, eds., *Management of Public Sector and Nonprofit Organizations* (Reston, Va.: Reston Publishing Co., 1984), p. 152.
5. Myron D. Fottler, "Improving Health Care Planning: Some Lessons from Immunization," *Long Range Planning,* 17 (5) (1984), pp. 88–95.
6. Kotler and Andreasen, *Strategic Marketing for Nonprofit Organizations,* p. 304.
7. Ibid.
8. Roger Fisher and William Ury, *Getting to Yes: Negotiating Agreement without Giving In* (Boston: Houghton Mifflin Co., 1981).
9. LaRue T. Hosmer, *Strategic Management* (Englewood Cliffs, N.J.: Prentice-Hall, 1982), chap. 9.
10. Ibid., p. 475.
11. Thomas V. Bonoma, *The Marketing Edge: Making Strategies Work* (New York: Free Press, 1985).
12. Rosabeth M. Kanter, "The Middle Manager as Innovator," in Richard G. Hamermesh, ed., *Strategic Management* (New York: John Wiley & Sons, 1983), chap. 27.
13. Ibid., p. 434.
14. Uyterhoeven, "General Manager in the Middle," pp. 408–422.

CHAPTER 18
Controlling Social Marketing Programs

1. Robert N. Anthony, John Dearden, and N. W. Bedford, *Management Control Systems,* 5th ed. (Homewood, Ill.: Richard D. Irwin, 1984).
2. E. Zigler and J. Valentine, "Speeches by Lyndon B. Johnson: Remarks on Project Head Start, May 18, 1965," in E. Zigler and J. Valentine, eds., *Project Head Start: A Legacy of the War on Poverty* (New York: Free Press, 1979).
3. June Solnit Sale, "Implementation of a Head Start Preschool Educa-

tion Program: Los Angeles, 1965–1967,'' in E. Zigler and J. Valentine, eds., *Project Head Start: A Legacy of the War on Poverty* (New York: Free Press, 1979). pp. 175–194.

4. Eduardo L. Roberto, *Strategic Decision Making in a Social Program* (Lexington, Mass.: Lexington Books, 1975).

5. Robert A. Rosenbaum, *The Public Issues Handbook* (Westport, Conn.: Greenwood Press, 1983).

6. Peter F. Drucker, *Management: Tasks, Responsibilities, Practices* (New York: Harper & Row, 1974), pp. 504–505.

7. Andrew W. Szilagyi and Marc J. Wallace, *Organizational Behavior and Performance*, 3rd ed. (Glenview, Ill.: Scott Foresman & Co., 1983).

8. Ibid.

9. A. R. Cohen et al., *Effective Behavior in Organizations*, 3rd ed. (Homewood, Ill.: Richard D. Irwin, 1984).

10. Ibid.

11. Zigler and Valentine, "Speeches by Lyndon B. Johnson," pp. 69–70.

12. Ibid., p. 69.

13. Rosenbaum, *The Public Issues Handbook*, p. 306.

14. Michael Harrington, *The Other America: Poverty in the United States* (New York: Macmillan Co., 1962).

15. Julius B. Richmond, "The Early Administrators," in E. Zigler and J. Valentine, eds., *Project Head Start: A Legacy of the War on Poverty* (New York: Free Press, 1979), p. 122.

16. J. B. Richmond, J. Stipek, and E. Zigler, "A Decade of Head Start," in E. Zigler and J. Valentine, eds., *Project Head Start: A Legacy of the War on Poverty* (New York: Free Press, 1979), p. 137.

17. George Brain, "The Early Planners," in E. Zigler and J. Valentine, eds., *Project Head Start: A Legacy of the War on Poverty* (New York: Free Press, 1979), p. 73.

18. Ibid., p. 74.

19. Richmond, Stipek, and Zigler, "A Decade of Head Start," p. 147.

20. Sale, "Implementation of a Head Start Preschool Education Program."

CHAPTER 19
Evaluating Social Marketing Programs

1. Philip Kotler, "Humanistic Marketing: Beyond the Marketing Concept," in A. F. Firat, N. Dholakia, and R. P. Bagozzi, eds., *Philosophical and Radical Thought in Marketing* (Lexington, Mass.: Lexington Books, 1987), pp. 271–288.

2. E. A. Suchman, *Evaluative Research* (New York: Russell Sage Foundation, 1967).

3. T. D. Cook et al., *"Sesame Street" Revisited* (New York: Russell Sage Foundation, 1975.

4. S. Ball and G. A. Bogatz, *The First Year of Sesame Street: An Evaluation* (Princeton, N.J.: Educational Testing Service, 1970); G. A. Bogatz and S. Ball, *The Second Year of Sesame Street: A Continuing Evaluation*, vols., 1 and 2 (Princeton, N.J.: Educational Testing Service, 1971); Cook et al., *"Sesame Street"Revisited*; J. H. Minton, *"The Impact of 'Sesame Street' on Reading Readiness of Kindergarten Children,"* unpublished Ph.D. dissertation, Fordham University, 1972.

5. Cook et al., *"Sesame Street" Revisited.*

6. D. T. Campbell and R. F. Boruch, "Making the Case for Randomized Assignment to Treatments by Considering Alternatives: Six Ways in Which Quasi-Experimental Evaluations in Compensatory Education Tend to Underestimate Effects," in C. A. Bennett and A. A. Lumsdaine, eds., *Evaluation and Experiment: Some Critical Issues on Assessing Social Programs* (New York: Academic Press, 1975).

7. David M. Rindskopf, "Structural Equation Models in Analysis of Nonexperimental Data," in R. F. Boruch, P. M. Wortman, and D. S. Cordray, eds., *Reanalyzing Program Evaluations* (San Francisco: Jossey-Bass, 1981), pp. 163–193.

8. D. B. Pillemer and R. J. Light, "Using the Results of Randomized Experiments to Construct Social Programs," in R. F. Boruch, P. M. Wortman, and D. S. Cordray, eds., *Reanalyzing Program Evaluations* (San Francisco: Jossey-Bass, 1981), pp. 225–236.

9. Cook et al., *"Sesame Street" Revisited.*

10. Ibid., p. 52.

11. Edward Zigler, "Project Head Start: Success or Failure?" in E. Zigler and J. Valentine, eds., *Project Head Start: A Legacy of the War on Poverty* (New York: Free Press, 1979), p. 496.

12. Ibid.

13. Herbert C. Kelman and Donald P. Warwick, "Ethics of Social Intervention: Goals, Means, and Consequences," in G. Bermant, H. C. Kelman, and D. P. Warwick, eds., *The Ethics of Social Intervention* (Washington, D.C.: Hemisphere Publishing Co., 1978), pp. 3–33.

14. Ibid., p. 25.

15. Cook et al., *"Sesame Street" Revisited*, p. 330.

16. Kelman and Warwick, "Ethics of Social Intervention."

17. June Solnit Sale, "Implementation of a Head Start Preschool Education Program: Los Angeles, 1965–1967," in E. Zigler and J. Valen-

tine, eds., *Project Head Start: A Legacy of the War on Poverty* (New York: Free Press, 1979).

18. Ronald G. Corwin, *Reform and Organizational Survival: The Teacher Corps as an Instrument of Educational Change* (New York: John Wiley & Sons, 1973), p. 216.

19. Ibid.

20. Kelman and Warwick, "Ethics of Social Intervention," p. 26.

21. Sandra S. Tangri, "A Feminist Perspective on Some Ethical Issues in Population Programs," in G. Bermant, H. C. Kelman, and D. P. Warwick, eds., *The Ethics of Social Intervention* (Washington, D.C.: Hemisphere Publishing Co., 1978), p. 365.

22. Herbert C. Kelman, "The Rights of the Subject in Social Research: An Analysis in Terms of Relative Power and Legitimacy," *American Psychologist,* 27 (1972), p. 999.

23. D. S. Tull and D. I. Hawkins, "Ethical Issues in Marketing Research," in G. R. Laczniak and P. E. Murphy, eds., *Marketing Ethics: Guidelines for Managers* (Lexington, Mass.: Lexington Books, 1985), pp. 55–70.

24. H. Watts and A. Rees, eds., *The New Jersey Income Maintenance Experiment,* vol. 2 (New York: Academic Press, 1977).

25. H. McKay, A. McKay, and L. Sinisterra, *Stimulation of Intellectual and Social Competence in Columbian Preschool Age Children Affected by the Multiple Deprivations of Depressed Urban Environments: Second Progress Report* (Cali, Colombia: Human Ecology Research Station, 1973).

26. David N. Kershaw, "Issues in Income Maintenance," in P. H. Rossi and W. Williams, eds., *Evaluating Social Programs* (New York: Seminar Books, 1972), p. 222.

27. Ibid.

28. Kelman and Warwick, "Ethics of Social Intervention," p. 19.

29. David N. Kershaw, "Comments," in A. M. Rivlin and P. M. Timpane, eds., *Ethical and Legal Issues of Social Experimentation* (Washington, D.C.: The Brookings Institution, 1975), pp. 28–29.

30. Kelman and Warwick, "Ethics of Social Intervention," p. 15.

31. Peter F. Drucker, *Management: Tasks, Responsibilities, Practices* (New York: Harper & Row, 1974).

Index